The Mary
The Story of No. 534
Neil Potter and Jack Frost

Revised and updated by Lindsay Frost

This book is dedicated
to the *Queen Mary* herself
and to the memory of the late
William Winberg

Shipping Books Press

First published by George G. Harrap & Co. Ltd in 1961 as The Mary:
    The Inevitable Ship
Second edition published 1971 as The Mary: Her Inception and History
This third edition published 1998
    by Shipping Books Press
    Market Drayton, Shropshire TF9 3ZZ
© 1961, 1971 Neil Potter and Jack Frost
© 1998 Lindsay Frost

British Library Cataloguing in Publication Data
    A catalogue record for this book is available from the British Library.

ISBN: 1 900867 02 8

Cover design by Linda Machin
Typeset by MJP, Doveridge, Derbyshire
Printed in the United Kingdom by Information Press, Eynsham,
    Oxfordshire

Contents

List of Illustrations

Acknowledgements

1961: Mr R. Hoare of the Ministry of Transport; Captain S.W. Roskill, R.N. (ret); Mr W.A. Jackman and Mr W.H. Newman. The staff of the Information Division of the Admiralty, of the Library of the Imperial War Museum, and of the *Daily Telegraph*. The immigration Branch of the Home Office and the Waterguard Division of the Customs and Excise. The authors, editors and publishers of the following newspapers for their permission to quote from their works: The *Daily Telegraph*; *The Times*; the *Daily Mail*; the *Daily Mirror*; the *Clydebank Press*; the *New York Herald Tribune*; *The Listener*; the *Architect and Building News*; Clive Bell, Raymond Mortimer. *My Life of Revolt*, David Kirkwood (Harrap); *Last Viceroy*, Ray Murphy (Jarrold); *The Blue Riband*, Charles E. Lee (Sampson Low, Marston); Sir Henry Clay, *Lord Norman* (Macmillan); Sir Keith Feiling, *The Life of Neville Chamberlain* (Macmillan); Sir Arthur Bryant, *Turn of the Tide* (Collins) and *Triumph in the West* (Collins); G.D.H. Cole, *History of the Labour Party from 1914* (Routledge and Kegan Paul); Sir Winston Churchill, *The Second World War,* vols III, IV, V and VI (Cassell); Dwight Eisenhower, *Crusade in Europe* (Heinemann); Harry S. Truman, *Memoirs, Vol 1 (Years of Decision)* (Hodder and Stoughton); Duke of Windsor, *A King's Story* (Cassell); Viscount Cunningham, *A Sailor's Odyssey* (Hutchinson); Christopher Sykes, *Orde Wingate* (Collins); and for permission to use Leonora Speyer's quatrain: *The War at Sea* by Captain S.W. Roskill (H.M.S.O.)

1998: Neil Potter; Captain Robin Woodall, R.D. R.N.R., Master,(Rtd), *Queen Elizabeth 2*; Captain Peter Jackson, Master, (Rtd.) *Queen Elizabeth 2*; Joseph Prevratil, President, *Queen Mary*, Long Beach; Andrea Owen, Liverpool University Archives; The late William Winberg, Curator, *Queen Mary* Archives, Long Beach; Brian Howell, Curator (1997), *Queen Mary* Archives, Long Beach; Geoffrey Coughtree and Anne Logan, former cabin staff onboard RMS *Queen Mary*; Alan (Bondy) Bond, former barkeeper, RMS *Queen Mary*; John Butt, Executive Cruise Director, Cunard Line; John Duffy, Hotel Manager Cunard Line; Stewart

Whitehill of U.I.E., Clydebank; Denzil Stuart of Denzil Stuart Associates, London; Christos Alexiou and Yannis Papaliossas, Radio Operators, RCL, 1994/95; Terry and Trish, former musicians, *Queen Mary*, Long Beach; Kathleen Crowl, *Queen Mary*, Long Beach. Linda and Peter for their patience. Dr Robert Dell; Edith Key; Barry Vaudrin; William H. Miller; Pete Smith; Claude Maluenda; David Williams; Peggy and Peter Frost; Paul Louden-Brown; David Hutchings.

Extract from the Cunard Brochure of 1965/66 reproduced by courtesy of Cunard. Abstract from the log of Voyage No. 516, reproduced by kind permission of Southampton City Heritage Services.

Thanks to the following for giving up their personal time to talk about the *Queen Mary*: Emily Twist, Rene Parthoens, Victor Van Wagenen, Helen Rees Lessner, Margaret Barrow, Paul Plauche, Charlie Read, Gordon Buyck, Margaret Bentley, Donald Meisel, Eugenia Carpenter, Peggy Stockhausen, Mary Riviello, Janet Ascheffenburg, Floyd and Helen Rickard, Rose Zidell, Margery Stich, George O'Neal, Selma Sapir, John Mace, Harold Parsons, Virgina Schelp, Joan Bates, Mandell Siegall, Chester Holl, Louis Guentert, Bill Carr, Irene Caplan, Pam Cowie, Jean Sutherland, Doreen Hughs, Ogy Carss, Arnold Brown.

Special thanks to Kerri-Anne (always the brightest star) and Jack.

Preface

The story of RMS *Queen Mary* is quite unlike any other maritime tale. To begin with, the actual construction of this huge vessel was an achievement of epic proportions. The first stages of building at John Brown's yard, Clydeside, Scotland, progressed well but the depression soon took its toll, biting like a savage dog into the well-established labour patterns which then existed in this industrial Scottish community. Suddenly, all work was stopped and Clydeside was plunged into a two-year period of despondency and destitution while the shipbuilding families resorted to desperate measures in order to survive. David Kirkwood, the Member of Parliament for Clydeside, and Sir Percy Bates, Chairman of the Cunard Line, mounted a clever war of wits against the British Government in an attempt to secure additional funds which would pave the way to the ship's completion. At first, all seemed to be in vain; then gradually, with the assistance of Neville Chamberlain and the Prince of Wales, a solution was reached which not only enabled the completion of "534" (the *Mary*'s yard number) but which also paved the way for the salvation of the crippled White Star Line.

As we all know, the massive liner went on to become more than just a ship – more of a legend, as she sailed across the Atlantic over 1000 times during her 30 years as an active ship, carried hundreds of thousands of troops throughout World War II and went on to a new career as a floating conference centre and hotel in Long Beach, California; a career, incidentally, which has now spanned almost as many years as her previous life on the ocean waves.

Her years during the golden era of transatlantic travel read like a star-studded saga of the wealthy, rich and famous though, of course, this ship was not merely the exclusive reserve of high society and the aristocracy. Thousands of tourist and third-class passengers would ride the grey Atlantic in this most magnificent of floating cities; some setting forth to explore North America or Europe, others forced to make the journey for official, or business reasons. Regardless, however, of their reason for sailing in the Mary, they all have one thing in common: she was without doubt the finest floating experience of their lives.

The first edition of this book appeared in Britain in 1961. It was the product of two clever journalistic minds. Neil Potter was a busy correspondent and Assistant News Editor on one of Britain's best known newspapers. Jack Frost, responsible for so much of the on-site research, was a successful journalist and one of the most well-loved figures on Fleet Street. The combined work of these two writers resulted in a volume which at the time could rightly be regarded as the definitive account of the *Queen Mary*.

Over thirty years have passed since that first publication and although the actual content and history of the ship's life to that point is still accurate, styles and times have changed since the 1960s. In order to bring the book into the 1990s, I have attempted to remould and restyle the original book with a view to the modern reader. I have also added new material, which was researched and written between 1992 and 1995.

I hope that now, in its new format and over three decades since it was first conceived, this the book shall continue to stand as the definitive account of one of the world's most loved ships – RMS *Queen Mary*, or: "534".

Lindsay Frost
1997

Forword

As a small boy, I always had a love of the sea and an ambition to go on the sea. Living in London during the Second World War did little to dampen that enthusiasm, as I was able to look at pictures and read about the great ships of that era. Amongst them was Great Britain's super-liner *Queen Mary*. Pictures and details of that great ship abounded in every book that I saw.

After the war, and moving to the home port of Cunard, Liverpool, I saw that ambition realized when I joined Cunard as an apprentice, and the prospect of serving on the *Queen Mary* became a reality. It was a wonderful moment when, in the 1960s I stepped aboard "The Mary" to sail as Junior Third Officer, and later as First Officer. Here I was on the ship had read so much about, able to absorb at first hand the mystique of the liner that carried the rich, the famous and the thousands of troops during her illustrious career.

I gathered all the information I could about the ship, including the definitive work written by Jack Frost and Neil Potter. Now, thirty-five years on, and having been in command of the successor to both the *Queen Mary* and *the Queen Elizabeth*, I feel very honoured to be asked to write this forword.

That the original book is being updated, is a tribute to the *Queen Mary* and will, I'm sure bring enjoyment to a whole new generation of readers who wish to know the history of that magnificent ship.

Captain R. Woodall, RD* RNR, (Retired)
Former Master Queen Elizabeth 2

About the Authors

Neil Potter, now in his seventy-sixth year, has been a journalist all his working life. He entered the profession when his failed eyesight prevented him from following his chosen career as a deck officer.

After a spell in Liverpool he moved to London. For twelve years he was a reporter and then Assistant News Editor on the *Daily Telegraph*. It was there, while on a voyage to New York on the *Queen Mary*, that he had the idea of writing the "biography" of the vessel.

He asked his colleague and close friend, Jack Frost, Shipping Correspondent of the paper, to join him in the venture.

For eight years he worked in television and then, twenty-five years ago, realizing the growth in the oil industry, became one of the most internationally respected oil writers, a role he continues to play today.

Jack Frost (1898–1974) was born in London. He entered journalism in 1914 as a tape boy at the offices of the *Daily Mail* in London's Fleet Street. He soon gained a hunger to work as a reporter and before long this ambition was realized, as Jack started a career that would make him something of a legend in journalistic circles.

He wrote as a crime correspondent for the *Daily Mail*, a motoring reporter for the *Daily Express* and then joined the *Daily Express* in 1938 as a correspondent covering both crime and shipping. Following the war, he returned to the *Daily Telegraph* as a shipping correspondent until he retired in 1963. Not happy to sit at home or tend the garden, Jack Frost continued to freelance as a shipping correspondent over the next decade.

Amongst the distinguished posts which he held was that of the Director of Press for Cowes Yachting Week and Chairman of the London and Southampton Press Clubs. In 1972, he was awarded the MBE for services to journalism.

Lindsay Frost, graduated in 1977 with honours in music and spent his early career touring Britain and Europe as a performer and writer.

In 1985 he joined the staff of Cunard Line and worked in several positions before achieving the coveted position of Cruise Director onboard the flagship *Queen Elizabeth 2*. With Cunard he spent eight years crossing the Atlantic and cruising to some of the world's most exotic and fascinating destinations working onboard *QE2*, *Sagafjord* and *Vistafjord*. It was during this time that he developed a fascination with the history of passenger shipping and began a second 'career' writing and lecturing. Since leaving Cunard in 1993, he has worked as a cruise director for Royal Cruise Line, Orient Line and Holland America Line.

1

"The Inevitable Ship"

The great, solid block that was the headquarters of the Cunard Steam-Ship Company stands on the Liverpool waterfront, beaten by the wind and the rain, bleached by the sun, frozen occasionally by the snow and facing the grey-brown waters of the Mersey River. This was the very heart of a shipping city where at one time, standing at the windows of that building, one could see ships of all nations passing by in procession at tide-time, almost as routinely as the green buses whose terminus was at the water's edge. Ferryboats would fuss across the river, dodging between the ships, almost like children running across a busy road. A sense of anticipation always filled the air as, every few days, a massive steamship would sidle up against the huge floating pontoons, ready to take onboard her frail human cargo; ready to pound her way across one of the world's most hazardous bodies of water, the North Atlantic Ocean.

One day early in 1926, a group of men gathered round a table in their office, behind a heavy dark-stained oak door along a discreetly quiet corridor on the fifth floor of that headquarters. It was only some 50 paces from the chairman's room.

This was one of the "secret" rooms – a planner's room. For these men were the company's design team; the men who, from their knowledge, from their experience and from their dreams, created ships. They designed on paper ships that eventually would become living beings. These men were unaware that they were about to initiate the birth of a ship that would become the most famous ship of its day.

They sat there, in front of them blank pieces of paper, beside them neatly sharpened pencils. For a moment no one spoke. All were lost in their thoughts, and anyway a little hesitant to begin. For where exactly do you begin to design a new ship?

One spoke: "Well, how long was the *Mauretania*?"

"790 feet."

"The *Aquitania*?"

"901 feet."

"Well, let's make this one a thousand feet and see what happens."

So they drew a line on their pieces of paper to represent a thousand feet. And so they were launched into a voyage of discovery. Thus was born the first thousand-foot liner in the world. Just as simple as that. Just as unscientifically as that, if you like.

That was the beginning, the birth, of this liner. That was the first faltering, hesitant step in her creation. There were to be a million and one other steps; a thousand and one more lines and drawings.

But it had all really begun as a dream a century and a half previously in the mind of a forty-year-old, taciturn, self-taught, self-made Quaker bustling about the quayside of Halifax, Nova Scotia. For in those days, when the sleek, fast American sailing ships ruled the Atlantic Ocean, that man, above all others, realized the possibilities of harnessing steam to drive a ship through the waters of the ocean. That was his dream, his burning ambition, and it was to lead to the formation of a company which has borne his name proudly through the years; and to the building of many notable ships all of which would, in their own way, make a considerable mark in the maritime world. Some of these vessels would become greater beings than mere forms of transport. They would become household names throughout the world. The 81,237 ton marvel *Queen Mary* was one such ship.

It was Samuel Cunard who believed implicitly in the future of steam in the face of general hostility, suspicion and virtual scorn, not only in his own country, but also in Britain. His faith, and his ability to persuade a handful of others, was to give Britain a dominating lead in the North Atlantic traffic and was, stage by stage, to lead to the building of bigger and faster vessels until the day dawned when the *Queen Mary* – the "inevitable ship" – had to be built. It was merely a question of natural succession, following the lines laid down by Cunard's policy, and the natural logical conclusion of his early faith.

This small, grey-haired man saw, in the days when mail services were irregular, that with steamships it would be possible to maintain a regular, steady service across the Atlantic. He saw that a guaranteed, regular timetable could be maintained with this type of ship propulsion, which would free ships from their utter dependence on wind and sea.

This was a revolutionary idea in those days; as startling as the first thought that it might be possible to put a man on the Moon. This would usher in the dawn of the steamship era, as sensational a change as we have witnessed so recently in our own times, with the beginnings of the computer age.

Cunard's ancestors had emigrated from Wales in the middle of the seventeenth century to Philadelphia and after the War of Independence his father, Abraham, had moved to Halifax, Nova Scotia. There, in the engineer's department of a lumber yard, Samuel had begun his career.

But before he was twenty-one he had left to help to form the firm of Abraham Cunard and Son, ship merchants.

By the time he was twenty-seven he had secured a contract from the British Government for the carrying of mails between Halifax, Newfoundland, Boston and Bermuda, a contract he fulfilled to the satisfaction of the Admiralty, in those days responsible for mail services. He had already demonstrated his faith in steam in a practical manner: his name headed the list of 144 people who subscribed the £16,000 to build the *Royal William*, a 160 ft vessel, with Birmingham-built engines capable of developing 200 hp to assist her sails. She had originally been engaged in trade between Quebec and Halifax, but was not a financial success. In 1838 she was sent to England, and sailed on August 4 from Quebec, arriving at Gravesend on September 9. She actually made the voyage from Pictou, Nova Scotia, where she coaled, to Cowes in seventeen days – a day faster than the speediest American sailing ship.

It was not the passenger trade which was to give Cunard his first opportunity to put his dream into actual practice. It was the carrying of mails. Up to this time they were transported in Government sailing ships and were very irregular. As early as 1830 Cunard had drawn up his own plans, which would enable the mails to be carried regularly in steamships. But the British Government at that time was not interested or convinced by the reliability of steam propulsion. It preferred to wait until some definite proof could convince it of its suitability for ships to carry mail.

So it was not until 1838 that it invited tenders for a regular service of steam-packets to carry the mails across the North Atlantic. But no one was very interested, certainly not in England. Cunard, however, realized immediately that here was his chance; this was his one hope to put his ideas into operation.

If none of the British financiers or shippers were interested, neither were they in America or Canada. In vain Cunard tried to interest people in both Boston and Halifax, where he was well known for his business sense and ability. But he failed. His one hope was to go to the fountain head. So he sailed for England, bringing with him a letter to James Melvill, Secretary to the East India Company, whose agent he was, and who were themselves interested in steam service out to the East.

He reached London, but again all those to whom he spoke were sceptical, hesitant, reluctant to put their money into his project. All his burning faith in the scheme could not convince them. He travelled north to Glasgow, taking with him a letter of introduction to Robert Napier, then a well-known marine engineer. He introduced him to George Burns, of the firm of J and G Burns. This Scotsman listened attentively, but was not at all convinced. He suggested he meet David MacIver, another shipping man, the following day for dinner. The experience of these men was only in coastal and short journeys across the Irish Channel.

This must indeed have been a historic dinner party. For there, over the table, Cunard, usually silent and not given much to talking, so convinced these two hard-headed Scottish shipping men that they agreed to cooperate with him. The company, the British and North American Royal Mail Steam Packet Company, was launched with a capital of £270,000 which was subscribed in two days by thirty-three men, Burns Bros taking 21 shares, MacIver Bros 16 and Cunard 135. With his plans formulated and his backing assured, Cunard put in his tender for the regular mail service between Liverpool, Halifax and Boston for a yearly sum of £60,000. His reputation as a mail carrier was known to the Admiralty from his earlier success on the other side of the Atlantic. His tender was accepted, and immediately he placed an order for the first of three ships which would be needed to maintain a fortnightly service between the ports; the cost of the three ships would total £96,000.

The first ship was the *Britannia*, 207 feet long, 34 feet wide, and of 1154 tons, a paddle steamer, to be built at Port Glasgow. Her engines were built by Napier and consisted of two cylinder engines of the side-lever type with a horsepower of up to 740, and an average speed of nine knots on a coal consumption of 38 tons a day. She had a cargo-carrying capacity of 250 tons, and passenger accommodation for 115.

She was launched on February 5, 1840. On July 4 of that year she sailed from Liverpool, and reached Boston in 14 days, 8 hours, at an average speed of 8 knots, and returned in 10 days at an average speed of 10.5 knots. Cunard himself travelled on the maiden voyage and received a tumultuous welcome.

Thus was born the first regular steamship service across the North Atlantic, and thus was the crown of prestige wrested from America, who even in the face of this challenge still pinned their faith in ships with sails. Later it was discovered that four ships would be required to maintain the two-voyages-a-month service, and the subsidy was increased to £81,000.

Eventually, of course, the Americans realized the dilemma they were in and that something would have to be done to meet this English competition. In 1849 Congress approached E K Collins, who had been king of the sailing-ship world, and offered him an agreement providing for a round twenty voyages annually, ordering him to build five steamships, each subsidized at the rate of £5,000 a voyage, which would bring him annually £100,000.

The battle was on – the battle for bigger, better and faster steamships, coupled naturally with safety factors. This battle was to continue well into the next century – equally fiercely, equally closely, not only between Britain and America, but with Germany, Italy and France all joining in, and the lead being seized first by one country and then by another. In 1846, when the original mail contract expired, the British Government announced its intention of renewing it on a more extended scale. A resolution was moved in the House of Commons favouring the proposal of the Great Western Steamship Company to undertake the service. But, among other things, they drew the line at sailing during the winter months, while Cunard offered a year-round service.

A committee of the House of Commons was set up to inquire into the relative offers, and Cunard obtained the contract. In the years that followed there was fought what was, at first, essentially, a Cunard–Collins battle, until, by the middle of the century Collins's steamships were able to win the prize for which America was clamouring, as a matter of prestige, by crossing regularly at twelve hours or ten hours faster than Cunard ships. But by 1858 the Collins Line had ceased operations.

For the remaining forty-odd years of that century more and more shipping companies, seeing the reward for speed, entered the fray. Ships of the Inman Line, the White Star Line, the American Guion Line, in turn all held that tantalizing record for the fastest crossing. And, to some extent unnoticed, quietly and efficiently, Germany was beginning to enter the race, though at first concentrating on the emigrant trade rather than that of first-class luxury traffic.

For a time too, Cunard dropped out of the race themselves. They stood on the sidelines, so to speak, and watched the developments that were taking place in marine design and marine engineering before taking the plunge and once more challenging the opposition. They contented themselves for this period with maintaining a steady second-class traffic. The company then underwent reorganization and was reformed with new capital of £2 million. Two years later Cunard became a public company.

The company built some speedy vessels, crack ships of their day – the *Umbria, Etruria* and *Oregon* – and in 1884 came back into the picture with a crossing at a speed of 18.14 knots. Five years later the Inman and International *City of Paris* crossed at more than 20 knots, and by 1894 the Cunard *Lucania* was speeding at an average speed of 22 knots from Sandy Hook to Queenstown (now Cobh), making the crossing in 5 days, 8 hours and 38 minutes.

But by the turn of the century the prize had slipped out of the hands of both Britain and America. Germany came into the picture with a vengeance. In 1897 NordDeutscher Lloyd's *Kaiser Wilhelm der Grosse*, 14,000 tons, crossed at an average speed of 21.39 knots on her maiden voyage and on her third round trip pushed her speed to 22.35 knots. One interesting clause in her building contract was that if she failed to maintain her guaranteed speed on her maiden voyage the company had the right to return her to the builders.

In 1900 the Hamburg-America Line's *Deutschland*, 16,500 tons, was averaging 24.37 knots. It is indicative too of the trends in passenger traffic that in 1898 North German Lloyd carried 24 per cent of all passengers landed at New York.

At the same time there was another threat to Cunard, this time from America. In 1902 John Pierpont Morgan organized his International Mercantile Marine, which brought together a number of British and other companies in one gigantic combine owning 120 liners. This plan was aimed at sweeping Cunard off the Atlantic.

The combine did not actually own the White Star ships but was the main shareholder. The sale of the shares was only permitted on the provision that the company's fleet should remain under British flag and management with British officers and crew unless the British Government agreed to a transfer to the American flag. Owing to over-capitalization, the combine was not too successful at first financially, but after a reorganization prospered. Faced with the determined German challenge and then the opposition from the IMM, Cunard was in a difficult situation.

In 1885 the Admiralty had set up a committee to consider the principles on which subsidies were being made to British companies for the retention of merchant ships as armed cruisers or troopships in wartime. The object was to secure greater horsepower and greater speed, and also to ensure that ships, once subsidized in this way, could not be resold to a foreign power without Government consent.

As a result of the report that was drawn up, the Admiralty entered into a contract in 1903 with Cunard to build two new ships capable of maintaining a minimum speed of not less than 24 knots in moderate weather. The company was to receive a subsidy of £150,000 a year and a loan of £2,500,000 at 2.75% interest towards the building costs, the assets of the line to be security, and repayment to be made over twenty instalments.

Cunard agreed to remain a purely British concern and not permit the ownership to be in the hands of nor the vessels of the company to be held by anyone other than British subjects. This contract was the direct result of the attempt by the Morgan combine to corner the North Atlantic trade. At the same time a new mail contract was negotiated for £68,000 a year.

This was Cunard's answer to the German challenge, and was indicative of its determination to regain the speed record and to keep it.

The orders were placed – one on the Clyde and one on the Tyne – for two ships which were to become household names, *Lusitania* and *Mauretania*. On her trials the *Mauretania* averaged 26.04 knots, and later over the measured mile reached 26.75 knots. She very quickly scooped up the record.

A few years later the Germans began to prepare yet another challenge. They built monster ships. The fabulous *Imperator* was built in Hamburg by the Vulkan Shipyard and launched in 1912, 52,117 gross tons and 919 ft long. The *Vaterland*, 54,282 gross tons and 950 ft long would follow soon after. The third giant was the *Bismarck*, still unfinished at the outbreak of World War I, 56,551 gross tons and 915 ft long. Both the *Vaterland* and the *Bismarck* were constructed by Blohm and Voss, also of Hamburg. All three of these ships were conceived and designed by the brilliant visionary Albert Ballin.

At the end of the War the competitors for the transatlantic trade stood back, licked their wounds, and took stock. A tremendous amount of tonnage had been sunk; Germany had been defeated, a Germany which just prior to the outbreak of war had built so many splendid liners for that trade. So the victorious Allies claimed those ships as part of the reparation payments. The *Imperator* and the *Bismarck* would now be owned jointly by the Cunard and White Star Companies who, despite the joint ownership, would each assume responsibility for just one of the ships. Accordingly they were re-registered and renamed the *Berengaria*, managed by Cunard, and the *Majestic*, managed by White Star. In fact, the *Imperator* was assigned to Cunard in direct compensation for the appalling loss of the *Lusitania* which had been torpedoed in 1915. The Americans retained the *Vaterland* and renamed her the *Leviathan*.

Shortly after the war, Cunard announced its decision to move its express traffic from Liverpool to Southampton. This was largely due to the steadily increasing volume of European emmigrant traffic. Eliminating the long overland journey north to Liverpool was a wise move. The new express service from Southampton was begun in 1919 with the *Aquitania*, which the company had built in 1914.

The westbound emigration from Europe to the United States and Canada was the business on which the North Atlantic lines were built up, especially the German companies. Before World War I the numbers varied between 500,000 and 1,000,000 per year. But in 1923, with the introduction of the quota system by America, the traffic was virtually finished. In 1913 there were 1,141,093 emigrants, but in 1931 this had dropped to 94,086, causing a loss in revenue to the shipping companies of some £7 million.

During the next seven years, Cunard replaced a number of its smaller ships, but no replacement was built for the express service, which was then being operated by the *Mauretania* (1907), the *Aquitania* (1914) and the *Berengaria* (1913).

It was soon quite clear that the Allied companies had prepared for themselves a formidable challenge. While they were operating the express service with old ships they had left the field clear for Germany to build up her passenger fleet from the very beginning in an era of new developments. Thus their rivals were able to take advantage of all the scientific progress which had been made during and after the war. In fact, in that very year, 1926, when Cunard was beginning its first tentative examination into the design of a new ship and discussing the problems, the Germans were actually ordering two new liners, the keels of which were laid down the following year.

Launched on consecutive days, one in Hamburg and the other in Bremen in 1928, the two liners completely swept the Atlantic and left

shipping men on both sides agasp in amazement at their performance –
the *Bremen* and the *Europa*.

In 1929 the 51,656 ton *Bremen*, 899 ft long, with a speed of 27.83
knots and looking and travelling like a destroyer with superb comfort,
crossed from Cherbourg to the Ambrose Light Tower, New York in 4
days, 17 hours, 42 minutes and turned around and came back in 4 days,
14 hours, 30 minutes at a speed of nearly 27.91 knots. The old
Mauretania's record, held so proudly and decorously for twenty years,
was gone, smashed completely. She, now oil burning, did make one
gallant effort to win the honours back and westbound on one day steamed
687 miles – equal to the best day's run of her German rival – and on the
eastbound voyage came within 3 hours of her time. The following year,
the *Europa*, delayed in her building by a fire, clipped 36 minutes off the
Bremen's time.

The effect of the competition of the new German ships can be readily
seen: in 1928 the British lines carried 31% of passengers, freight and
mail, earning £11,461,000, while Germany carried 17% at £6,319,463.
The total traffic of all countries was £36,912,000.

By 1931 Britain's share of the trade had dropped to 22.25%, worth
£5,562,000, while Germany's had risen to 25.75%, earning £6,463,093.
The total earnings had dropped to £25,050,327.

In 1926 Britain carried 52.5% of the first-class traffic and 50% of
other classes. Five years later she was carrying only 33.25% and 38.25%.
Germany, on the other hand, was carrying 28.75%, compared with 9.25%
first-class passengers, and 20.5%, compared with 11.75% of other classes.

If there is any doubt that the trend of the trade was to the newer and
faster express vehicles, the following table shows it. The figures are for
all passengers carried.

Ship	1928	1929	1930	1931
Berengaria	37,062	36,853	23,472	13,408
Aquitania	28,033	29,363	27,895	21,992
Mauretania	16,922	18,842	15,806	12,560
Bremen	–	24,960	49,759	42,157
Europa	–	–	38,123	43,291

The Cunard company first thought about its new liner in 1926. Sir
Thomas (later Lord) Royden and Sir Aubrey Brocklebank, chairman of
the Technical Committee, began to be actively engaged with the
management and the technical superintendents in the planning of the
new ship. Indeed, Cunard certainly had to begin to think of finding
some answer to the challenges which were beginning to develop and
come to fruition in the next few years.

The Compagnie Générale Transatlantique brought out the *Île de France*
in 1926, and it was known that they were planning a super liner. Italy put

the largest motor ship in the world, the *Augustus*, into service, as well as the steamers *Rex* and the *Conte di Savoia*. America was planning two new ships, and the White Star Line laid down a new liner at Belfast.

This was to be the *Oceanic*, whose keel was laid at Harland and Wolff's yard in 1928. She was to be 1000 feet long, a monster diesel liner, whose engines would develop 200,000 shp and, with four propellers, would drive her through the seas at an average speed of 30 knots. Because of the world depression, construction work had not gone very far when it was suspended. Eventually some of the steel was used in the building of another ship for the same line.

In the meantime the IMM planned to sell all its British holdings, particularly the White Star Line. In 1926 a syndicate headed by Furness Withy and Co was in the market for the purchase, but the deal fell through. Towards the end of the World War I, the Royal Mail Steam Packet Company had offered to buy the White Star Line, but President Wilson had banned the sale for reasons of state.

Eventually it was bought by the Kylsant Group, and in 1927 a new company was floated to finance the purchase with a capital of £9 million, of which 5 million 6.5% preference shares, guaranteed by the Royal Mail Steam Packet Company, were issued at once and immediately oversubscribed. Four million pounds worth of ordinary capital was subscribed at par by the Royal Mail and its associates.

So it was by 1926 that Cunard had begun the design stage of its new ship. She would follow the natural progression of developments then taking place in marine engineering and in naval architecture.

Great steps forward had been made in both these fields. Cunard was quick to realize that there were possibilities in these developments in relation to transatlantic services. They meant that for the first time two ships could be built which would maintain a weekly express service between Southampton and New York, doing the work done previously by three ships.

So far, these were mere ideas, vague and uncorrelated. They had to be translated from the thoughts of the directors through the skill of the designers to a complete ship design; practical and economic. This was to be the problem for the next four years. No one quite knew what ultimate size the ships would be, nor how fast they would be. But whatever the final result, they would be the ships to meet the demands of the two-ship service, both in size and speed. They would, in fact, be the inevitable ships.

2

No. 534

During the next two years those planners, who had begun by drawing a line on a piece of paper, worked continuously on the design project. They worked in secret, although from time to time there were rumours that Cunard was planning something revolutionary in the way of ship design. At an extraordinary general meeting, held on October 17, 1927, Sir Thomas Royden, the chairman, said the company "must be prepared for further developments as circumstances demand." The meeting was called to move an increase in the capital of the company to £8,100,000 by the creation of 1,100,000 new ordinary £1 shares.

He said in the course of his speech: "It cannot be said that the ordinary capital of the company, even with the proposed addition, is unduly high in relation to the value of the tonnage it owns. As an illustration of this, I might point out that the company's ordinary capital, now issued, does not represent even the combined cost of one new express steamer, one of the 600ft class, and of one of the 520ft class."

The first stage in designing a new ship consists of the management supplying the naval architect with the basic requirements. These depend on the service, which influences the type and number of rooms and public rooms; and the schedule it is desired to maintain, which influences the proposed speed and machinery.

From this broad picture the naval architect's department works out the approximate main dimensions, the approximate weight, stability, and the approximate power with the superintendent engineer, and sketches out the general lay out. This is, apart from cooperation with the engineers, a naval architect's problem, and there is very little consultation with other departments. A sketch design is submitted to the management, and building cost is worked out against the ship's earning capacity. During the first half of this century it was mainly a trial-and-error stage, based on calculations, estimates worked out on the basis of the management's requirements and the architect's experience, knowledge and skill. Now, as we race through the 1990s, the computer age is well upon us; design factors are more clearly defined and performance results infinitely more predictable. However, during the 1930s it was not unusual for four or five designs to be worked out before the ship could become an economic possibility.

The trend of development in the design of Atlantic liners since the coming of steam had been towards larger and faster ships; the larger ship being more comfortable due to its being less affected by the elements, while the increased speed shortened the trip. Experience had shown that on occasions, after being converted to oil burning, these ships could turn round in eighteen hours in port. If, therefore, it was reasoned, the passage could be reduced to five days it might be possible for two ships on a fortnightly turn-round to do the work that three vessels had been doing.

The distance to be covered in a year would be about 145,000 nautical miles. So it was clear that the ship should be fast, strongly built to face North Atlantic weather, have powerful and reliable machinery, with a sufficient reserve of power to make up any lost time through bad weather, and would have to run without any major repairs for eleven months of the year. Furthermore, reliable boilers would have to be chosen, as there would be no opportunity for boiler-cleaning in port.

A schedule was worked out which gave the following results:

Westward Passage

Leave	*Time*	*Arrive*	*Time*
Southampton	Wednesday noon		
Cherbourg	Wednesday 6pm		
		Ambrose Channel	
		Light Vessel	Monday 6am
		New York	Monday 9am

Number of hours in New York – 50
Steaming time from Cherbourg to Ambrose – 112 hours

Eastward Passage

Leave	*Time*	*Arrive*	*Time*
New York	Wednesday 11am		
Ambrose Channel			
Light Vessel	Wednesday 12.30pm		
		Cherbourg	Monday 9.30am
		Southampton	Monday 3.30pm

Number of hours in New York – 44.5
Steaming time from Ambrose to Cherbourg – 112 hours

The speed required for the 112 hour passage on the various tracks used across the Atlantic according to the season would be between 27.61 and 28.94 knots.

The whole problem of speed with such a ship could be calculated, and this showed that the faster the ship, particularly in the higher speeds, proportionately less voyage time was saved by an increase in speed and at the same time the power required to propel the ship increased rapidly and uneconomically.

An increase of speed from twenty to twenty-two knots on the voyage to New York would save only fifteen hours. To increase the speed from twenty-eight to thirty knots would save four hours and the horsepower required to step up the speed by those two knots would be enormous and probably completely uneconomic.

This table indicates this point:

Speed	Voyage time			Time saved	
Knots	*Days*	*Hrs*	*Mins*	*Hrs*	*Mins*
27	4	18	49		
28	4	14	43	4	6
29	4	10	54	3	49
30	4	7	20	3	34
31	4	4	0	3	20

Mr J Austin, the superintendent engineer, produced a paper for the Technical Committee to consider which outlined some of the problems to be discussed in these early stages.

The decision as to the size of the ship can be arrived at by taking into account the requirements of the service, the capacity of the builder's yards, the facilities for launching, the depth of waterways from the builder's yard to the open sea, the facilities for docking and undocking at terminal ports of call, and the facilities for dry docking. It is probable that a thousand-foot ship with calls at Plymouth would not be possible. The speed of the ship depends upon the time in which it is desired to make a passage between Southampton and New York and Southampton. At the present the following are the average times and speeds for the passages out and home and the total fuel consumption for each of the three express steamers:

	Ship	Distance (*knots*)	Hours steaming	Speed (*knots*)	Consumption Port to Port (*tons*)
OUT	*Mauretania*	3,257	137.95	23.62	3,872
	Aquitania	3,250	151.03	21.50	4,058
	Berengaria	3,244	146.58	22.12	5,099
IN	*Mauretania*	3,297	133.88	24.62	4,087
	Aquitania	3,296	145.75	22.62	4,052
	Berengaria	3,294	143.75	22.90	5,059

In addition to these actual steaming times given above, an allowance of four hours should be added for embarkation and disembarkation of passengers and baggage at Cherbourg.

Assuming the proposed dimensions of the ship should be:
      length   1000 ft
      breadth   110 ft
      draught   38 ft
the fuel consumption for a speed of 22.75 knots would be 7,720 tons, 27.5 knots would be 11,550 tons.

He enumerated fourteen different types of machinery which could possibly be used for propelling the liner. These ranged from direct-drive turbines with Scotch boilers to the new diesel-direct drive. There were three forms of fuel to be considered: coal, oil, or pulverized coal. He pointed out, as a warning, that if oil were adopted as the best type of fuel, then they "would always have to bear in mind the possibility of oil shortages," and suggested that the ship might be generally arranged so that in the case of such an emergency it would be possible to convert her to coal burning. He set out his own views on the types of machinery which were worth serious consideration. Some he dismissed as being totally unsuitable or unreliable.

Quietness of running and the fact that the vessel had to include all the amenities of a first-class hotel, as well as being propelled across the Atlantic at high speeds, were so essential that the greatest care had to be taken in the design and manufacture in order to eliminate noise and vibration.

He thought that diesel engines were not developed enough to justify their adoption for the horsepower required in a ship of this type. Certainly, in the early part of this century this type of engine had not been developed to anywhere near the same standard of efficiency that exists today. A single-reduction, geared turbine with high-pressure water-tube boilers should be considered, "as it had been used by the battleship *Hood*." He himself favoured the same machinery with Scotch boilers. The turbo-electric system might be given serious consideration, but he warned that "marine engineering establishments in this country will not favour this machinery, as their works are laid out for the manufacture of steam and diesel machinery."

These factors all contributed to the particulars which the design team needed, though they did not at this stage necessarily need such detail about machinery. Eventually the naval architects worked out that the main dimensions would be 1018 ft overall length (965 ft between perpendiculars), 118 ft moulded breadth, and a gross tonnage of approximately 80,000 tons, designed for an average sea speed of 28.5 knots.

From these discussions and the sketch plan the design team moved to the final stage, taking the project up to the placing of the building contract. During this stage the builders were called in for in-depth consultation. The length of time needed for these discussions was expected to be between eighteen months and two years. Here the closest collaboration between all departments and the naval architect was required. A study was made of the detailed ship layout, and it was here that the architect had to be something of a skilled diplomatist. To this day, it is too easy for each operating department – deck, engine-room, and catering – to think only in terms of its own requirements and not consider the ship as a whole. It is not uncommon for members of a ship's department to consider, albeit silently, that their particular area is the most important on the ship. The engineers realize that the ship cannot move through the water without their services; the passengers cannot eat without the experience of the chefs or the waiters; neither ship nor passengers would have any idea where they were going were it not for the skill of the navigator and, in any case, what would the poor passenger do to pass the time without any entertainment?

It was at this stage also that crew numbers, machinery spaces, kitchen arrangements, bedrooms, public rooms, storerooms, cargo-handling, baggage-handling, offices, shops, the hospital, mooring arrangements, and the hundred and one other aspects of the necessities of this massive ship were worked out.

The design now became the combined effort of several departments working closely together with the naval architect holding the balance. At the same time his own department were making a more accurate estimate of weight, centre of gravity, stability, and so on. It was during this stage that the first experimental tank tests took place.

From these tests a more accurate power estimate could be reached. When this had been calculated consideration was given to the method by which this power could be generated and applied to the actual ship.

Various ideas were discussed and drawings made for the board to see. The directors considered drawings for both a three-class and a four-class ship. At one time there was a suggestion of making her all one class; a 'hotel liner', with passengers paying a different rate according to the location of their cabin but all using the same public rooms. It was felt that in this manner many more passengers could be carried, as there would be no need for so many public rooms. This has, in fact, been the inevitable result of natural shipboard social evolution on *Queen Elizabeth 2*. For although this younger vessel was initially conceived as a multi-class ship, nowadays the only distinction in "class" is in cabin and restaurant allocation.

The designers produced plans for a number of ships, varying in size and specification, but all within the broad terms laid down by the directors. All the time they had to bear in mind the necessity for hull strength. While the hull had to be strong enough to withstand the storms and gales of winter in the North Atlantic, at the same time it had to be 'flexible'. For a ship must 'bend' with the waves, it must have a certain amount of 'give' in it, otherwise it would be most uncomfortable to travel in. Imagine a ship poised on the crest of a wave of a length equal to her own length, or alternatively supported at her ends by two such waves, the trough being in the middle of her length. This produces what is known as "the maximum hogging and sagging moment" likely to be met.

Prior to the advent of computers, this was by no means easy to calculate. The length of a wave is not an easy thing to measure with any accuracy, and there is no precise line of demarcation between waves and swell. When the Cunard design team was at work it was assumed that average waves did not exceed 600 ft in length with 800 ft as the maximum, and that swell might extend up to a mile. But shortly after they had begun work reports were received of waves up to 1050 ft in length and 50 ft high in the North Atlantic.

These men were pioneers, exploring far beyond the limits of known human knowledge in ship design. Furthermore, the weights and stresses went far beyond the normal range of standard tables laid down for their guidance. It is a comparatively 'easy' matter to design a ship that is a mass of materials; but these men were creating a ship with a soul. They wanted a ship that was sea-kindly, smooth-sailing, gracious and comfortable, yet capable of withstanding storms and able to maintain a clock-like schedule year-round on the hazardous North Atlantic. One of the designers said, "You could, of course, spend the whole of your life working out the stresses alone, and even then you might not get the ideal solution. Our whole aim was structural safety, which meant strength while at the same time not making the hull to heavy. In this we were greatly aided by the new steel with a high yield point, which had recently come out and which meant in theory we could reduce the main scantlings. But, always aiming at strength with safety, we did not cut them down by anything like the amount we could have done. We erred on the side of safety even if it meant having a little more weight than was, on paper, necessary."

It was a condition of these experiments that the hull form should be one which would enable the liner to maintain the required average speed in rough weather, with comfortable conditions for passengers, even if it were not the most efficient form in smooth weather.

In due course the most suitable hull form was chosen, and it was discovered that a shaft horsepower of 158,000 would be ample for the service speed. But it had been decided that it was necessary to allow ample margin to make up time lost on the voyage through fog or rough weather. It was also decided to have four outward-turning propellers.

These would be driven by four separate sets of turbines, with each set capable of being operated independently ahead or astern. This independent operation had not been practical with the direct-turbine drive ship. It was anticipated that this would be invaluable in manoeuvring a ship of this size.

Two of the units in the forward engine-room drove the outer propellers and the two in the after engine-room drove the inner propellers. The design of the machinery and boiler installation was carried out in John Brown's works at Clydebank.

The layout of the propelling machinery is one of the main factors in determining the design of a ship. It must be so arranged as to exclude all noise, smell and heat from passenger accommodation and from public rooms, which are directly above. It must also meet the requirements of the watertight subdivisions of the ship. Across the ship the space in the boiler-rooms was limited by the double skin provided as a protection against collision. These structural features, with the disposition and size of the main machinery, auxiliary machinery and boiler-compartments, together with spaces required for public rooms, practically dictated that the ship should have three funnels. The positioning of the funnel hatches and the engines was crucial and had to be arranged in conjunction with the layout of the passenger accommodation, whilst all the time considering the outward appearance of the ship.

Saturdays and Sundays meant nothing to the designers. Work went on all the time. Solutions came at odd moments. One particular designer said that he was stuck for an answer on how to deal with a space some four inches square on the drawing. "Try as I might I could not get the answer. That night I went for a long walk and puzzled over it unsuccessfully. I went to bed and slept.

"Suddenly in the middle of the night I saw it all in front of my eyes as clearly as if it were drawn on a piece of paper. I always emptied my jacket pockets on to my bedside table when retiring. I must have reached out and found a pencil and the back of an envelope. I hurriedly copied the solution down and fell asleep again.

"In the morning I went to the office as usual, not remembering anything of this. Once again I puzzled over the problem and then I put my hand in my pocket and found the envelope with the answer. I had no recollection of drawing it at all."

The design of the main dining room caused much thought and consideration. Such points were raised as whether the room should be round or square? How many people should it seat? How were they to be seated? Should the tables be round or square? The catering department was asked for its views on accessibility and what would provide the best arrangement for service. Three model seating plans were drawn up.

Eventually, after two years of planning, gradually, slowly, the design was perfected, and with the cooperation of the builders reached a stage where the company felt it could place the shipbuilding order. Shortly after this, when they were ready to go ahead, the directors were appalled to learn that the ship, as planned, would cost £6,500,000. The plan was therefore shelved until such time as shipbuilding costs had dropped and made it much more of an economic possibility. But planning work continued at Liverpool. The design team continued with their detailed drawings.

The directors then decided to call a conference of engineers to discuss the proposed engines of the ship. On Thursday, December 6, 1928, behind carefully guarded doors on the fifth floor of the headquarters of the company, ten men, all sworn to secrecy, met.

The Cunard experts had studied all the published information on every type and design of engine; these men had all their own experience, from both shipyard and seagoing, to draw on. But now the company chiefs paused and wondered if they really had got all the latest information. Perhaps, they felt, if only they could ask the opinion of the leading experts in the country, it might put their minds at rest. There was a precedent for this, as the experts of the day had been called in when the machinery for the *Mauretania* and *Lusitania* had been under consideration.

As Sir Aubrey Brocklebank, who was the company director virtually responsible for the ship at that time, put it to the meeting, "We have been assailed with lurking doubts that perhaps we are a beat behind the times with our machinery." Even so, some of the directors opposed the conference on the grounds that information might be given to a rival, especially, as Sir Aubrey put it, "We have only one ship to be scrambled for." He had his way because, "given a real engineering problem I knew engineers well enough to be sure they would come from the ends of the earth to give their best advice."

He said that the original design for the engines was for single-reduction, geared turbines, the brainchild of Sir Charles Parsons, in which a reduction gear box is placed between the turbine and the propeller shaft for the purpose of allowing both the turbines and the propeller to run at speeds of revolution for maximum efficiency; high speeds of revolution being required for turbine efficiency and low speeds for propeller efficiency.

But in recent years there had been advances made in the design of diesel-electric and turbo-electric engines. The Americans were particularly interested in diesels, and were making a lot of use of them.

Sir Aubrey said that the company wondered whether, perhaps, one of those types of engines would give the company better results. One of their main considerations, naturally, was for fuel economy – a vital factor in liner operation. A saving of 0.1 lb of fuel per shp would mean a saving of £56,000 a year on the fuel bill. As Sir Aubrey said, "I know that Mr Austin, the superintendent engineer, is apprehensive that in future years someone may round on him for burning more fuel when a more heroic policy might have reduced consumption."

Then, rather like a university professor setting a group of students a theorem or equation to solve, he stated the known facts. He pointed out that really the problem resolved itself into "whether we adopt single-reduction, geared turbines, diesel-electric drive, or turbo-electric machinery."

He said that they were anxious not to have to fit too much solid, permanent ballast and therefore the question of stability in relation to the weight of the engines and boilers and the placing of them in the ship was extremely important. The main factors to be taken into consideration, in possible order of importance, were:

reliability;

ability to make successive trips for long periods with only thirty-six hours in port;

simplicity, ease, and reliability in manoeuvring;

freedom from noise and vibration;

cost of upkeep;

cost of fuel.

He himself favoured the single-reduction, geared turbine with Scotch boilers because of their proved reliability, and he doubted whether water-tube boilers could be efficiently maintained with only thirty-six hours in port. Diesels, he said, frightened him.

"We have also got to consider a possible accident, and we are far more concerned in keeping the ship afloat than in the most elaborate systems of [life]boats; and we feel that the inherent stability coupled with the maximum subdivision gives us a far better chance of keeping her upright so that one side is not thrown out of action through a bad list. The new German ships [*Bremen* and *Europa*] have the elaborate-boat solution. We prefer to concentrate on the ship.

"In conclusion, gentlemen, it should always be borne in mind that the continued ability to arrive at the other end and at the right time is the most important factor of all."

Then there was silence in the room as they pondered on these words; each thinking, calculating in his mind, arranging his ideas on this fascinating engineering problem.

There was little discussion on the actual type of engines to be fitted into the ship. Everyone agreed that the only suitable type was single-reduction, geared turbine. It was decided to fit the vessel with four Parsons impulse/reaction single geared turbine sets, driving four screws. Each turbine set consisted of one high-pressure, two intermediate and one low-pressure turbine arranged in series and coupled through gears to its respective propeller. There would be two engine rooms, each of which would house two of the turbine sets. The two in the forward room would drive the outside screws, whilst those in the after area were linked to the inboard propellers. Each turbine set was designed to produce 39,500 shaft horsepower to each propeller, the total power amounting to 158,000 shp at a service speed of 29 knots.

The conference was then asked by Sir Aubrey to consider the type of boilers which should be fitted. Here again he explained the main background against which the situation should be considered. The essential requirements were reliability; cost of upkeep and cleaning; fuel consumption; effect of heat through the decks on both passenger and crew accommodation; expectation of life; the ability to carry out the necessary cleaning and repairs in thirty-six hours between voyages over a long period.

Very soon it was clear that the opinion of these experts differed very strongly from the views of the company and its engineers. The company was in favour of Scotch boilers. Mr McL Paterson, the naval architect, went so far as to challenge the conference by saying that if water-tube boilers were installed, the whole design of the ship would have to be scrapped and started over again. He said that with water-tube boilers there would be a loss of weight in the bottom of the ship which would affect the whole stability. It was claimed generally that Scotch boilers could run for six months without being cleaned, and this was making a strong impression on the company.

Admiral Skelton pointed out that the Navy had run water-tube boilers in a ship for thirteen years without any trouble. The meeting eventually decided to ask the advice of Sir Charles Parsons, who had been unable to attend.

On January 11, 1929, another meeting was held in Liverpool, and Sir Charles attended. It was felt that Scotch boilers with their slightly lower efficiency but much greater reliability would be "the most suitable within the conditions laid down by the company."

If water-tube boilers were fitted their much smaller weight, as compared with Scotch boilers, would bring about complications. In order to get the required stability, it would be necessary to add very considerably to the beam of the ship, with the result that the ship would then be too wide for any of the existing dry docks at Southampton, New York, or Boston.

By July 1929 a difference of opinion had developed between expert advisers as to the type of boiler to be used. Recent developments, which were supported by the company's experience with the *Berengaria*'s behaviour under new conditions of water-softening, indicated that water-tube boilers were the right thing. This was further supported by the fact that all the modern big ships on the North Atlantic had water-tube boilers, including the *Bremen*.

As stability would be largely affected by the question of whether water-tube or Scotch boilers were installed, and as the layout of the proposed ship was based on the assumption that the boilers would be Scotch, this latest change of view threw all the designers back almost to where they had started. So the whole position was gone into again on the basis of water-tube boilers.

Eventually, the liner was fitted with 24 Yarrow type five drum water-tube boilers which would supply steam to the main engines at a pressure of 400 lb per square inch and a temperature of 700°F (370°C). These boilers were placed in four boiler rooms and grouped in three rows, with two boilers per row in each boiler room. The overall system comprised a total of 160,000 water tubes. Furthermore, three auxiliary double-ended "Scotch" boilers were installed in a separate boiler room, producing steam at 250 PSI and at a temperature of 200°F (93°C). This steam was directed to turbo generators which provided power for all the ship's services.

The fuel used to power these boilers was "Bunker C" marine grade oil. The ship would carry around 8,000 tons of this thick, tar-like fuel, stored (or bunkered) in double bottom and wing tanks. Consumption amounted to approximately 1,000 tons per day.

Boiler technology was to progress rapidly throughout the following decades. The *Queen Elizabeth*, launched in 1938, would require only twelve boilers to generate the same amount of power, whilst there were a modest three boilers in *Queen Elizabeth 2*, launched in 1967. All three vessels had similar service speeds.

The naval architects still had to try to solve the problem of stability. The technology available decades later would lead to the extensive use of aluminium in shipbuilding. By using steel for the lower superstructure of the vessel and the lighter aluminium for the upper part, it would become much easier to ensure overall stability and avoid "top heaviness". At the time when the *Queen Mary* was under construction, however, only steel was available.

Oddly enough, it was a new method for waste and sewage disposal which helped considerably in restoring the stability necessary as a result of the weight loss in the bottom of the ship caused by the installation of water-tube boilers.

In view of the height of the ship many new problems arose in the sanitary arrangements. Prior to this design the disposal of waste in ships was by means of two systems, one for sinks, baths and washbasins and the other for sewage. But the Cunard designers felt that it should be feasible to develop a one-pipe system for use in ships. Visits were made to a number of hotels, and details were obtained from America of specifications of various methods used in skyscrapers, offices and hotel blocks. Mr Austin made a careful study of the flow and surge of liquids in a ship in the motion caused by waves at sea. He erected a large scale model of his proposed sewage system at the top of the Cunard Building at Liverpool. By using glass tubes and coloured liquids he was able to convince the directors that it was possible to use a one-pipe system.

The *Queen Mary* was the first ship to have this system installed, and the saving in weight by using copper for the pipes instead of galvanized iron and the reduction in the number of pipes (especially high in the ship), not only cut the cost, but offset very considerably the loss of weight low down caused by the installation of water-tube boilers.

Stability is always a crucial matter in a ship's operation and the consumption of large quantities of fuel and water can seriously affect the vessel's weight displacement. The *Queen Mary* would burn over 1,000 tons of oil per day, drawing it from the vast double-bottom tanks deep down in the liner. Naturally the ship's stability would be affected and so a clever plan of ballast-pumping was worked out. As fuel and water tanks became empty and therefore much lighter, so water ballast was pumped in to maintain the correct weight displacement and so maintain stability.

In the six months from May 1930, when they were informed that they had won the shipbuilding contract, to 1 December 1930, when the contract was actually signed, the designers and shipbuilders of John Brown's worked in the closest cooperation with Mr McL Paterson, the Cunard naval architect, and his team and Mr J Austin, the superintendent engineer. Most of this work, after the calculations, was taken up with tests on models of the proposed liner. These took place in their special testing tank, four hundred feet long and twenty feet wide, in a glass roofed building, in the Clydebank yard.

Sixteen model liners were made true to scale in varying shapes and designs. The tank was equipped with apparatus by which waves of varying length and height and of head-on seas could be accurately reproduced, while overhead towing gear could make the ship travel at any speed the designers wanted. She could be made to sail in a smooth Atlantic sea, or pitch and toss and roll in a heavy swell or at the height of a sixty mph gale with waves the equivalent of sixty feet or more.

Everything and every movement was microscopically recorded by delicate instruments. The bows of several well-known Atlantic liners and other ships were tried on some models to see how they fared or fitted in with the rest of the hull design in creating a "sea-kindly" ship. Sometimes the designers used plain wax models of just the hull; other times they used models with complete superstructure, deck houses, funnels, ventilators and lifeboats in order to get the correct and complete picture of what her behaviour might be. Many times the height and shape and design of the funnels was changed.

Films were taken of the water movement and projected on to screens for the designers to study. In all some 8,000 experimental trips were made up and down the tank by the various "liners", 17 ft long, while every movement was watched, recorded and studied.

Towards the end of the experiments a small electric motor and four propellers were fitted to one of the models, so that she became self-propelled. This enabled her to be set free to roll and pitch among the waves and give the designers a better idea of her behaviour. They were particularly anxious to learn the effect of head on waves and speed on the behaviour of the model; the amount and character of pitching induced by these waves; and the sea-worthiness of the model; and especially in which designs the weather decks were free from water. In all, the models travelled some one thousand miles up and down the testing tank.

At the same time, in a specially designed wind tunnel, a scale model was tested which was fitted with a device which discharged smoke into the funnels and which concurrently drew air into the model ventilating system and then circulated the air.

Air currents of varying strengths and direction were played about the model, and after many trials, alterations and discussions a funnel design was fixed which, it was felt, would eject all the smoke and fumes clear of the ship and the sports and promenade deck.

More than a thousand experiments were conducted on 24 in diameter models of the propellers themselves, apart from the tests made on propellers fitted on models. These were to determine the relative direction of rotating the propellers and the pitch, formation and area. Other tests were carried out to determine the angle of the propeller bossing. Again, while we may bask in the technological wonders of the late twentieth century, when all the above can be calculated in less than a second by fast "thinking" computers, we should regard the architects, scientists and designers of these earlier years with some reverence. The *Queen Mary* was the result not of computer technology, but of human endeavour; of toil and tears; of affection and heartache.

Even when all the calculations and tests had been made Sir Percy Bates was not completely satisfied with them. In July 1930 he asked Lloyd's of London if they would send a team to the yard to check on all the calculations and designs. It was not that he did not trust his designers. This was his policy of safety-first in all and was followed in every stage of the building.

They checked the estimates of weight, centre of gravity of the steelwork, the output of machinery, and everything else. Everything was checked, tested and rechecked. Nothing was left to chance. It took the Lloyd's men several weeks of hard, concentrated effort to audit the design figures, at the end of which they reported to Sir Percy that they could find no fault with them.

So it came about that the shipbuilding contract was signed. The size of the ship as ordered was not dictated in any way by a desire on the part of the company to have a Big Ship for her own sake. It was controlled simply by the necessity, within their plan, to provide sufficient passenger accommodation and propulsion to operate a two-ship weekly express service across the Atlantic. "The *Queen Mary* represented the smallest and slowest ship which could fulfil those conditions and accomplish such a regular service."

3

No Dry Dock – No Ship

Although British shipbuilding had enjoyed a flourishing growth from 1910 to the end of World War I, there was to be a long period of decline in the industry from the early 1920s until 1935. The war had itself demanded the expansion of the big yards and had necessitated the construction of many military ships. Then, following the losses of the War, the world's merchant fleet grew rapidly over a four-year period up until 1923. When it became apparent that, at the end of the War, the necessity for warships would be replaced with a need for a steady supply of merchant vessels, John Brown went to work and secured agreements with no less than five shipping lines: Canadian Pacific Railway (a joint arrangement alongside Harland and Wolff and Fairfield), the Royal Mail Group, the Orient Steam Navigation Company, the Coventry Syndicate and Cunard. Foreseeing a large boom in merchant shipbuilding, the parent company, John Brown and Co, Sheffield, injected a vast capital sum of £316,000 into the facilities at Clydebank.

To begin with, it seemed as though these improvements would reap great benefits. Starting in 1918 the Royal Mail Group placed seven orders with John Brown; Cunard ordered two new large passenger ships, the *Franconia* and the *Alaunia*; and Canadian Pacific ordered the *Montcalm* and the *Montclare*. However, these orders had been placed in the midst of post-wartime inflation and, by the end of 1920, the drop in orders and the effects of Government deflation had started a serious decline. Furthermore, throughout the next two years, the pressing economic situation would render the upkeep of the shipyard's payrolls almost impossible to maintain under conventional methods and so, alongside the suspension of work on the *Franconia* and *Alaunia*, the workers at John Brown's were given the option of redundancy or agreeing to a work sharing system whereby the men would only work on alternate weeks. This was not a successful scheme however, and by 1922 the yard's workforce had dropped by over half, from around 9,000 to a mere

3,653. This drop in employment is more than just a statistic – Clydebank's very life blood flowed as a result of two main industries – John Brown's Shipyard and the Singer Sewing Machine factory. The "creation" of over 5,000 redundancies gave rise to despair and malcontent that ate its way through the small industrial community like some loathsome virus. Post-war optimism had given way to a grey, sullen blanket of despondency.

Through the 1920s orders for navy ships were predictably cut to a minimum. In fact, as a result of the signing of the Washington Naval Treaty of 1921 (under which Britain relinquished much of its naval superiority), orders for no less than four big battle cruisers were cancelled. John Brown's would not launch another British naval ship until 1929. The picture for merchant ships was not much brighter: between 1922 and 1928 John Brown gained only 23 orders for new vessels and on some of these the yard actually sustained severe financial losses. By 1930, John Brown had no new ships on the ways. To make matters worse, the parent company, John Brown Steel, Sheffield was now on the brink of bankruptcy.

It was against this backdrop that on May 28, 1930, the Cunard Company told John Brown's that it had been selected as the builder of the proposed liner. The contract had been won against all odds. At a time when it was virtually impossible to obtain any shipbuilding orders, John Brown's had gone all out and achieved probably the most important shipping order of the decade. Furthermore, Cunard itself had pushed back all boundaries by designing and ordering such a huge ship in the midst of a particularly depressed economic climate. Other leading British shipbuilding companies – Vickers, Armstrong Whitworth, and Harland and Wolff – had submitted tenders but had been rejected. John Brown's had built many Cunard ships, as well as large liners for other companies and many large naval ships. Sir James McNeill of John Brown's said "We got the order because we had the 'know how.'" He was, naturally, reluctant to expose the appalling financial condition that the yard was experiencing at this time. It is fair to say that the securing of this particular contract singularly paved the way for the restoration and survival of both John Brown's of Clydebank and the parent company in Sheffield. Without the contract, the shipyard would almost definitely have had to close. On December 26, 1930, Cunard paid an advance of £250,000 to John Brown's, thus alleviating much of the yard's overdraft and relieving the pressure from the Union Bank.

This order was, however, "subject to certain vital questions," which were still under consideration, being settled before the shipbuilding contract could be signed and orders could be placed for materials.

Six months were to elapse before the contract was actually signed while these problems were ironed out. Sir Percy Bates regarded these problems as an inescapable challenge and a matter of enormous significance to the status and future of the Cunard Line. As he was to say later, "To have failed to make the contract to build No. 534 would have implied a definite surrender, a failure to be true, both to the company's historic past, as well as its undoubted future." Little did he know that in the years that lay ahead, this liner would become far more than a giant piece of shipping hardware. She would ultimately be a symbol of solidarity and triumph over the terrible social, political and economic odds which were soon to be dictated by the worsening depression.

The main problem to be settled concerned the insurance of the liner while she was being built, together with the future full sea risks when she was operational. It was at that time one of the most stupendous transactions ever undertaken by the marine-insurance market.

The normal insurance market would not be able to provide cover for anything like the whole cost. Therefore Cunard approached the British Government and asked if they would help to bear the additional burden.

On July 4 the shipbuilding committee was told that an official letter had been received from the Treasury "approving in principle" the provision of the insurance facilities "for which we have asked." There was also an official minute from the new unemployment panel, presided over by Prime Minister Ramsey MacDonald, to the same effect.

This new unemployment panel had followed the revolt within the Labour Party, expressing dissatisfaction at the way in which the unemployment problem was being handled. MacDonald had moved J H Thomas from his position in charge of unemployment policy and had himself undertaken general supervision of the Government's policy in regard to this problem, which was exercising so much of their thoughts.

The outcome of these negotiations with the Government (during which the representatives of Lloyd's were consulted), was the Cunard (Insurance) Act, passed in December 1930. This was designed so that the Government would assume responsibility for the balance of the risk of the ship's insurance value over and above the amount which the normal market could absorb. The value of the liner for insurance purposes during building was fixed at full price payable by the company, exceeding £4,000,000. The market could only assume £2,700,000 of the risk, which was more than had ever been insured on a similar risk before.

There is hardly any doubt that Cunard were indirectly assisted by the worsening unemployment situation in Britain at the time. To have scrapped No. 534 because of the absence of adequate insurance would have resulted in the loss of several thousand jobs in Clydebank. It would also have resulted in acute embarrassment for a Labour Government which was already under considerable pressure. This was not to be the only occasion when the Government would step in and assist in the building of No. 534.

Many underwriters considered the terms of the policy fixed by the Act as inadequate. The Act fixed the premuim rate at thirty shillings (£1.50) per £100 insured for a period of three years, after which the risk was to be continued if necessary at the rate of sixpence (2.5p) per £100 insured per month. It was also said that many underwriters were annoyed that the Government had only consulted Lloyd's and not the representatives of the Underwriters' Association.

At that time no one imagined that the work of construction would be suspended in December 1931. During the suspension, as the structure was practically all of metal, there was comparatively slight risk. No one knew during that period when work was stopped what the position would be at the end of the three-year period, which expired in December 1933. It was generally believed that the risk would continue at the rate of sixpence per £100 insured per month according to the Act.

After work had been restarted the market was approached to adjust the insurance to allow for the suspension period. Negotiations were carried out by the chairmen of the Institute of London Underwriters and Lloyd's Association of Underwriters in their markets and terms agreed which were communicated to the Government. These amended terms, which were accepted, extended the initial policy to June 30, 1936, at an inclusive additional premium of ten shillings (£0.50) per £100 insured and if construction was not then completed the continuation rate of sixpence per £100 insured per month would operate. The Act did not lay down the terms for full sea-trading risk other than that, subject to certain conditions, it should be "reasonable."

While these negotiations on the question of insurance were taking place *The Times* was to cast doubt on the wisdom of building such a liner. In a leading article on September 22, 1930, it wrote, "Is it wise that Parliament should be asked to lend a hand on a project planned on so colossal a scale that private enterprise could not find the means to carry it through?"

The leader went on to discuss the possibility of disaster to the liner and the effect it would have on the market.

"The real question is whether so large and so elaborate a masterpiece is really needed to convey passengers across the Atlantic. The possibilities of the vessel's being an economic failure have to be faced."

The article doubted the wisdom of "building a ship which strained to the utmost the existing resources of shipbuilding insurance. It is impossible not to admire the Cunard Company's ambition, and analogy is against the crying down *a priori* of any great undertaking, but in this case there appear to be obstacles in the way of a kind never before experienced in shipbuilding."

There were other problems to be decided apart from the ship design and her insurance. Before it could be put into service, when completed, three other inter-related problems had to be solved.

There had to be new and improved docking arrangements, both at Cherbourg and New York, with all the facilities to make them capable of handling the passengers, baggage, and all the refuelling, watering and victualling of such a large ship. Furthermore, there had to be accommodation to dry dock the liner at Southampton for her overhauls. In fact, without these requirements it would be impossible to put such a ship into service. Once the main design of the liner was agreed upon, and while the detailed planning continued, the directors turned their attention to these aspects of the problem.

In May 1930 the company began to make tentative inquiries about the possibility of dry-docking facilities at Southampton. They pointed out to the Southern Railway Company, owners of the docks there, that by 1933 they would need a dock capable of taking a vessel up to 1075ft long; that it would have to be 124ft wide at the entrance, with a minimum depth of 40ft.

Southampton at that time had two dry docks, one on land, so to speak, and the other a floating dry dock; but both too small for such a ship.

Thus began seven months of negotiation. For the railway company did not want to build a new dock at that time. They were already embarked on a vast new reconstruction programme of quays and they did not feel ready to go ahead with what they considered to be a dry dock for just one ship, as all other ships could use the existing facilities.

Sir Percy Bates had said, "Use the unsigned contract as a lever with which to move the Government. Nothing must leak out to the press. We still have a difficult game to play with the Government, and publicity of the wrong kind would seriously hamper us in playing it."

The railway company expressed the view that work could not begin on their projected dry dock for some eight to ten years and it would take between four and five years to finish.

Sir Percy Bates wrote to Sir Herbert Walker, general manager of the railway company:

> The real point which touches us most acutely at the moment is the question of the provision of dry-dock accommodation at Southampton.
>
> I understand from local enquiries that the Southern Railway propose to take four years digging the dock, which, of course, would be too late for our ship. I do not know whether any acceleration of the programme could be arranged, but if it could not it would be necessary to arrange with the Southern Railway to put sections into the existing floating dry dock, a far less satisfactory place for such a big ship than a proper dry dock dug on land.

Sir Percy was determined to get his new dry dock at Southampton and the history of the subsequent negotiations illustrates well his ability to negotiate firmly and determinedly. From time to time he toyed with the idea of moving the terminal port away from Southampton. He even considered the idea of building a completely new port on the South Coast; he deliberately let it be known that it was just possible to squeeze the liner into the Gladstone dry dock at Liverpool. He used all these hints and suggestions, always timing them appropriately. But he knew that from every point of view Southampton must be his ultimate goal.

One night, after a friend of his had dined with Sir Herbert, a report reached Sir Percy that the railways considered the existing dry-dock facilities "quite sufficient for the present requirements of shipping at the port. He [Sir Herbert] pointed out that it practically meant they were being asked to spend some millions of pounds for the docking of one vessel, which might bring in a revenue of £5,000 per year. He seemed to think it was an impracticable proposition." This was just the type of challenge that Sir Percy Bates enjoyed.

Sir Percy made arrangements to meet Sir Herbert personally. This meeting took place on June 18 over the dinner table at the Oriental Club in London. Sir Percy reported back to the company the following day in these terms: "He fully appreciated the great advantage to his port of its becoming the base of the new ship, but wished to be informed just how important the question of dry-dock facilities was to us. I told him it amounted to 'no dry-dock, no ship.'"

Sir Percy, on his return, had drawn up figures showing what he estimated the revenue to the railway company would be:

Tonnage dues

	£
30,000 net tons at 1s 3d*, less 5% 23 voyages	41,000
Dues on cargo at 5s 6d a ton: 1000 tons per round voyage on 23 voyages	6,000
Dues on passengers at 1s 6d per head: 23 round voyages at 850 each way per voyage	2,900
Rail fares to and from London	26,000
Rail costs for carriage of cargo and baggage	1,500
Cross-Channel freight	2,000
Drydocking charges: 2 dockings of 1 week each	88,400

All the time these negotiations, these talks, and this exchange of correspondence was going on the liner design was nearing completion. In fact, the company was almost ready to sign the building contract.

By September Cunard really began to exert pressure. The first salvo in this final assault was fired on September 15 when Sir Percy wrote to Lieutenant Colonel G S Szlumper, assistant general manager of the

* The figures here are expressed in the UK currency used at the time: Pounds (£), Shillings (s) and Pence or Pennies (d). A Pound consisted of twenty shillings, and each shilling was worth twelve pennies. In 1971, the country's currency was changed with the result that a Pound simply consisted of 100 "new" pence (p).

railway company, in these terms: "We are now rapidly reaching a point at which the contract will be signed and it is of vital importance that the position of the graving dock facilities should be cleared up completely."

He was told that there were now three alternatives: the alteration of the floating dock, the alteration of the Trafalgar dry dock and excavation of an entirely new dry dock.

While these negotiations were continuing the company had also been dealing with the Government on the question of obtaining their support and assistance in insuring the new liner. The Government were about to announce to the House of Commons that agreement had been reached and work could begin on the ship. Naturally the Government did not want to be told at the last minute that they could not make the announcement, which they were counting on to alleviate the worsening unemployment situation, particularly at Clydeside.

Continually Cunard pressed the railway company for an assurance, even in general terms, that the dock would be ready by October 1933. But the railway company were not going to be hurried into making any decisions, irrespective of the threat that there would be no new ship unless they gave this assurance. On October 16 they replied to Cunard that the board had considered the matter and "were unable to give the general assurance you seek."

Four days later Sir Percy wrote:

> I regret that on the financial side the expected return does not seem attractive, and in the absence of Government assistance in this connection I wonder whether due allowance has been made for the fact that the new steamer might be expected to make anything from twenty to twenty-two voyages in a year.
>
> I should have thought that fact, with the added advantage to you of her increased size, would made her a very profitable substitute for the *Mauretania*, even without taking into account the very heavy increase in railway fares that such a steamer might be expected to bring to your company.

All the time, Sir Percy had been in close contact on this question with Sir Thomas Bell of John Brown and Company, the builders, with whom by now they were working closely in the design of the ship. Sir Thomas had told him that at any time he was prepared to enter into the fray and see what he could do himself. On November 4 he sent a detailed note to Sir Percy of talks he had had in London.

> Saw Foley [an official of the Board of Trade] and gave him details of amount of wages which would be spent and the number of men who would be employed during the next three years on Clydebank and throughout the country if the Cunard Insurance Bill goes through on Monday.
>
> Told him the Government spokesman would not be in a position to tell House that the contract can be signed and work given out, as the Cunard chairman informed me yesterday that on no account can he consider signing

the contract until he can receive definite assurance that it will be possible to dry dock the proposed ship at Southampton by the end of October 1933.

Foley said he was going to a Treasury conference with the Treasury Grants Committee and other people on the Government grant.

He wanted to know why assistance was required for such a necessary thing as a dry dock in a big shipping place.

I then explained to him that while a dry dock pays a private owner who carries out all the repairs, it cannot pay a dock company who only obtain the dock dues and nothing else, and really it is an absolute essential of a shipping port, it really bleeds the harbour dues and quay dues and is not able to give anything like adequate return for the amount expended.

He said the Treasury withdrew their objection but "the whole matter depended on the railway company not making exorbitant demands in the form of a grant."

I then went to see Szlumper and told him I wanted to see Walker. He asked "Why?"

"Well," I said, "what I have to lay before him is this: from what I can gather, the government have every hope of getting the bill passed on Monday, November 10, sanctioning the Cunard insurance requests, but now that this fresh point has come up of there being doubt about the Railway Company providing the requisite dry-docking facilities the Government will find themselves in a curious position in that they will not be able to assure M.P.s that this much desired work to relieve unemployment can at last be commenced, and that this is due entirely to the Southern Railway not seeing their way to provide the requisite dry-docking facilities."

He said at once, "Oh, if that is the case Sir Herbert will certainly desire to see you."

I saw him at 3.15, and his first question was, "Am I to understand that the Cunard Company have not given out the order for the boat and that they will not do so until they receive assurance from us that we will provide the requisite dry-docking facilities by October 1933?"

I assured him such was the case.

"Now," he said, "I am going to take your word for this and telephone at once." He wanted to know why it was so essential to try and rush him into making an assurance this week.

He gave me some figures that the cost would be in the nature of £1,500,000 depending on depth, while it would cost £800,000 for a new floating dock. He went on, "I am going to have very great difficulty indeed in justifying such expenditure. Is 45ft depth essential?"

To which I replied that provision must certainly be made for docking a damaged ship trimming heavily by either bow or stern.

Sir Percy telegraphed Mr Foley:

As regards dry dock I have not yet got the assurance that I require out of Southern Railway and I should like you to understand that *no dry dock no ship*.

BATES

Things moved quickly after that.

Just before the next board meeting he sent a telegram to Sir Herbert Walker:

> In view of Cunard board meeting to-morrow will appreciate anything you can tell me about Southampton dry dock position.

He received the following reply:

> Your telegram. Glad to say have received offer from Development Grants Committee which will enable me to recommend to my board next week that we proceed.
>
> WALKER

On November 27 Sir Herbert sent another telegram.

> My board at their meeting agreed to provide necessary dry-docking facilities for your new boat. Am writing in confirmation.
>
> WALKER

In his letter Sir Herbert said they would build a new permanent graving dock, but he would be glad to receive from Sir Percy some assurance that "your company will continue to use our docks at Southampton and to make use of the new dry-docking facilities."

On December 1, Sir Percy wrote:

> I understand that as a physical feat it is possible for you to have the dry dock ready by the time required – namely, October 1933, and it is in reliance on your willingness as well as your ability to arrange this that we are proceeding to sign the formal contract for the ship.
>
> I am assured that the date of completion of the ship remains unaffected and we are relying on the Southern Railway to see that the dock is ready to receive her. In giving such an assurance, you will realize that we can be no more precise than is the Southern Railway with regard to the completion of the dry dock. At the same time I can personally assure you without any reservation whatsoever: (1) that at the present time the company has no intention of changing its base port on the Channel; (2) that I know of no circumstances which might make the company wish to do so.
>
> It is quite realized that in the event of the dock not being ready you will come under no formal obligation to the Cunard Company in that respect, but I must impress upon you that a very serious state of affairs will arise should this unfortunately be the case.

It was decided to build a dry dock 1200 ft long, 135 ft wide and 48 ft deep, with a wide area outside the entrance for the ship to swing into it. An immense enclosing bank round the site had to be built to keep the enclosed area more or less dry by pumping during the excavation work.

Enormous quantities of chalk were brought by rail from the railway company's own quarries at Micheldever. Dredged material was added to the bank by an ingenious special craft, the "Bankwell." Originally employed when work was being carried out on the first section of the docks-extension scheme, her great utility was again proved in the construction of this encircling bank.

The whole site was surrounded by interlocking sheet-steel piling, driven through the embankment and the foreshore to reduce soaking by the tidal waters to a minimum. Piles were driven along a total length of 7000 ft, and thousands of tons of steel used. The tidal waters were permitted to ebb and flow over the enclosed area through special sluices while the bank was being formed. When the bank was finally completed timber doors already prepared were fitted one by one and dropped into position on the sluices.

Excavators removed 1,500,000 tons of earth to a level of 90 ft below the final quay level. Three large steam shovels cleared the soft mud day and night until harder subsoil was reached.

When one end had been completely excavated concrete laying was begun, so that the processes were going on simultaneously. The whole work was carried on between June 1931 and April 1933 so that if work had not been stopped on the building of the liner the dry dock would have been completed and ready in ample time for the new ship to have used before going into service. Altogether some 750,000 tons of concrete were used in the construction of the floor and walls. It can be emptied of its 180,000 tons of water in four hours.

Some idea of the enormous national importance attached to the building of this liner, and therefore the construction of the dry dock, can be appreciated by the fact that, on July 26, 1933, King George V and Queen Mary sailed into the enormous basin in the royal yacht *Victoria and Albert* to perform an opening ceremony. The dock was named after the King and became the "King George V Graving Dock." Over 60 years later, it is still in use. The last occasion when a Cunarder utilized the services here was in November 1996 when *Queen Elizabeth 2* underwent her most recent refit. The ship was to make a visit to the dock following problems with the new propellers and vane wheels.

At the same time as Cunard were negotiating with the Southern Railway, the French authorities at Cherbourg had proved much more amenable. They went ahead with their plans for new quay accommodation, working amicably with the Cunard experts. In June 1930 Captain Ward, marine superintendent, and Mr McL Paterson travelled across the Channel to examine their proposals for the quay, to check what facilities they were providing for gangways, cranes, fuel oil and fresh water. No great difficulties arose.

On the other side of the Atlantic, however, it was for some months a very different story. The New York Harbour Authority were planning vast improvements, but the discussions over the plans and the cost were very prolonged.

Sir Ashley Sparks, Cunard's resident director in America, made every effort to obtain some idea of what new rental the company might have to pay. But he was unable to get any firm figure.

Sir Percy Bates wrote to him,

> We cannot afford for twenty-five years to pay New York Pier rents based on to-day's level of values, costs and wages if, as looks possible, there is to be a severe readjustment in wages and passages rates.

By August 1930 he was writing:

> You make my flesh creep in every letter as to the price we would have to pay, but refrain from figures. I would like to know the figures which are talked about, even though we know we shall not have to pay them.

He was told what Sir Ashley called "the fantastic figure" of $3,000,000.

He wrote again:

> Things are queer just now. I feel that a period is coming to an end and the change may embrace the whole level of passage money across the Atlantic, the scale of living on both sides, values of all kinds, and even the price of piers. If the price of piers alone is maintained and perhaps increased in the face of a general slide in other quarters it seems to me as though we may have to consider providing a 'Southampton' to the 'London' which calls itself New York.
>
> Ships of the kind we are projecting are a certainty because the prospect of a weekly service with two ships only is too alluring to be discarded.
>
> Such ships would have to live for twenty-five years and it might be better to face a year or two's discomfort rather than make a bad bargain with the Dock's Commissioner which would affect their whole life. I am writing wildly, perhaps, but you are to blame with your repeated reference to the extreme prices of piers.

Sir Percy suggested that perhaps they might consider using Boston as a terminal port with free rail travel to and from New York. At another time he suggested it might be worth considering incorporating all the other similar shipping lines into one company to operate from one pier which would be a "ferry stage for Europe for the elite traffic."

Eventually after discussions with the dock engineers about the length of the pier and the depth of water required (as this involved blasting through solid rock), agreements were reached in January 1931 for a thousand-foot pier at a rent of £48,000 a year.

So it came about that the formal shipbuilding contract was signed in December 1930.

On December 27, the hull plate was laid and named Job No. 534.

One of the shipyard executives at that time described the scene:

"It was a particularly raw, foggy winter's day and the electric lights under the cranes of the building berth had to be put on soon after half past three in the afternoon. But so strong was the grim enthusiasm of managers, foremen, and workers in their determination to have something to show at the end of that first day after all the months of waiting that work continued in the wet and in the darkness well into the night."

The unusual length of the liner encroached on to the normal working space of the yard, so a bridge had to be erected under the giant bows in order to facilitate the running of trains and other traffic bringing material to the ship.

The first rivet in the hull was put in by "the man in the bowler hat," the late Donald Skiffington, yard director at the time. Born in Clydebank, son of a carpenter, Skiffington was often considered to know more about the construction of ships than probably any other man in Britain. He had either built, or had a hand in building, more than three hundred ships on Clydebank, from battleships like *Repulse, Hood, Vanguard* and *Duke of York* to liners like *Queen Elizabeth, Empress of Britain* and *Caronia.*

By January 1931 the whole of the keel had been laid, and the lower ribs and frame were in position. Three shifts of workmen toiled on the vessel day and night, and the skeleton of the hull was completed by the late spring.

It was calculated she would be ready for launching by May or June 1932, and ready to go into service, as Sir Percy wanted, by 1934. By November 1931 80% of the hull plating had been riveted into place; thousands of plates of high-tensile steel ranging from 8 to 30 ft in length and weighing from 2 hundredweight to 3 tons had been curved and cut and fixed, and the lines of the bows began to merge with the flow of her graceful sides.

Meanwhile, depression was spreading through the country. Strangely, however, it seemed if those working on the liner were completely oblivious to this financial and social onslaught. Perhaps bewitched by an overwhelming sense of pride and a desire to achieve the construction of this magnificent ship, they simply chose to ignore the advance of this depression.

Despite the grave economic climate, Britain was still gripped by a powerful urge to fight off foreign competition in matters nautical. Remember, France's wonder, the *Normandie,* was also on the stocks, a fitting reminder that the island nation could not rest on its laurels. Earnestly, doggedly, they went about their tasks, For some time now the directors of Cunard had been getting worried at the financial situation in the country and at the problem of raising money in the markets. They had already spent £1,500,000 in building the liner.

4

Skeleton on the Stocks

The date: Thursday, December 10, 1931.
The place: Cunard head office, Liverpool.
Location: Boardroom, fifth floor.

The directors of the Cunard Company gathered under an umbrella of secrecy and anxiety. This is not destined to be a happy pre-Christmas meeting. They were worried men. In many ways this would be one of the most important meetings in the history of the company.

Fifteen days before Christmas they gathered to look at the provisional figures for the years' trading. For the first time for many years the company would not have a net profit out of which to pay the second half-year's dividend on the Preference shares; nor any dividend on the Ordinary shares. They were faced with the almost unbelievable fact that the gross revenue of the company for the year was calculated to be nearly £2,500,000 down on 1930.

At the very time that the company had placed the order for the new liner, a year before, transatlantic traffic was facing a serious decline. The financial situation in both America and Europe was reflected in the numbers of passengers travelling. As Sir Percy Bates had said, "the numbers carried were less, and there was evidence that these classes of passengers desired to economize in their travel. If it had not been for very strenuous efforts which were made by the management and the staff to economize in the general operation of the company the large decline in traffic and revenue would have had a far more serious effect on the net revenue."

The company had always been operated on the lines which had been laid down by Mr John Burns, later the first Baron Inverclyde, when he was chairman of the company. Speaking at the launching of the *Etruria* in 1884, then the most powerful steamship in the world, he said, "I have been told that it is an anomaly in shipping to talk of bad times and yet to build such immense ships. There is no courage in entering upon great enterprises in prosperous times, but I have faith in the future and confidence that the Cunard Company will hold its own upon the Atlantic."

In fact, things had become so bad that, within a few months, the chairman was to announce that all the staff, both ashore and afloat, had accepted a reduction in their "remuneration" and that it would apply "from the directors down." This, with other economies, was expected to save the company at least £1,780,000 in a full year.

By 1931 the total British earnings from passenger traffic had fallen from £9,115,895 in 1928 to £3,965,57, partly due to foreign competition. The total earnings for all countries dropped from £27,846,000 to £18,153,164.

Traffic in all classes fell from 1,069,079 in 1926 to 686,456 in 1931.

A few days before the meeting the company had warned the Board of Trade confidentially that it was almost certain that they would have to stop work on the new Cunarder.

The directors met to decide on that problem. It was true the company had a million pounds in cash in the bank; but at the same time their ships had not earned enough to set aside anything for depreciation, and there, slowly rising on the stocks at Clydeside, was their new ship, which was costing money every day; money which the company could not get nor raise in any way.

The way to finance the building of such a ship is normally to pay for it out of money set aside each year against depreciation, by borrowing on the finance market, and by the liner's earnings in the first five years of her life. But the international crisis in the 1930s had changed the whole financial background and made the continuous use of this type of finance increasingly difficult. In fact, it was at that time impossible to borrow money on the finance market for such a project.

The situation in the North Atlantic was serious. The decline in passenger and freight traffic seemed to have no limit; the trade outlook for 1932 was very grave. There was a glut of tonnage in the trade, and the company was faced with the competition of other fleets "in the building and running of which, with Government assistance, the earning of sufficient profit and their annual depreciation charge may no longer remain a matter of primary importance."

In other words, Cunard – alone among the big companies battling for what little traffic there was in the North Atlantic – was operating as a purely commercial venture. All other countries' fleets were receiving, in some form or another, subsidies from their Governments.

The director's meeting proceeded and the decision was reached that work must stop on No. 534 at noon on Friday, December 11. To Clydeside this meant a black Christmas: three thousand men directly employed on the building were sacked; ten thousand men and women employed on subsidiary contracts for electrical equipment and the hundred and one items which go into the creation of a liner were also affected. Men in rolling-mills, forges, foundries, throughout the country; men at work-benches, at lathes, men building massive castings, or men creating delicate machinery parts; all were jobless, thrown on to the labour-market at a time when unemployment was rising at an alarming rate.

Other contracts for work which were just about to be signed were left unsigned and in abeyance.

At seven o'clock the next morning a notice appeared at John Brown's yard under the signature of Sir Thomas Bell, managing director:

> Notice is hereby given to all employees in Clydebank Shipping Yard, engine and boiler departments, that all work in connection with Contract 534 (the Cunarder) is to be stopped as from noon, December 11.
>
> The services of all employees will therefore terminate at noon to-day. The owners express their profound regret that special circumstances have necessitated the total suspension of all construction work on the hull and machinery of this important project.

Later that same day, in the House of Commons, Mr Runciman, President of the Board of Trade, rejected a suggestion that the Government should intervene so that work might proceed.

> I am afraid that any idea of direct Government financial assistance is out of the question. The question of direct Government assistance was not raised, and if it had been raised it would not have been possible to give financial assistance.

The directors prepared and issued to the shareholders a long detailed statement explaining their reasons for this momentous decision and the financial background of the company. At the same time they explained the breakdown in the long negotiations to buy the Atlantic fleet of the White Star Line. In their statement the company said their reason for anticipating the annual meeting was "the impact of the national crisis."

"World conditions, which, of course, govern the traffic in the Atlantic as elsewhere, have now arisen on an unprecedented character, which, in the opinion of the directors, render some postponement advisable as a proper precaution."

The *Daily Telegraph* City Editor wrote:

> The announcement proved somewhat of a shock in the City. Nevertheless, the wisdom of the decision was not questioned. The financing of an expenditure of £4,500,000, a simple task in prosperous times, has become impracticable owing to the heavy shrinkage in the company's revenue, a large part of which is normally set aside for depreciation and applied to the construction on new tonnage.
>
> It is satisfactory to be assured that all bills of exchange with which the construction of the new liner has hitherto been financed will be duly paid off as they mature, the company's liquid resources being ample for that purpose.

David Kirkwood, Member of Parliament for Clydebank, telephoned Sir Thomas Bell as soon as he heard the news and asked some specific questions. He rose in the House of Commons later that day, December 11, to read the telegram he had received in reply. After telling of the notices posted in the shipyard it went on:

> I would add that had work continued it would have involved placing orders in the near future for nearly two and a quarter million pounds for the whole of the ship's internal passenger accommodation. So in the circumstances all must agree that it was their bounden duty to at once call a halt. You naturally ask how long this stoppage will continue. Unless the Government are prepared to co-operate with the Cunard bankers to take on a share of what otherwise would be transacted in the Bill Discount Market the stoppage can last for three month, six months, or even twelve months, for no one can tell how long it will be before the Bill Discount Market will once more be functioning normally.

The World at large learned of the decision in their morning newspapers, which reflected the sense of doom and a shadow of despair. The *Daily Telegraph* wrote in its leading article:

> From the moment that particulars about her were made known the British people took her to their hearts as the boat that was to recapture the lost Blue Riband of the Atlantic now worn, because worthily won, by the German *Bremen*. The decision to stop work will be felt as a direct blow to national pride.

It went on to describe it as an "industrial catastrophe."

> It is not indeed stated in the circular whether the Government help towards the construction of No. 534 has been solicited. If it has there is no obvious reason why it should be refused to the Cunard ... Even as an emergency measure for the prevention of unemployment a Government loan or guarantee of cheap money would be a far sounder business proposition than most of the "unemployment schemes" in which public money has been sunk. Unless therefore considerations arise which do not appear at first sight, here is an obvious case for Government help.

The public response was overwhelming. The Cunard Company was inundated with offers of financial help from people all over the country, all anxious to see the liner completed.

Sir Percy Bates said, "We are not a proud people and we would accept aid from anywhere if we could get it on proper terms. But we must know that that kind of thing is going to be effective before committing ourselves to approval. There is no immediate prospect of resumption. At any rate I cannot see it for the moment, unless we can find some fairy godmother. I cannot conceive the possibility of an early change in the situation."

Two days later the company directors met again, urged by thousands to launch a public appeal; to issue new ordinary capital in small sums. But the directors expressed the opinion that this was unworkable because of the technical difficulties of dealing with over a million new shareholders and the disproportionate cost of transfer and other charges.

Mr W Thorne, M.P., general secretary of the National Union of General and Municipal Workers, sent a letter to the Prime Minister:

> At our executive meeting the question of the hold up of the completion of the Cunard liner was discussed and I have been authorized to say that in the opinion of my executive the Government should supply the necessary money needed to complete the work at a reasonable rate of interest.

He himself led a deputation of trade unionists to the Board of Trade, at which they suggested that the Government should guarantee to Cunard a loan representing the difference between the normal cost of discounting bills and the existing abnormal rates or that a loan for a long term at easy terms should be given to the company.

It was calculated then that the approximate cost to the National Insurance Fund in paying out unemployment benefit to the laid-off workers would run at something in the region of £13,000 per week.

The effect of the stoppage on Clydeside and on the local families can be gauged by the fact that half of the total wages being paid in the area came from the work on this ship. It was to be the saddest Christmas that Clydebank had known for many a long day.

By January 1932, of the 3,640 men who had been working on the ship, a mere 422 were left in the yard. The average number of employees throughout 1933 was a mere 675. The vast majority of these men were black-coated workers such as foremen and draughtsmen. There was also a handful of senior craftsmen for maintenance work.

The situation was deplorable, not only in Clydebank, but all over the nation. The idle hull of No. 534 would fester on the stocks as a symbol of a collapse in British shipbuilding. The situation would worsen and orders for new vessels would plummet. In fact in 1933 the total tonnage of new vessels completed in British yards hardly exceeded 130,000, something like 5% of the industry's potential.

For two years there was no hope. The great skeleton stood there in a township which became almost like a graveyard. The majority of the working population of Clydebank depended on the shipyards or the Singer factory. Half of Singer's workers were laid off, so there was no hope there.

One or two did manage to find work, mainly as canvassers for popular newspapers, which at that time were waging the big circulation battle with door-to-door canvassing and offers of free gifts as a feature of the campaign.

Clydebank became a town or workless men and of women striving to keep the home going, to feed the family, to clothe them and, above all, to keep the men's spirits up. Untold tales of sacrifice went on behind the front doors of those houses which lined the streets that ran down to the river's edge. One half never knew how the other half lived. No one really knew how anyone survived.

Clydesiders do not talk of those days. These were days which touched their pride, and they are a proud, independent people. Clydebank became a town of people who no longer lived. They just managed to exist, day after day, week after week, with all the dreary monotony and forlornless that is bred from life without seeming hope.

They rationed themselves, in food and in clothing. They faced the autumn rain and the bitter Scottish winter cold stoically. In these months they thronged the cheaper cinemas of Glasgow at threepence-a-time matinées, to keep warm and to save light and fuel.

But it was not just the shipyard workers who felt the pinch. It was everyone; shopkeepers, for example, found it almost impossible to make ends meet, so emaciated was the local cash flow. Many people lived by barter, "taking in each other's washing." Yet so carefully did these housewives manage, so disciplined were their lives, that there was very little debt nor were there many defaulters in paying the rates. Somehow they managed to find the money and pay it out each week. There was always the dreadful, dreary routine of the dole queue, but at least this provided money.

Along the foreshore they searched for driftwood; waste ground was scavenged for firewood. There was the continual steady tightening of the belt, and the continual staying in bed to keep warm.

And all the time David Kirkwood, who lived among these people, who regarded them as "his family", fought and fought his long, desperate struggle, as a staunch ally of Sir Percy Bates, in their battle to persuade the Government that work must be restarted.

The world economic situation which had forced this decision on the company was no new thing that year. In 1929 the American stock market had crashed, a tumbling, tormenting Niagara Falls of a crash. Speculators and ordinary people, lured by that enormous ebullience of American confidence, had bought shares and continued to buy. Now the crazy edifice had collapsed.

In the face of this domestic crisis the United States began to withdraw their finance from Europe, precipitating a world economic crisis with its consequent closing of markets and resultant unemployment, and import restrictions which were reflected in British exports.

In England, MacDonald's second Labour Government took office in 1929 with Snowden as Chancellor. They had fought the election, among other points, on promises of dealing with the unemployment situation. But unemployment steadily increased. In eighteen months it more than doubled.

In June 1929 there were 1,163,000 registered – 9.6% of insured population. In June 1930 there were 1,912,000 – 15.4% of insured population. In December 1930 there were 2,500,000 registered – 20% of the insured population.

G D H Cole, in his *History of the Labour Party*, says:

> The Economic Advisory Council, of which I was a member, discussed the situation again and again, and some of us, including Keynes, tried to get MacDonald to understand the sheer necessity of adopting some definite policy of stopping the rot. Snowden was inflexible, and MacDonald could not make

up his mind, with the consequences that Great Britain drifted steadily towards a disaster of whose imminence the main body of Labour M.P.'s and of the Labour Movement were wholly unaware! All these troubles came to a head only in 1931, but they were there in 1930 to be seen by those who were prepared to look facts in the face.

There was much criticism of Labour's failure to tackle the unemployment problem, and by July 1931 the figure had risen to 2,750,000. In that same month there came the May Committee report, prepared by Sir George May, retiring chairman of the Prudential Insurance Company, which had been set up to recommend practical reductions in national expenditure and which said that cuts of £96 million should be made, including a 20% cut in unemployment benefits; increases in contributions to the Fund; the means test; and cuts in teachers' salaries.

This created the belief abroad that Britain was insolvent, and the insecurity of the British currency led to a run on sterling. The Bank of England borrowed £50 million from the Americans and French, but that did not last very long. A loan of a further £80 million was being negotiated, and in August a National Government was formed and the loan came through. In September Britain suspended the Gold Standard, and there was a General Election in October.

In December 1931, during a debate in the French Chamber on a bill to give a substantial measure of financial aid to the Compagnie Générale Transatlantique, the French Minister of Marine suggested that if the Cunard Line would give up their "super ship" the French would do the same. The following day the Cunard issued a statement in reply which said that "no communication has reached them either from the French Government or the French company."

Some short time before M Lavel, the French Prime Minister, had visited Germany, and it was known that shortly after his return discussions took place between the German and French steamship companies with regard to limitation of tonnage in the trades in which steamers of both countries were employed. They were seeking some economic collaboration and international understanding of limiting the tonnage for each service to fit the needs of the traffic and limit the number, size and speed of ships to be constructed over a period of years.

On January 27, 1932, Cunard issued a further explanatory statement in the form of a circular to shareholders. In this it stated that if certain financial facilities were granted by the Government, "it would undoubtedly be of material assistance in enabling the work on the ship to proceed at an earlier date than may otherwise be found possible." It stressed that the company had "never lost faith in their ability to operate the liner" in such a manner as would enable her to pay her way.

Referring to criticisms that the liner was to be a "luxury" ship the company said that naturally the standard would be most modern. "The cost of the decoration of the passenger accommodation of such a ship is a very small percentage of her total cost, and it is estimated that the greatest saving which could be affected as between the bare necessities and the best modern accommodation would amount to less than five per cent of the total cost of the ship."

The company stressed once again that the reason for building the new liner was that she was "necessary for the company's express services and was therefore ordered in the natural sequence of events. Ships have to be replaced as they grow old if the company's business is to be maintained.

> The last express ship built by the Cunard Company was the *Aquitania*, which commenced its career in 1914. Since that date the French line have built the express liner *Paris* in 1922, the larger and faster *Île de France*, of 43,000 tons, in 1926, while the ship at present under construction for the same company is reported to be of a similar tonnage as No. 534.

The statement pointed out that both the Germans and Italians had built new liners.

> It is obvious therefore that there is a demand for vessels of this character which requires to be met, otherwise they would not be built. If Great Britain is to maintain its place in the forefront of shipping the task of building such a ship as No. 534 has to be undertaken.
>
> The first of the projected new ships ought to be ready to take her place in the service in 1934 unless the company makes a definite surrender of the paramount position, and risks the transfer of the British mails to foreign and faster competitors.

In tracing some of the financial background of the company it stressed that in the past the Government had given them favourable facilities in the matter of finance, and pointed out that the agreement under which the *Mauretania* and *Lusitania* were built came to an end as recently as November 1927 when the last instalment of the loan was repaid.

> Throughout the period of the loan every instalment was paid on the due date.
>
> The construction was suspended, not on factors inherent in the Atlantic trade, not on factors domestic to the company, but on international factors which were "hampering the ordinary financial machinery of commerce."
>
> To sum up, No. 534 is being built because the Cunard Company will need such a ship; and for no other reason whatsoever. She will be such a ship because, being needed, no other sort of ship is wise to build. In other words, for the Cunard Company she is the inevitable ship and therefore we ordered her.

In April 1932 Sir Percy spoke to the shareholders at the annual meeting in Liverpool.

> Work on the ship is still suspended and I am unable to say at what date it will be resumed.

The hull is very far advanced, and only five months' work is required to make her ready for launching. In the meantime not only is the structure, which is being carefully watched, perfectly safe, but advantage is being taken of the delay to apply more permanent preservatives to the steel than in the case of any other ship built within recent years. Long views are essential in the North Atlantic, and though we have met with obstacles at the beginning of No. 534, we consider she is necessary to the continued welfare of the company. We will get work restarted as soon as we can see our financial way clear to her completion.

If we thought in the least that any international monetary complications would so disturb the ordinary financial machinery we should, undoubtedly, have asked the Government for financial help at the time we arranged the Insurance Act. I believe that at the time the two things together would not have been more difficult of accomplishment than the one was by itself.

But on February 2 Mr MacDonald, the Prime Minister, was again repeating in the House of Commons that the Government could not undertake to give direct financial assistance. Throughout that year on 1932 they maintained this attitude. By 1933 Neville Chamberlain was Chancellor of the Exchequer and he was maintaining that the door had not been shut "to assistance in some form or another" which would enable the liner to be completed. But it would be dependent upon certain conditions, which included among them the consolidation of existing British interests.

So the long struggle continued by careful and delicate negotiation. Much of the discussion and talks were conducted behind the scenes in correspondence and meetings. All the time Sir Percy Bates battled and struggled and negotiated in his efforts to get work restarted. All this time Clydebank had been a township of dole queues, means tests, hardship and hunger. To make life less tedious and to help preserve the sanity of the thousands of idle men and their women, mutual-service associations sprang up everywhere. These held classes in mechanics, dress-making, woodwork, cooking, languages, home-making, arts and crafts, music, physical culture, and a hundred and one other subjects. Throughout this period the workers acquired a reputation, which extended far beyond the city limits, for steadfastness in adversity, for initiative, and for resourcefulness.

But all the time there was the grim struggle to live. Here follows a picture of what life meant. It is a report from the Clydebank Press on Friday, January 6, 1933, when two deputations appeared before the local education committee to appeal for extra nourishment for the children. The kiddies were described as "so undernourished that they were not even able to pull along the heavy boots which the authority had provided for them with clothing."

Mrs Brogan, one mother, described the situation to the committee as "the terrible state of affairs when the mothers have to beg for a little extra nourishment and suitable garments to clothe their children.

"The children of Clydebank are really very undernourished," she said, and instanced that there was nothing left in the family purse after paying rent, coal and gas to give the children the necessities they should get.

By the middle of the week an unemployed man's income was absorbed, and existence depended on a pennyworth of vegetables. "It is quite true to say that unemployed people's children go to school with half a slice of bread and margarine and sometimes a drink of tea if there is such a thing in the house. At the dinner hour they come in to a penny bone and a pennyworth of lentils and sometimes a pennyworth of vegetables. At tea-time they have bread and margarine over again. That is my own experience."

Another member of the deputation, Mrs Robert Hughes, asked that the Education authority should consider providing a hot meal to each child of unemployed parents and low-paid workers.

All that year the situation did not improve.

On December 15 a deputation from the local branch of the National Unemployed Workers' Movement at the monthly meeting of the Clydebank Town Council asked for a three shilling extra relief at Christmas and New Year to all unemployed adults, with 1s.6d. for each child of unemployed parents and two bags of coal for each unemployed householder for Christmas and the New Year weeks. Provost Stuart pointed out that according to the Acts relating to these matters in Scotland, it was not competent legally for the Town Council to grant either of these requests.

David Kirkwood, the local MP, did not spare himself in his continuous fight to get work restarted on the liner's hull. He wrote letters, made speeches, visited shipbuilders, ship owners, Cabinet Ministers and financiers. He pleaded, cajoled, begged and threatened.

"For two years the skeleton in the yard of John Brown's had been an obsession to me," he wrote in his autobiography. He saw MacDonald, Chamberlain, Snowden, Runciman, Sir Percy Bates and Sir Thomas Bell. But he made no real progress.

> For more than two years "534" had been engraved on my heart. In the morning I woke wondering if something could be done that day to bring the skeleton to life again. During the day I made myself a nuisance to all and sundry. They said I had a bee in my bonnet. In the evening I would try to plan something new for the morrow.
>
> I was utterly selfless in the agitation. I never thought of public opinion, whether for or against. I had set my heart on seeing that ship built, and all the determination and dourness in my nature rose to help me. My pertinacity was not resented. I was often put off, but I never received a rebuff. I admit that I was a worried man. I annoyed them. I pestered them. Never once was I the object of unkindness or discourtesy. On the contrary, I was treated at first like a man with a mania. Then with sympathy. Then with encouragement. I talked with men whom I had never before met, many of whom regarded me

as a vehement and noisy partisan.... During those two years I had to hold in my heart more secrets and confidences than in the whole of my life.

We think of prison as a place where men are shut in. It is worse than prison for men to be shut out of work.

And their wives – those heroic women of the tenement and the Guild – had seen their men depressed and nervous. They had long ago eaten up their little savings. They had struggled with untold splendour of sacrifice to pay the rent, to keep up the spirit of the men. To them the sight of the closed gate and the horrid framework beyond had been a blight.

Kirkwood never gave up the struggle. One day in lobby of the House of Commons Lady Astor approached him and said that the Prince of Wales was going to Scotland to see for himself what conditions were like there and he wanted to talk to Kirkwood about it.

At first Kirkwood refused to see him. Later he received a formal invitation to a reception at Lady Astor's London house. The card said "Decorations." He told Lady Astor that he had no clothes other than the ones he was wearing and no decorations but "my specs."

Lady Astor telephoned him and said: "The Prince of Wales says it is not your clothes but yourself that he wants to talk to, and that if you wear your serge suit that is your best decoration."

So he went, and there he met the Prince of Wales, who said, "We can't talk here. Let's go into the library." There they talked frankly and openly of the conditions on Clydeside.

The Prince said to Kirkwood: "Well, how are things on the Clyde?"

"Very bad."

"What do you think can be done?"

"I want you to come down to Clydebank and see the Cunarder. That ship means work. It means life. It means prestige of the British Empire and the Blue Riband of the Atlantic."

"Well, tell me about it all."

And so Kirkwood did.

For thirty minutes he spoke. When Lord Astor came into the library to remind the Prince that there were other guests he ignored the request and remained with Kirkwood. For a further twenty minutes he listened to this man who was fighting for the lives of his constituents, for the people of Clydebank; for the future of British shipbuilding.

Kirkwood recalled, "I felt, as I feel when I see an expert engineer at work, that I had been in the presence of a man who had a big job to do, and is earnest to do his job well."

The Prince went to Clydeside and saw for himself. He came back and talked to the Government about the problem of getting work to the area and, in particular, of getting work on the liner restarted.

Gradually, slowly, through all the different negotiations, a solution was emerging.

5

Atlantic Merger

For more than two years the battle to get work restarted on that gaunt outline of ribs which dominated the shipyard town like some skeleton of doom had continued. Some of the campaigners wanted work to begin to aid the unemployment situation in the country; others wanted it so that Britain might once again hold her head high in the Atlantic trade. But Neville Chamberlain, then Chancellor of the Exchequer, while equally anxious for work to restart to ease the unemployment problem, had already made it perfectly clear that the effect on the total unemployment figures for the country as a whole would not be much more than negligible.

Chamberlain throughout was determined that, faced with the growing competition from foreign liner companies, there was not room for two big British companies acting in opposition to each other in the Atlantic trade. Moreover, he was worried about the situation of the White Star Line, which was in grave financial difficulties. He wanted to see one united company, strong, determined, vigorous and financially sound, capable of withstanding the ever-growing competition and of re-establishing British prestige.

He wrote in his private diary "My own aim has always been to use the 534 as a lever for bringing about a merger between the Cunard and White Star Lines, thus establishing a strong British firm in the North Atlantic trade."

This was, of course, no new suggestion.

The Oceanic Steam Navigation Company, trading as the White Star Line, had been bought back after the War from its American owners, although it had always remained under the British flag, by the Royal Mail Steam Packet Company, who still owed the Americans more than £2 million.

In July 1930 Mr Runciman, President of the Board of Trade, had initiated negotiations for the sale of the North Atlantic fleet of the White Star to Cunard.

In October 1930 the voting trustees of the Royal Mail Company asked the Cunard directors to investigate the possibility of an amalgamation. Cunard made what is described as "a substantial cash offer" for some of the White Star Atlantic fleet. This was in the neighbourhood of £3,250,000, partly in cash and partly in the assumption of liabilities.

The Treasury had already investigated the financial structure and situation of the White Star Line. On January 5, 1931, Sir Montague Norman, Governor of the Bank of England, was asked by the Treasury to come to the assistance of the company and see what he could to alleviate the worsening plight.

The company was not in a position to carry on without a temporary advance to cover its operating loss, at least until the summer season restored its takings. It could not afford to complete the new 27,000 ton motor ship *Georgic*, being built at Harland and Wolff's Belfast yard. It could not raise any further credits from its commercial bankers and it was in debt to the Treasury, which was not itself prepared to give further credit.

There was, therefore, a grave danger that if the company was unable to maintain its payments a receivership would be insisted upon. Norman arranged a temporary advance on security of the shares the company held in the Shaw Saville and Albion Line. However, on May 11 1931, he had to report to the Treasury that further help was needed, and he proposed an advance of £1 million, out of which the previous advance was to be paid, provided that the accountants approved the security and the Treasury approved the transaction in writing. This temporary solution (and it could clearly only be such) solved the problem for the immediate moment.

Norman called in Sir Frederick Lewis, chairman of Furness Withy, to advise him. He felt that some permanent reorganization was urgently called for. Sir Frederick considered the matter and produced the advice that the chairman of Cunard should be approached with a view to the company buying the White Star Atlantic fleet. In the meantime Norman asked the Treasury to continue the Bank's credit until the negotiations were complete.

This was June 1931. This time the Cunard directors suggested buying certain ships of the Atlantic fleet with Cunard Ordinary shares at a share valuation to be fixed by an accountant, based on an amalgamated balance sheet of the Cunard Company and its subsidiary companies, in which the Cunard Atlantic fleet was to be valued on a basis comparative to the values placed on those of the White Star Line. Sir Percy Bates has described the negotiations in these words:

> This basis was designed to enable the Cunard Company to take over the White Star fleet on terms fair to the Cunard share and debenture stock holders, while at the same time giving the White Star interests their fair share of any earnings the future might have in store for their ships under Cunard rationalization.

One of the conditions of the purchase was that the Treasury should repeat the financial terms under which the *Mauretania* and *Lusitania* had been built for No. 534 and her projected sister ship. It was suggested that the Bank of England should "facilitate finance for the new ships." The voting trustees, in a statement, rejected the cash offer.

The *Georgic* was not included in this offer, as at that time only £300,000 had been expended on her, and it was represented to the Cunard directors that if Cunard took over the fleet it was advisable to suspend her construction in view of the fact that tonnage already existing on her berth was considerably in excess of traffic requirements.

Once again this offer was refused. There was no other possible buyer in the market, which meant that there was no chance of an early repayment of the Bank of England's loan.

Sir Montague Norman had therefore to take the responsibility for a reorganization of the White Star Line with Sir Frederick Lewis as chairman and indefinite extension of credit. Once again, in October 1931, Cunard was pressed to make an offer on the basis of Income Debenture stock, which, it had discovered, would be a form of security satisfactory to certain of the White Star creditors.

In the meantime the trading position in the North Atlantic had become worse, both in traffic and prospects, and all classes of traffic were showing an alarming decrease. In 1931 686,456 passengers were carried both ways, compared with 1,002,353 the previous year. This time it was put to the Cunard Company that rationalization was in the national interest.

Fully sharing this view, the directors made another offer on October 26, 1931, for the fleet, including the *Georgic* when completed. This was £500,000 in cash and the balance in Income Debenture stock with an overriding guarantee of not less interest in such stock up to 4.5% than any dividend paid on Cunard Ordinary shares. Once again the Bank of England offered to facilitate finance for the Cunard new ships.

This was after they had carefully assessed the possible earning capacity of the fleet as a going concern in relation to its size and the prospects of traffic. The Oceanic Steam Navigation Company's published accounts for 1930 showed a loss of £379,000 before any charge for depreciation.

As Sir Percy said later, "It was clear that some considerable time would be necessary to stop this drain," and, as he told the shareholders, "while the form of the offer relieved the White Star interest of the risk of losses continuing, it placed that risk squarely upon the shoulders of the Cunard Company, at the same time securing to the vendors repayment of Income Debenture stock in whatever measure Cunard rationalization of the fleet was successful."

Yet again this offer was refused.

They were asked to take over the ships at a much higher valuation than they considered reasonable, on terms of repayment which they considered detrimental to their shareholders, and also with other special terms for the purchase of the *Georgic*, which involved assuming liability for a bank loan of £670,000 and accepting £453,000 worth of bills to be drawn by the builders on Cunard at a time when these bills could not be discounted. Sir Percy felt that to modify their original proposals on these lines would be to lead his company "into a position of jeopardy." While fully realizing the grave danger of Government-assisted tonnage being placed on the Atlantic in competition with their own ships, the company decided it had no other course than to allow the negotiations to fall through.

In August 1933 the Bank of England and the Treasury reconsidered the position, and the White Star credit was continued, as there was obviously no hope of repayment, and to have insisted on it would have involved a receivership. This was the very thing that the original advance had been given to prevent.

On March 2, 1932, Sir Percy told Mr Runciman he would make this offer, though it was really in the nature of an exploratory proposal: the Government to finance two new Cunard ships at 2¾%, then cash for the *Georgic* £1,350,000, the balance in Income Debenture stock, "the amount of the latter to show some improvement on earlier offers."

This was the first time the company actually suggested the Government should provide the finance for the new ships, as all previous offers had laid down that the Bank of England should "facilitate it."

The discussions, formal and informal, on all levels continued. All the time Sir Percy was pressing the Government for financial assistance to get work restarted on the liner. All the time the Government, "backed with that persuasion which naturally arises in those who have the power of the purse," as Chamberlain was to phrase it, was trying to bridge the gap between the two sides. They let it be known that some satisfactory agreement between the two companies was an essential preliminary to any offer of financial help towards the completion of No. 534.

In the meantime, however, a new step had been taken which was aimed at facilitating an agreement. In October 1932 Neville Chamberlain and Mr Runciman asked Lord Weir to conduct a confidential inquiry into the trading and financial position of the British shipping companies operating mail and passenger services on the North Atlantic and, more importantly, to make a special survey of building and operating subsidies paid by foreign Governments.

Lord Weir who had been Minister of Aircraft Production in World War I, and had been concerned with shipping all his life, knew Chamberlain well and had had many talks with him on this subject. Knowing only too well how a Government committee can take a long time to produce a report if it is overloaded with members, he insisted on carrying out the survey himself.

From his flat in the Adelphi in London, by the River Thames, he carried out his work, and in eight weeks delivered a secret report. He talked to Sir Percy Bates, to Lord Essendon, chairman of the White Star Line, and received considerable statistical and financial evidence from Mr Foley of the Board of Trade.

The Weir Report, of which only four copies were made, and which was marked "Most Secret," was one of the most important reports in the history of British merchant shipping. It paved the way for the overcoming of the deadlock in the merger negotiations and provided a basis for Government assistance for work to begin once more on 534.

It had, of course, always been a keystone of British industrial policy up to that time, particularly in relation to shipping, to be opposed to Government aid in any form of subsidy.

The British Government regarded the Weir Report as absolutely Top Secret for many years. However, Lord Weir himself spoke freely of its content a short time before his death in 1959. He recalled his work on the report very clearly and felt very keenly on its importance as a complete survey of the situation at that time.

"I was delighted when I was approached to make the survey," he said, "because I felt so keenly on the whole business. It was fairly clear to me, before I even delved into the subject in detail, that this was the sort of enterprise which the Government, at that time, should encourage. It was the very sort of stimulus which was needed, not only for the shipping industry, but for the whole of Britain, which was then languishing in a state of doldrums and needed a good fillip to give it back its courage and raise its heart again.

"I was so impressed with the amount of aid which was clearly being given by foreign Governments to competitors of British shipping in the North Atlantic trade. It was so obvious, when one studied the situation closely, that our shipping companies, Cunard and White Star, were facing what was developing into a very grave threat. It was an impossible situation, and one which could lead eventually to their being swept off the Atlantic and virtually out of business in the luxury traffic. No one seemed to really realize how serious this threat was.

"Of course, to-day every one knows just how much money was being poured into foreign companies, but in those days it was not generally realized.

"America, for example, was absolutely pouring finance into shipping, to such an extent that it was impossible almost to see how it could be economic. Ship owners could get building subsidies, operating subsidies, and mail contracts were at a far higher rate than any British vessel, something like four times as much a round voyage.

"In France the situation was that there was State assistance in the same manner, for building, for operating, and for mails, as well as a number of beneficial relaxed duties and carriage rates for shipbuilding material.

"In Italy there was State assistance, and in Germany, although the situation was somewhat confused, there was definitely State aid in some form or another.

"It was my firm belief that the British Government should guarantee a building loan to the Cunard Company on condition that the two companies merged into one united front against this opposition. I had spoken to both Sir Percy Bates and Lord Essendon, the respective chairmen, and they both assured me that they realized this and were quite convinced the merger should go through if only they could sort out their differences on the terms of such a merger. It was there that they were bogged down.

"I told the Government that the Cunard policy of the two-ship express service was thoroughly sound and at the same time economic. The company's finances were in a very strong state because of the company's policy over the years; while those of the White Star were in a very poor state. I also stressed the tremendous importance from a prestige point of view of new big British ships steaming into New York harbour."

The Weir Report provided a basis for the resumption of negotiations, and with the aid of the Treasury advisers and experts a solution was eventually reached, though this was to take another twelve months. Under the agreement the Cunard Company and the Oceanic Steamship Company both sold their North Atlantic fleets and assets, including 534, to a new company, to be called Cunard White Star Ltd, in consideration for shares in the new company, Cunard getting 62%, 22.8% being issued to the Northern Ireland Government, and 15.2% to the trustees for the Oceanic Debenture holders.

The Government then proposed to lend the new company £9,500,000. This was divided into three portions:

1. £3,000,000 to complete 534.
2. £1,500,000 working capital.
3. £5,000,000 for a future sister ship.

Various classes of Debenture stock were issued against these advances.

But the battle was by no means ended. For Neville Chamberlain there began the difficult task of steering the Government's North Atlantic Shipping (Advances) Bill through the tortuous channels of Parliament. After these years of stalemate, while being pressed on all sides to get work restarted, the Government, having at last reached agreement, found itself bitterly assailed from both sides of the House of Commons.

After years of depression, unemployment, hunger marches, cuts in unemployment benefit, they were confronted with what seemed to them to be a National Government sponsored plan to loan £9,500,000 to a private capitalist enterprise to build one large liner and possibly another one at a time when many of them had been refused help for specific schemes of public works in their own areas aimed at relieving unemployment. One member, from Clydeside, was to suggest that it would be a far better plan to divide the £9,500,000 million among the unemployed, as that would bring "far greater happiness to a far greater number of people."

No one could really be surprised that, in view of the general atmosphere of the times, Labour members glibly rolled off their tongues such phrases as "sumptuous floating palaces," "rich man's ship," and a "millionaires' ship." The Government were criticized too for advancing such large sums of money on "gambles" in private enterprise without what was termed any "adequate security" and without any representation on the board of the new company. Some members wanted to go much farther indeed and nationalize the whole of the shipping industry, while others wanted the money spent on building a fleet of tramp steamers.

This was the language of Labour at the time. It is perhaps surprising to find some Conservative members joining in decrying the plan on the grounds that the era of the big ship was over; that there were simply not enough millionaires left in the world to fill her; and no one else would sail in her. One member went as far as to claim that big ships could not possibly play an role in the event of war. "Nobody in their wildest moments would imagine that a 72,000- ton ship could be of any military use at all."

All this storm Chamberlain, well-informed, well-briefed, knowing precisely what he was doing, was to deal with calmly, firmly and factually. He knew, as indeed many of the opposition members themselves knew, that they dare not sacrifice their political future by voting against a measure which would to some extent relieve unemployment in one of the worst-hit areas, as well as in many other parts of the country and, at the same time, give a boost to the national spirit. We must bear in mind that, whilst the actual hull itself was the nucleus of this massive project, the effects of the suspension of the construction of 534 ricocheted throughout the entire country. Hundreds of businesses in Britain had been dependant on contracts resulting from this vast shipbuilding enterprise. They, like the shipyard itself, were now anxious, if not desperate, to see a resumption of work.

Chamberlain was asked if the Government had changed its mind about public-works schemes.

Captain, later Lord, Crookshank, a Conservative member, had this to say:

> We remember the race to build better and more formidable and more luxurious vessels transporting across the Atlantic Tudor villages disguised as smoke rooms, ships containing shops, swimming baths, squash racket courts and everything of that kind on the assumption that you were going to

get a very rich clientele. We always studied the American multi-millionaire. I do not know whether there are any left. Who [he asked] is going to travel in this ship?

If the Chancellor of the Exchequer suddenly came down and said, "Well boys, here is £9,500,000 to play with. What shall we do with it?" there is not a boy in the class except the Hon. Member of Dumbarton Burghs [Mr Kirkwood] who would hold out his hand and say, "Build this vessel."

There were accusations that the Government was engaging in economic warfare against other countries. "It is trying to recapture the prestige of the Atlantic to smash another nation. This ship is built to smash Germany."

Sir Joseph Nall restored some sanity to the discussion.

This question of the North-Atlantic-passenger business has reactions throughout this country. To the American tourist or visitor coming to Europe the nationality of the particular ship or the line which owns the ship is very often of little importance. The particular ship, on its merits as a ship, is what affects them. What is of importance to us in this country is that if those visitors or tourists are attracted by a ship which belongs to another European country they land in that country and may only afterwards come here.

It is in the national interests that we should attract to these shores an ever-increasing volume of shipping traffic from the United States.

I well remember, a little over a year ago coming back from New York in the *Mauretania*. I do not think I have ever felt so depressed at the position which this country seemed to be occupying as, upon a Sunday morning, in a fairly still sea, with a mist, the *Mauretania* was running almost parallel with the *Île de France* when away in the mist appeared the *Bremen*, which in an hour had overtaken both ships. The old *Mauretania*, still the fastest of the British ships on the North Atlantic run, was over twenty-five years old.

Mr Chamberlain answered the queries as to who was to travel in the ship by saying:

Anybody who has travelled recently on the Atlantic will have observed that the ships which have the fastest rate of speed are those which carry the largest numbers of passengers, and those passengers are not necessarily millionaires. On the contrary, the big and fast is designed to carry a very large number of what one might call the intermediate class who would jump at the opportunity of going by a route by which they could get to their destination quicker than by any other.

On the charge of cut-throat competition with Germany he replied:

Why are we to be the only country which is never to engage in competition and which is to suffer every country to smash us, throw our ships out of commission and make no effort on our side to hold our own and engage in competition with others on equal terms?

David Kirkwood, in one of his most lyrical speeches made in the history of the House, said this:

I welcome this new ship, not only for the good which it will bring to my own constituency but for what I really believe it means to the shipbuilding and engineering industry of this country. I believe that as long as this ship, known as 534, lies like a skeleton in my constituency so long will depression last in this country, because as it lies there in Brown's yard, it seems to me to shout "Failure, failure" to the whole of Britain.

It has been here and elsewhere said that there is not the traffic on the North Atlantic to warrant such a tremendous expenditure. One would think that the individuals who run this business were apprentices. They are the most astute businessmen not only in this country but in the world.

He then painted this picture of a Britain at work on the giant liner, filling in the details with such colour and life that it might almost be a Breughel painting.

Sir Thomas Bell, managing director of John Brown and Company, realized at once that this was a gigantic undertaking and that it devolved upon him to build the best that Britain could produce. He tapped all the skills and all the technique at his command in Britain and the result has been that in the deserted hours of the night heavy lorries have been lumbering over distant roads bringing materials from every part of England to Clydebank for the construction of this ship.

Giant castings and forgings have come from English foundries and forges. Seven turbo-generators are being built now in Rugby; they are powerful enough to supply light and public service to a large town. Walsall is sending 400 tons of high-pressure tubes. When the Bill goes through today and the word goes forth to go right ahead with the ship the Potteries will have to make her 200,000 pieces of crockery; Sheffield will have to make her 100,000 pieces of cutlery, having already supplied heavy castings and forges up to a weight of 1,000 tons.

The cases for the rotary turbines, some of the finest casting that has ever been done, have come from Sheffield, milled and machined in Clydebank to the limits of 1000 up and 1000 down, in which will be placed hundreds and thousands of blades set by hand by Scottish engineers to the thousandth part of an inch. Liverpool has an order for £10,000 worth of glass for myriad windows of the ship. The propellers come from a Millwall foundry in London. A Darlington forge supplied the stern frame, one of the greatest engineering feats in casting that has been accomplished in the history of the world, a casting weighing 190 tons. When it was leaving Darlington by rail they had to take it on a cylinder and it closed up the whole way. It took six hours to convey it twenty miles to Middlesbrough where it was transhipped. Practically all Darlington turned out to see the wonderful feat of transport of 190 tons along that railway. The casting was then transhipped to the Clyde. I have seen those pieces myself in their place.

Sir Thomas Bell points out the wonderful formation of the stern part and the stern frame, the contour and finish of it and how it fits in as if it had been a forging and not a casting at all.

Hundreds of Southampton men have carved out of the earth a dock, the greatest dock in the world, in which the ship may rest, the world's greatest maritime achievement. Among other things that will be required, and these all come from England, are miles of anchor chains, miles of carpets, miles of curtains and tens of thousands of electric globes and bell pushes. The ship will require equipment for 15,000 meals every day while at sea. From 9,000 to 10,000 men will be employed right away all over the country. Within a week in Clydebank alone anything from 1,000 to 1,500 men will be started.

Eventually both the House of Commons and of Lords voted and the Bill was passed on March 27, 1934. One week later, on April 3, 1934, work began again. This was the rebirth of a community which had "died" when the order to stop had been given. Despair was gone; the future held high hopes. Men and women all over Clydebank wept unashamedly; Church services of thanksgiving were held.

The first message of hope was received by four hundred men.

Dear Sir,
    Please report to Messrs John Brown and Co., Clydebank, on Tuesday April 3, 1934, at 7.40 am ready to start work. Please hand the enclosed introduction card to employer.

At seven o'clock that morning the workers began to arrive at the yard, and not long before eight o'clock, to the tune of "The Campbells are Coming", they were led by the Dalmuir Parish Pipe Band into the yard to where the skeleton of the great ship lay.

All Clydebank turned out to watch them; it was like the marching of an army released from a beleaguered city. One thousand men poured through the gates as the hooter sounded. Four hundred men had been officially told to report; six hundred were actually at work, the other two hundred being selected from the "daily market" as the need arose.

By the end of the week 1,500 men were employed and later 3,500. And the man who had done so much in that long long fight to get the men back to work was not there. David Kirkwood lay at home in bed with influenza. "This is the best tonic I could have had, though I would have liked nothing better than to have seen the men go back to work and wish them good luck," he said.

One of the first jobs to be tackled was to get rid of the birds which had nested in the scaffolding and in the gantries of the cranes during those silent months. For thousands and thousands of rooks had made their homes there. Then 130 tons of rust which had accumulated had to be removed.

In January of 1934 Sir Percy had asked Lloyd's Register to make a special survey of the hull, boilers and machinery as they then existed. This resulted in a report which was completely satisfactory, showing that no deterioration had taken place and that the impression, held in some quarters, that the hull had sunk or become distorted was entirely without foundation, The alignment of the hull on the berth was perfect.

Shortly after work was recommenced on the liner, the Chairman of John Brown's, Lord Aberconway, resigned his post. He died shortly afterwards, aged 83. He was succeeded by his son.

There was one more attempt to prevent the merger. The International Mercantile Marine Company of America sought an injunction to prevent the merger on the grounds, among others, that the directors of the Oceanic Company (White Star) had no right to transact the merger. It claimed that, "having regard to the default of the Royal Mail Steam Packet Company in discharging the interest on the outstanding balance of the purchase price of the Oceanic Company, due to them, the Marine Company, they should be regarded as the sole owners of the shares or, alternatively, the trustee companies were bound to exercise the voting rights conferred by the shares to veto the agreement."

It said that 534 would be "a grave liability on the company" and the directors had "wrongly allowed themselves to be influenced by a desire to see this big ship built for a relief of unemployment."

On May 8, 1934, Mr Justice Eve gave his judgement in which he dismissed the application with costs.

The situation was that on January 1, 1927, the Royal Mail Company agreed to buy the whole of the issued shares capital of the Oceanic Company, 5,000 fully paid up shares of £1,000 each, for £7 million.

This was to be payable in bond in this way:

£2 million cash on or before February 1, 1927;

£1,250,000 before June 30, 1928;

£1,250,000 before June 30, 1929;

£2,500,000 before December 31, 1936.

Pending the payment of the balance of the purchase price and the interest, the 5,000 shares should be held by the Midland Bank Executor and Trustee Company and the New York Trustee Company. The trustees, among other things, to permit the Royal Mail Company to exercise in relation to the management and general business of the Oceanic Company the voting rights conferred on the Oceanic shares.

"The plaintiffs are not only not the holders of the shares but they can never be. They are merely unpaid vendors who so far have received all they are as yet entitled to under the contract for sale.

"They have no *locus standi* to impeach the conduct of the Oceanic business, either on the grounds of its being *ultra vires*, or a misuse of the company's statutory powers."

On May 11 the new company, Cunard White Star Limited, was registered with a working capital of £10 million in £1 shares.

At the first meeting of the directors on May 17, Sir Percy Bates was elected chairman.

6

Secret of a Name

At ten minutes past three on the afternoon of Wednesday, September 26, 1934, one simple sentence, spoken by Queen Mary, lifted the veil of secrecy which had guarded the name chosen for number 534. Speaking calmly and clearly, her voice picked up by the microphones and carried to listeners all over the world, she said, "I am happy to name this ship the *Queen Mary*. I wish success to her and to all who sail in her," as the bottle of Australian wine crashed against the port bow.

For the first time a reigning Queen of England had consented to name a merchant ship and in the presence of the King and the Prince of Wales. And so it was that the vessel which had become known throughout Britain as a symbolic number 534 was christened with a name which took its place in history, and become so affectionately known to thousands of sailors and passengers simply as "The Mary."

When the ship was nearing completion a hundred and one names were suggested by members of the general public, who wrote to the company and to the newspapers. *Clydania, Leonia, Scotia, Brittania, Galicia, King George V* and *Hamptonia* were but a few of the names offered.

For many years there has been handed down a story claiming to give the facts of how the ship came to be named *Queen Mary* by a misunderstanding on the part of King George V. This story relates that it had been the original intention of the company, in keeping with the Cunard tradition of having the names of their ships end in "ia", to name her *Queen Victoria*.

Lord Royden, a director, and a personal friend of the King, told his fellow directors that he would ask him for a royal consent at an appropriate moment. He bided his time. One day when out grouse-shooting the chance came. King George turned to him and asked how his ship was progressing. Lord Royden said it was coming along very well and he wanted permission to name her "after the most illustrious and remarkable woman who has ever been Queen of England."

The King replied, "That is the greatest compliment that has ever been made to me and my wife. I will ask her permission when I get home."

Charming and amusing though this story is, it is pure myth.

Here follows the true story of how the ship came to be named, and how it very nearly was not named, *Queen Mary*. The launch was fixed for September 26, 1934, and the Queen had consented to perform the naming ceremony. But, as yet, there was no name.

The question of a name was considered by Sir Percy Bates and his colleagues on the board. They took two factors into consideration: the intended honour of Their Majesties' presence at the launch: and the necessity to reconcile the opposing wishes of the two parent companies, Cunard and Oceanic.

For many years the names of Cunard ships had been of a particular type with the termination, "ia", and the same was true of the Oceanic Company with the termination "ic". It seemed to the board of the Merger Company a very happy event if the formation of that company could be signalized by a name definitely marking a breach with the past and the beginning of a new era for the future.

A number of names were suggested; the name *Queen Mary* was first written on the back of a menu card. This was provisionally chosen but there were complications. It was known that there were already two ships of that name on the British Register, and, on approaching the Board of Trade, Sir Percy was advised to come to some compromise with the owners of one of the vessels, Williamson Buchanan Steamers Ltd, whose ship was one of a small fleet of passenger steamers engaged mainly in tourist traffic on the Clyde and on the Scottish lochs. The other ship belonged to a Colonial Government and presented no difficulty.

On July 2, 1934, Sir Percy called on Mr E W Macfarlane, of Williamson Buchanan Steamers, at his office in Glasgow to ascertain whether he would be agreeable to change the name of his ship in order that No. 534 might be given that name. Mr Macfarlane was very sympathetic, but pointed out that he found great difficulty in agreeing, as the passenger traffic on the Clyde was highly competitive, and while his company was doing well they were having a pretty hard time of it competing with the railway steamers and MacBrayne's. He felt it would be definitely unsafe for him to risk his trade by changing the name of his newest ship.

Sir Percy felt he could go no further at this meeting. He asked Sir Thomas Bell, of John Brown and Company, the shipbuilders, to see what he could do on the matter. Sir Thomas contacted his friend Captain Williamson, who had until recently been associated with Williamson Buchanan Steamers, and together they had an interview with Mr Macfaclane on July 4.

They pointed out the advantages that might accrue and the favourable publicity which would ensue when it became known why they had changed their ship's name to, say, *Princess Elizabeth*. But Mr Macfarlane remained adamant, and little progress was made. He did, however, promise to consult his chairman, Captain Buchanan. Subsequently Captain Buchanan made the suggestion that their ship's name should be changed to *Queen Mary II*, as this would involve only the addition of the Roman numeral to the name.

Sir Percy then told the Board of Trade of the result of these talks and asked for their concurrence in Captain Buchanan's suggestion. The Board, in their reply, stated that if Mr Macfarlane should apply for the alteration of the name of his ship to *Queen Mary II*, they would agree, and the name *Queen Mary* would then be available for Cunard White Star. The way was now clear for an approach to be made to the King and Queen for their consent to Her Majesty's name being given to No. 534.

Sir Percy explained the circumstances to his friend, Sir Warren Fisher, secretary to the Treasury, who promised to see Sir Clive Wigram, the King's private secretary. On July 21 Sir Percy received a letter from Buckingham Palace over the signature of Major Harding, assistant private secretary, informing him that his proposal as regards the name of No. 534 had been approved by Their Majesties. In his letter of thanks Sir Percy added, "It is a great relief to me to know this now, as I might have had great difficulty in suggesting a suitable alternative."

As a tangible mark of the company's appreciation, a portrait of the Queen was presented to Williamson Buchanan Steamers to be permanently hung in a prominent position in *Queen Mary II* during the working life of that ship. The eighteen-by-fifteen-inch portrait was in water colours, by A T Nowell.

Years later, the smaller steamer is still in existence and has again been renamed *Queen Mary*, since its giant namesake was moved to the United States and therefore removed from the British register. The little *Queen Mary* is permanently moored on the River Thames in London, not far from Charing Cross, where she fulfils a role as a floating restaurant and bar.

After naming the liner, listeners in Sydney, Paris, New York and Cape Town, as well as all over England, heard the Queen whispering as she thought, "Now I press the button?" and the reply, "Yes, that's splendid." For her voice had been picked up by the microphones and echoed round the world.

As she pressed the button the thirty-thousand-ton empty shell of the white-painted liner began her journey to the waters, with the sound of creaking timbers and cheering, shouting, delirious Clydesiders echoing over the shipyard.

Fifty-five seconds later she was afloat, proud and untamed, yet checked and held like a wild stallion in a corral, by two thousand tons of drag chains, many of which had been borrowed from other yards, and then seized by seven tugs, to be manoeuvred into her fitting-out basin.

It was shortly before the launch that two of the leading members of the design team walked through John Brown's yard and suddenly, as they put it, "We turned a corner and there she stood, this massive, magnificent ship we had created, towering above us, like some skyscraper. We were awed into silence. Then we both looked at each other and the same thoughts crossed our mind and we began to speak at the same moment. 'What have we done? Are we tempting fate? Will this massive structure of steel ever float on water?'"

That day was to give them their answer, unhesitatingly. John Masefield, the Poet Laureate, had written a poem for the occasion, entitled "Number 534", as even he did not know her true name. It was said that because of their very great personal friendship Sir Percy Bates had asked Rudyard Kipling to write a poem, but he had refused on the grounds that he could never write to order, and that anyway, "Let Masefield do his own job; he used to be a sailor."

In this poem Masefield writes:

> ... a rampart of a ship,
> Long as a street and lofty as a tower,
> Ready to glide in thunder from the slip
> And shear the sea with majesty of power.
> I long to see you leaping to the urge
> of the great engines, rolling as you go.
> Parting the seas in sunder in a surge
> Shredding a trackway like a mile of snow,
> With all the wester streaming from your hull,
> And all great twanging shrilly as you race
> And effortless above your stern a gull
> leaning upon the blast and keeping place.

Few people knew then, or know to this day, that the launch was very nearly postponed and that it was, indeed, rain which saved the situation.

The night before the launch a strong westerly gale blew up, and Donald Skiffington spent the whole night in the yard watching and waiting to see what happened. He was almost on the point of advising the board that they must tell the King and Queen that there was no point in their leaving Balmoral as, with the wind in that direction, it would be folly to launch the ship. But the rains came and the wind dropped.

It was raining on that September morning. It wasn't the gentle autumnal rain coming down, soft and gossamer-like, from the Highlands. It was cold, lashing rain that poured down from the grey sullen skies. There was no wind.

This was the day the world had waited for, not merely the world of the shipyard, which had lived with the ship night and day, watched her grow up from the merest beginnings to her present stature, but the world at large, all of the world. On this day people, some of whom had never even seen a ship, and certainly would never travel in this ship, waited for that supreme moment of triumph when she would move slowly down the slipway and float proudly on her natural element, leaving the land forever.

The King and Queen had travelled by train from Ballater, the station for Balmoral, where they were staying. A special royal suite had been erected in the yard, 35 ft above the ground, with five rooms, built on the starboard side of the liner. They walked along a tubular steel gangway, 20 ft high and 8 ft wide, to the bow for the ceremony.

The launching of such a ship was a fascinating and awesome process. Throughout the morning workmen made their final preparations. Swinging their hammers in unison, they rammed home the countless finely tapered wedges which had lifted the hull a fraction of an inch above the position in which it had been built. When there was no doubt that she was resting in her cradle the launching triggers were cocked, and it was these six triggers that the Queen actually released when she pressed the button.

Once the triggers had been cocked with a special device to ensure that none of them would be released before the appropriate moment, the blocks and shores on which the vessel had been built were finally removed. The upper surfaces of the great slides, the better part of a 1,000 ft in length and over 100 ft in width, had received their final coating of 150 tons tallow and 50 tons soft soap. The removal of the keel blocks and shores was commenced five hours prior to the launch and was carried out at a steady rate from ten o'clock in the morning.

The actual launching of the liner took precisely one hundred seconds. This was the result of five years of hard, concentrated study, calculation, experiment and test. Somehow it seemed as though it was not meant to really happen, as if man was daring to push the limits back too far. The *Queen Mary* was, at the time, the largest moving man-made object ever constructed. To some it seemed an absolute impossibility that she would actually be able to move. Yet, at the moment the Queen pressed that tiny button, the massive bulk of "534" slowly, reluctantly, began to creep at an imperceptible rate down the ways. For an instant, a silence fell on the huge crowd as breath was held in fearful anticipation; is she moving? Yes; no... yes! She's on her way! Sir Thomas Bell, then managing director of John Brown's, recalls the ceremony:

> The pressing of the button releasing the launching triggers was succeeded by a hush of expectancy. For a few seconds, seconds that seemed like minutes to some of us, nothing happened, until at last a welcoming creaking of timbers was heard, followed by a movement, just perceptible and no more. Then, almost immediately afterwards, we found ourselves watching the great structure moving majestically down the launching ways, its towering mass gradually gaining speed and going faster and even faster. It was really awe-inspiring to see such an irresistible force in action and to know it was utterly beyond all human control.

Down the ways she slid and, as she accelerated to full launch speed, the cheers of thousands cut through the infernal din, for the launch of a giant liner was a noisy business. The raucous argument between timber, metal and concrete generated a terrifying racket as the tons of soap and tallow lubricant were stripped and dragged off the launch ways and the massive timbers crashed and snapped, leaving a trail of debris in their wake. As the monster entered the Clyde, a host of massive drag chains joining hull to launch ways were pulled out in unison to their full length. As they snaked angrily along the dock, they kicked up filthy clouds of rust and dust, adding another dimension to air which was already reeking with the stench of burning timber and scraped and gashed metal. As they reached the pre-determined tension, they snapped in succession at exactly the right moment, arresting the ship's movement and slowing her to a halt.

Sir Thomas Bell:

> The climax was reached when the stern plunged in to the water, driving a great wave before it. Soon afterwards the bow was making its graceful curtsey to us all, telling that all was well.

Mr (later Sir James) McNeill, of John Brown's, said later that the most important factor of the vessel's safety on launching was the estimate of the distance she would travel after leaving the ways and the exact path of the stern.

During a discussion by naval architects some years later, in which the launch was described as "one of the greatest engineering feats of the century," it was revealed that Mr McNeill and his team had calculated the liner would travel 1,194 ft at 11 ft 6 in water level. They were wrong. She actually travelled 1,196 ft! It must be remembered that, as in the very building of the liner, this was a unique launch; for no ship of this size or this weight had ever been sent down the slipway. So once again no one knew exactly what would happen.

As early as March 1930, when the tender for the construction of the ship was under consideration and before Cunard had actually told Brown's that they would be the builders, a group of men began their first study; began their first tentative calculations on paper to determine the date of the launch and the method. Because clearly it was no use Brown's tendering for the building if they were not going to be able to launch her.

The measurements were: 1,000 ft long, 118 ft beam, and 135 ft from keel to the top of the superstructure, with more than 30,000 tons hull. This had to be moved from its cradle on land to its rightful place in the water – safely.

At first the group carefully examined the case for the adoption of four launching ways. But this was very quickly dropped, after investigation, in favour of the conventional two ways.

Then began the paper calculations. Complicated mathematical calculations were worked out, discussed, argued over, pondered over.

Later, when the actual launching time came nearer, all the reliable records of local tide behaviour from 1929 to 1933 were supplied to the team and a forecast of the tides was made. The date September 6 was selected. Eight weeks prior to this date the actual tides and weather conditions were checked and observed from day to day. The depth of water was expected to be 8 ft, but an abnormally high tide occurred that day and there was actually 11 ft 6 in. It was worked out that the ship could be safely launched with a wind up to 30 mph, which was unlikely to occur.

After the problem had been worked out on paper the tests were transferred to the realms of a scale model. A model nearly 17 ft long was made, with propellers, bossings, and all launching appendages complete, the propellers being in the locked position as in the actual launching.

Exhaustive tests were made to discover what actual distance she would travel after leaving the ways and the exact path of the stern. To ensure that proper conditions of water-flow around the model would be exactly reproduced, the river bed was represented by a false bottom fitted in the test tank outwards from each of the ways, and the actual contours of the river bed along the line of the launch were moulded in clay contained in a large shallow tray of sheet iron fixed to the box girder forming the false bottom. Cameras were sited all along to record the launching and the model's actual behaviour.

At the same time a great deal of work had to be done to the river itself. More than 5.5 acres of land opposite the shipbuilding berth were bought by the Clyde Navigation Trustees to widen the river.

The launching of the ship with a length of more than 1,000 ft and a weight greater than any formerly experienced necessitated prolonged dredging operations. Dredging then began and went on for a long time across the river in the line of the launch, as well as the deepening of the fitting-out basin in which she was to lie.

This meant widening the river by 100 ft in a two-mile stretch. The first of these widenings was undertaken during the building of the ship. At the end opposite the Dalmuir Sewage Works the work was begun after the launching and went on ceaselessly until the spring of 1936.

Unforeseen snags occurred, and it was found that there was an outcrop of rock under a portion of the river included in the river deepening which necessitated the employment of a rock breaker for several months augmented by drilling and blasting operations to remove that rock. This was done during the summer of 1935 and completed by the end of the year, in all several thousand tons of rock being removed.

The dredging required in the channel itself to secure the safe passage of the ship to the sea on one tide was a formidable undertaking and engaged the whole of the dredging plant of the Trustees almost continuously during the time the liner was being built and fitted out. From first to last millions of tons of soil were removed from the river and deposited at sea.

For the actual ceremony grandstands were built in the fields at

Inchennan on the opposite side of the Clyde from the slipway. Seats were booked in August for fifteen shillings, and special trains were planned to bring the spectators.

At one time the town councils were warned that a wave at least 8 ft high was expected to sweep up the Clyde. This, it was claimed, would sweep the public right of way on Clydeside. It was recommended, in the interest of public safety, that this right of way be closed. It was therefore decided to close the road east of the river Cart, opposite the yard. In the event all the precautions were justified. A number of people in the fields did get their feet and legs wet when the wash wave came over the river as the liner took the water. Later the local council thanked John Brown's for their advice and help. More than two hundred thousand people watched the launching, from the shipyard, from the opposite banks, and from the Anchor liner *Tuscania*, which was used as a grandstand.

Sir Percy Bates, reading an address of welcome to the King, included these words:

> British shipping of all kinds has been going and is still going through a period of acute crisis. The right attitude on our part is surely neither to complain nor to acquiesce, but to take the course of true confidence and adventure. That, Your Majesty, is the justification and inspiration of this new ship, and her launching by Her Majesty the Queen is the happiest send off for her on her high mission.

King George, in one of the finest speeches he made, had this to say:

> The sea, with her tempests, will not readily be bridled, and she is stronger than man; yet in recent times man has done much to make the struggle with her more equal.
>
> To-day we come to the happy task of sending on her way the stateliest ship now in being. For three years her unaccomplished hull has lain in silence on the stocks.
>
> We know full well what misery a silent dockyard may spread among a seaport and with what courage that misery is endured. During those years when work upon her was suspended we grieved for what that suspension meant to thousands of our people.
>
> We rejoice that with the help of my Government it has been possible to lift that cloud and to complete this ship. Now, with the hope of better trade on both sides of the Atlantic, let us look forward to her playing a great part in the revival of international commerce.
>
> It has been the nation's will that she should be completed, and to-day we can send her forth no longer a number on the books, but a ship with a name in the world, alive with beauty, energy and strength,
>
> Samuel Cunard built his ships to carry the mails between the two English-speaking countries. This one is built to carry the people of the two lands in great numbers to and fro so that they may learn to understand each other. Both are faced with similar problems, and prosper and suffer together.
>
> May she in her career bear many thousands of each race to visit the other as students and to return as friends.

We send her to her element with the goodwill of all the nations as a mark of our hope for the future. She has been built in fellowship among ourselves. May her life among great waters spread friendship among the nations.

The Queen was presented with a casket of hand-wrought and chiselled steel, mounted in gold and silver gilt, on behalf of John Brown's.

Sir Percy Bates, in reply, said, among other things:

When I was here last week I felt almost staggered at the seeming audacity of our imagination, when built in steel, yet I am sure our imagination was true. The *Queen Mary* is planned for success, and to plan for anything short of success must lead to certain failure.

Some of you will understand steel work, and to those I have no need to talk. But to those of you who are not accustomed to regard it as a craft of beauty, to those I say that there is not beauty only in that hull, but beauty in the detailed work in the steel that forms it. I will go further, and say, without fear of contradiction, first that good work possesses its own beauty, proportionate to its excellence, and second that no better work in steel has been done in any hull.

He concluded by referring to the fact that the "proof of our dream" would be when the liner, with her sister, was engaged on "her proper work," and said these words:

When that time comes the ships, their builders, their owners, His Majesty's Government, and all the many workers who will have shared in this great enterprise may have earned some right to the words of the epitaph of the men of the Press who died in the war, coined, I think, by a great poet. It runs, "They served their day," and if some day this can be said of this ship and her begetters, all will have deserved well of our country and justified the good wishes of to-day.

Time indeed was to show how prophetic these words were and how "her begetters" justly and rightly deserved that right to praise.

Once in the fitting-out basin there began the equally gigantic task of transforming this inanimate empty metal shell into a living being, a floating hotel, a ship which could sail across the Atlantic and in which people would live for five days at a time.

From Norwich came electric motors; from Darlington the stern frame and rudder and propeller shaft brackets, from Sheffield heavy forgings: Dartford sent a refrigeration plant, and air compressors came from Peterborough. Wallsend-on-Tyne built the oil-pumping and heating units, while Manchester sent the sprinkler and fire-alarm equipment. Pumps for oil-fuel pressure feed came from Bath, and silver solder for blades from Newcastle. Suppliers all over the country sent wood of every description. All these and the countless other parts and pieces, employing thousands of men and women in their construction, had to arrive at the dockside exactly when required, otherwise there would have been chaos.

All this seemingly impossible jumble and mass of material and equipment had to be fitted into its own place in the liner. The heavy machinery was the first to be placed, being lifted on board in sections and joined up in the ship.

So all through the seasons of the years the work went on. By December 1935 the twenty-four massive water-tube boilers, providing power for the enormous 100-ton turbines, had been placed in the four boiler-rooms, divided and cut off from each other by water-tight doors, and protected from the sea outside not by one skin, but by a double-skinned hull, in places 20 ft thick. A water-tube boiler really means that instead of a vast cistern filled with water, the boilers consist chiefly of miles of steel tubes around whose extensive surface areas the gases from the oil-fired burners can produce the necessary heat. The three "auxiliary" Scotch boilers had also been installed, in a separate room. These provided steam for the seven turbo-generators which would supply 10,000 kilowatts of electricity to the "hotel" and all its refrigerators, heaters, telephones, lights bulbs and so on. All had been connected.

On one day in December the furnaces were lit for the first time and, as it has been put, "Workmen toiling on her superstructure, the hundreds about the yard and the watching people in the little streets around saw a wisp of brown smoke curling upwards from the fore-funnel of the great ship, whilst below, unseen, the "lighters" were climbing up the drip catchers on the boiler fronts, opening aperture after aperture in the upper boiler faces, thrusting in a flaming torch and turning on oil and air cocks."

Not that all matters technical were confined to the engine room! Drysdale's of Glasgow manufactured hundreds of the pumps required for refrigeration, sewage and other purposes. Kelvin, Bottomley and Baird produced the ship's compasses. Three colossal steam-powered whistles were installed on the *Queen Mary*. Two of these were fitted to the front of the forward funnel and one on the middle funnel and it was said that they could be heard from a distance of ten miles. Safety was an important issue and the *Queen Mary* had the best equipment available. She was fitted with a total of 66 watertight doors, 38 of which could be remote-controlled by the officer on the bridge. All doors could be operated manually. With these doors, it would have been possible to completely isolate a damaged area of the ship, thereby preventing the spread of flooding. For the extinguishing and containment of fire, a sprinkler system was fitted. Highly sophisticated for its time, this system consisted of a large number of sprinkler heads which could operate independently of each other and, when activated, would trigger an indicator light on a control panel on the bridge. Providing for the worst possible scenario, considerable work had also been devoted to the ship's lifeboats. To begin with, all the boats, built by Hugh McLean and Sons of Glasgow, were motorized; this was a first in British passenger shipping. The two forward boats, the rescue or "crash" boats, were 30 ft in length whilst the majority measured 36 ft in length. They could accommodate a total of 3,266 people, in excess of the ship's actual capacity.

Later the decks were covered over and the work of fitting out the public rooms and the staterooms began. Four thousand miles of electric cable and wiring had to be fixed, mostly to be covered with polished woods and panels. Then came all the furnishing and fittings, the wash-basins, the taps, the baths, the showers, the curtain rails, the doors, tables, chairs, the hundred and one household articles which turn a room from a bare, empty space into a comfortable living accommodation.

Seemingly, no expense was spared in providing the very best for Britain's finest liner. Much of the furniture was designed and built by the London firm of Waring and Gillows; Priestley Brothers of Halifax were responsible for the hundreds of blankets, made from the wool of six thousand sheep; the General Electric Company supplied the electric lights; the pianos were by the Steinway company.

In the period during which the company ordered the liner and work was suspended, the situation in the North Atlantic passenger trade was depressing, to say the least. In 1930, the year the *Queen Mary* was ordered, 67,000 less passengers were carried in all classes by all ships. All liner companies were worried about the situation and the future, and it says much for Cunard's confidence in the prospects that the liner was ordered at such a time. By 1931 what was officially described as "an alarming situation" was disclosed when the year's figures were collated.

First-class passengers in both directions were 34,000 less than in 1930, which itself had shown a drop of 27,000 from 1929. All classes were down:

> cabin class fell by 62,000;
> second class fell by 34,000;
> tourist class fell by 67,000;
> third class fell by 120,000.

Altogether a total of 317,000 less passengers, which, it was estimated, meant a loss in revenue to all the lines of some forty million dollars.

In 1932 all classes but tourist and third showed the continuing decline, the reduction in all being 43,000 and the following year a reduction of 175,000 ocurred. The number of sailings in this period showed that the total round trips were steadily cut in an effort to combat the falling traffic.

1930	2,125
1931	1,770
1932	1,493
1933	1,411
1934	1,280

In fact, 1934, the year of the liner's launching, was called "the most disastrous year in living memory," when there were only 64,565 first-class passengers against the 162,300 of 1928. There was a total number of passengers carried of 460,000 in all classes, compared with more than 1,000,000 in 1928.

The fares charged by the steamship companies operating on the North Atlantic were controlled by the Atlantic Conference, which was an organization in which were represented all the liner companies. It was founded in 1908 to end a rate war and with the aim of bringing stability into the trade.

In October 1935, Cunard White Star Limited announced to the Conference that the new liner would be entering service the following year. Discussion was then begun on the rates to be charged for passengers. The company and the other lines had for a long time been unable to agree on the proper relationship between first class and cabin and, to cut the Gordian Knot, Cunard gave notice that it wanted the *Queen Mary* entered under the cabin class agreement and not first class.

This startled the Conference, which rightly regarded the liner as the last word in a luxury vessel. For this meant that the rate for the top class would be fixed at a lower basis than for a ship like the *Normandie*, with whom she would compare in age, size and speed.

But, as usual, Sir Percy Bates was following a carefully thought-out scheme to clear up a number of anomalies which had developed in the rates applicable to liners. The term "cabin class" had been introduced before 1914, and applied to the top class of ships whose owners had decided to adapt them to carry two classes instead of three. These were ships which, although still popular, were ageing and no longer had the same appeal to first-class passengers and were not quite the equal of more modern vessels.

Companies quickly realized the possibilities of using the designation "cabin class", and began to build ships specifically as cabin class. They were, in effect, first-class liners, despite the fact that they were not quite as large or as fast as some of those in the first-class category. As Sir Percy Bates, who had fought this anomaly for some years, was to say, "this naturally enabled a Company to obtain a competitive advantage over all ships classed as first. By entering the *Queen Mary* as a cabin class ship we have taken the earliest remedy that was available to us without the certainty of a rate war. The *Queen Mary* is not yet running and thus time for discussion has been afforded."

He referred to the fact that the term "luxury liner" had gained the public eye and ear. "Luxury, of course, there is in the *Queen Mary*, but the luxury of one age is the commonplace of the next, and the term should not be misused to obscure the economic factors of the ship which caters for all classes of travellers."

Discussion there certainly was at the Conference, but to no avail. The rate awarded to the *Queen Mary* dissatisfied Cunard White Star Limited. In accordance with the Conference rules, they appealed. As there was a disagreement over the appointment of an arbitrator, the company withdrew its appeal and said it would accept the original award.

Whereupon NordDeutscher Lloyd gave notice of appeal, and the ship was later awarded a higher rate. The company, on hearing this news, telegraphed to the Conference that it would accept this rate and amend its circulars accordingly.

> But the Conference is fully aware of the constantly recurring difficulties which have gone on for years in connection with the grading and classification position, and the unsatisfactory state of affairs is confirmed and emphasized, not only by the failure of the arbitrators to give decisions in the case of the *Statendam* and *Columbus*, but by the process of reasoning in the award of the Court of Appeal in the *Queen Mary's* case. Until a general agreement for top class is reached in which all ships are graded in accordance with recognized Conference factors of age, size and speed, the present difficulties and anomalies will continue. In the interests of the Conference it will be agreed on all sides that the situation should be clarified and, in the hope that it will assist in bringing about a fair adjustment of the whole question, we hereby give the necessary six weeks notice to retire from all agreements, which we are confirming by registered letter.

This was the text of a telegram sent by the company to the Conference and was, in effect, what Sir Percy meant by the opportunity for discussion. No one, apart from the general public, believed that the company had any intention of resigning from the Conference.

It was realized by the shipping companies that they must have an immediate discussion on this matter, and arrangements were made for a meeting in London in January 1936, which was postponed by the death of King George V and later opened and then adjourned to Paris.

Eventually at the Paris meeting the Conference decided to abolish the term "first class" altogether from its agreements, and "cabin class" became the top rating, applying to accommodation in the largest, fastest and latest ships on the North Atlantic.

On March 5, 1936, King Edward VIII visited the liner in the fitting-out basin. He himself wrote of the occasion:

> The completion of the 81,000-ton liner *Queen Mary* was an important item in the public events of 1936. Eighteen months earlier, I had seen my mother launch the great ship from John Brown's yard on the Clyde. Early in March, while the vessel was undergoing her final fitting out before being delivered to the Cunard White Star Line for service on the North Atlantic run, I travelled to Glasgow with the object of calling the world's attention to this stupendous product of British industrial skill.

This was to be no formal ceremonial visit. It was again a wet day and the King wore a black overcoat with a large fur collar and carried his bowler hat as he walked on board up the workmen's gangway.

All the scaffolding had been removed inside the ship for the occasion, so that he would have an opportunity of seeing what the liner would really look like. It was re-erected after he left.

Immediately he was on board he told the company officials that he wanted the tour programme altered. Bluntly he said he didn't just want to see the first-class accommodation. He wanted to visit the third-class accommodation and, furthermore, he also wanted to see the crew accommodation. "I am sick of looking at lounges. Where do the men eat and sleep?" he said. This caused something of a delay and officials had to hurriedly amend the itinerary.

When he saw the dog kennels on the sports deck he remarked, "All very well, but where are the lamp-posts for them?"

He walked more than seven miles during his three-hour tour and went everywhere and saw everything from the bridge to the depths of the engine room; he tested the chairs in the lounge; he turned on the taps in the cabins; he discussed the decorations with Mr Skiffington; he talked to the Captain, Sir Edgar Britten; he took no notice of the official party and frequently got himself "lost" so that he could talk to overalled workmen or ship's engineers. In the engine room he asked for one of the engines to be started and then he balanced a coin on the edge of the casing to test the lack of vibration.

He said of the third class, "This is more comfortable than the first class of twenty years ago."

After his exhaustive tour of inspection he had this to say: "She is a mammoth vessel – a ship built for utility." As he left the yard word had spread of his desire to see everything in the ship, including the crew quarters. A Communist party meeting was being held at the dock-gate and the speaker was just saying, "And when the revolution comes..." when the King's car drove slowly by. The orator, carried away by his own enthusiasm, shouted, pointed to the King and cried "and there goes the man who will lead us."

Just as his car was drawing away from the liner's side the ship's whistle was sounded for the first time, echoing across the hills in salute.

The *Queen Mary* had the doubtful distinction of being recorded in Lloyd's List of Wrecks and Casualties on her very first sailing day, for she was aground in the Clyde, though in no danger and only for a short time. The Clyde Navigation Trust denied this at a meeting later, but as far as Cunard was concerned, she was recognized as having been aground.

Lloyd's casualty report said, "Lloyd's agent at Glasgow telegraphs March 24, as follows, 'Steamer *Queen Mary* passed Princes Pier, Greenock 2.10 pm reported to have touched South Bank at Dalmuir, but no damage reported.'"

It was at 9.45 on the bright spring morning of March 24, 1936 that the 81,000-ton liner was eased gently out of her fitting-out basin and nosed and nuzzled into position to make her way to the open sea for the first time.

This was a poignant moment. She was leaving the place of her birth after the Clydesiders had lived with her in their midst for more than five years. They had watched her grow and become almost an integral part of their lives, and it was a proud but sad moment of parting.

Only two of her twenty-four lifeboats were carried, the others having been sent down river ahead of her, and the barest minimum of fuel was loaded because of the difficult task of manoeuvring her in the narrow, twisting, turning, navigable channel and the small amount of water underneath her – a few feet in some places.

This was the one and only time she was to make the journey. The Clyde Navigation Trust, as we have seen, had spent the period between the launching and this day continually dredging the channel. Divers went down repeatedly to ensure that her keel was clear of mud and any other obstructions. The last descent was made on the morning of sailing.

For a month before this moment her giant engines had been tested in secrecy and with her propellers uncoupled. Instruments had been placed in passengers cabins and public rooms to record the vibration.

The two pilots, fifty-six year-old Captain Duncan Cameron, pilot-in-charge, and forty-four year-old Captain John Ligurnia Murchie (he had been born at sea in the RMS *Ligurnia*), had decided to advance sailing time by an hour because of a strong, gusty south-east wind.

As her great whistle boomed out four times across the Clyde Valley, workers all over John Brown's yard dropped their tools as if they had heard the starting gun for a race, and rushed to the water's edge to see "their" ship sail away. There were tears in the eyes of many who had lived and worked with her so long. One elderly workman stood silently watching as the tugs got her into position, and said, "Good luck to you, my girl," and walked away.

She entered the main stream stern first, and was manoeuvred into an oblique position until her bows lay downstream, part of her length taken by the mouth of the River Cart. She was then eased into mid-channel and shortly afterwards her own engines took control and she moved off at six knots. Thousands of spectators had flocked into the Clydeside during the night and all along the Clyde Valley right down to Gourock. It was estimated that one million people had come to see her go; they had come by special train from all over Scotland and England, by plane, by car, by bicycle and on foot.

Schools were closed for the elder children; shops were shut. On the previous Sunday some 600,000 people had visited the area, on both banks of the river, just to gaze at her. More than 10,000 people were shown over the liner, the last visitors not leaving until nearly midnight.

The night had been lit by their camp fires and brightened by their songs, and now they crowded the fields at the water's edge and jammed the hillsides and perched in trees to see the "stately ship" sail. Eleven aircraft flew overhead as the tiny tugs delicately manoeuvred her out of the basin and headed her for her fourteen-mile journey to Gourock.

Slowly, so slowly, she began her majestic journey. At Dalmuir a gust of wind caught her, swept her stern across the river so that she was diagonally across the river with her stem almost against one bank and her stern scraping the shores of the other while spectators on the banks chatted to those onboard. It was reported that she was aground again abreast the Dalmuir Light.

Captain Cameron was the coolest man on the bridge. He never turned a hair. Later he said, "We 'skidded.' They often do that. I knew there might be a little trouble and was prepared for it. I simply brought the ship to a standstill. It was nothing to worry about. You have to do that sort of thing to nurse a vessel of that size around the bends. Nothing like it has ever been attempted before."

So she steamed on and reached Gourock, where she anchored until 2.30 in the morning of March 26. She carried out adjustments to her magnetic compass, which involved turning the ship in two or three circles to obtain a true bearing and to rectify errors due to the metal work. Here, too, anchor tests and other trials were carried out.

All day and far into the night, when she was brilliantly floodlit, she was circled by tugs and pleasure steamers packed with some 30,000 sightseers. She refuelled for her journey to Southampton and took on her remaining twenty-two lifeboats.

She still, at this juncture, belonged to John Brown's, and the shipyard had provided many of the crew, apart from officers. In Southampton, she was to enter for the first time the giant dry dock which had been built for her and the projected sister ship. There she would have her hull thoroughly examined, checked and painted with anti-corrosion and anti-fouling paint, and her propellers changed before returning north for her formal acceptance trials.

Captain E W Harvey, Southampton's dock master, was responsible for the dry docking. He said, "These big liners keep you guessing. But I am quite happy about her." He had visited her at Glasgow and carried out an inspection of her so that he could assess the problem.

She arrived off Cowes ahead of schedule and anchored there for six hours before moving up Southampton Water to the dock, followed by a flotilla of craft of every sort. Three quarters of a million people watched her from the banks, many having come from far parts of England in special trains. As she began this journey she was welcomed by the outward-bound German liner *Bremen*. Dressed with flags, the German shipped radioed:

Our heartiest congratulations for the completion of our youngest and biggest companion at sea. May our first meeting be the beginning of a long, good co-operation.

COMMODORE ZIEGEBEIN, OFFICERS and CREW

Captain Sir Edgar Britten replied:

Please accept from myself, officers and crew our warmest appreciation of your kind message. The *Queen Mary* will, we all feel sure, be a worthy successor of those fine ships which have preceded her in the waters of the North Atlantic and of which your noble vessel is one of the brightest examples. Kindest Greetings.

She was actually dry docked in twenty-five minutes.

Shortly before the liner had left the Clyde Cunard White Star had taken the unprecedented step of appointing another captain to her, Captain George Gibbons, to assist Captain Sir Edgar Britten. He had spent some time with the liner in Glasgow helping Sir Edgar in the hundred and one final details before sailing and he made the voyage to Southampton. Later it was decided that there was no need for two captains and that the master and Staff Captain could cope with any problem. Captain Gibbons therefore returned to the command of the *Brittanic*.

On April 1 questions were asked in the House of Commons about that voyage down the Clyde. Mr Chamberlain said that the liner had arrived in an entirely satisfactory condition.

The propellers which were to be fitted to the liner for her speed trials had been lying at Southampton and in chalk or indelible pencil had been covered with the signatures of thousands of people from all over the country. People from Bath and Walton-on-Thames; from Cardiff and Liverpool, Torquay and Portsmouth, and even from across the seas had autographed them. Five members of the Farnborough, Hampshire, Cycling Club had inscribed their names and that of their club. After a thorough check, the ship moved to the Ocean Dock to take on stores for her trials.

Later, sailing reports came in that she had been sighted "steaming fast" up and down the Irish Sea off the coast of the Isle of Man. For the next few days she carried out trials and tests of many kinds. It was reported that she had steamed at more than 30 knots and had reached 32.84. Some observers, stop-watches in hand, rather like racing touts, claimed she reached an even higher speed and passed the 33-knot mark.

On April 19 John Brown, later managing director of the shipyard, stood with a stop-watch on the bridge and timed how long it would take to bring the liner to a stop. At 150 revolutions a minute it took 10 minutes, 30 seconds from the time the engine room telegraph was moved to "stop," and at a speed of 21 knots it took 4 minutes, 1 second to alter her heading 180 degrees. Ten years later these statistics were to be called for in a court of law as evidence as to how quickly she could stop or turn.

It was during these trials that Lord Burghley, the British Olympic runner, in evening dress, ran just over 400 yards round the Promenade Deck in under 60 seconds. This was in answer to a challenge from a number of guests. A plaque was fixed to record this achievement, but it disappeared during the war years.

And so the builders' task was ended, and there is a simple document which states:

12 May, 1936. Handing over of S.S. *Queen Mary*, Southampton 12 Noon.

Probably no one realized that while this great new ship was inaugurating a new era of transatlantic travel and naval architecture, she was also marking the end of one particular aspect of ship design. She was the last of the great three-funnel liners.

7

Design and Décor

This huge ship was a new venture in marine design, revolutionary in a multitude of ways. With her immense prestige value, with the eyes of the world watching every development, the Cunard Company realized it was presented with an artistic challenge.

This was the beginning of a new era in transatlantic travel; a new era in standards of accommodation in public rooms and in staterooms and cabins. The directors were desperately anxious to avoid any suggestion that this was simply "a luxury liner." Sir Percy Bates hated the expression. But Cunard publicity referred to her as "Britain's masterpiece."

A committee was set up, which functioned rather like the Hanging Committee of the Royal Academy for its Summer Exhibition. Some bitter critics of that body would say that this committee made some equally startling decisions.

Sir Percy Bates invited Mr B V Morris, an American architect and interior designer, to be his personal adviser on the general scheme of decoration. Mr Morris had designed the Cunard Building on Broadway, New York. In view of the large numbers of Americans who would be travelling in the ship, Sir Percy clearly wanted to get some first-hand ideas from an American on their particular likes and dislikes when travelling. Mr Morris came over to England and stayed with Sir Percy at his home in the Cheshire countryside. There for the first time he studied the preliminary plans for the liner.

He immediately made an number of suggestions, pointing out that the design of the promenade deck prevented the passengers walking completely round the ship, as it was shaped like an inverted letter "U", with the smoke room in the open end. This was later changed so that it was possible to walk right round. Years later, however, the layout of the promenade deck reverted to its original design and many passengers complained again that it was impossible to walk right round. Morris criticized the elevator system as being inadequate. He questioned the desirability of calling the main lounge by that title, mulling over such names as "Lounge", "Garden Lounge'" and even "Social Hall".

After these preliminary discussions Sir Percy decided to engage him on a full-time basis. There must have been many occasions later on when he wished he had laid down more explicitly Mr Morris' powers and not given him such wide terms of reference. For Morris became so interested and immersed in his project that he was continually sending long, detailed cables across the Atlantic and despatching plans and suggested alterations across the ocean in other Cunard ships. Indeed, it must have seemed at times that it would have been considerably simpler to have engaged him in 1926 when the liner was first thought of. In the end the company had to cable and write to him that he must stick to the plans as approved by the board. They "strongly deprecated any departure from them."

Later Morris, realizing the difficulties of working at such long range, suggested the appointment of a London architect to work with him. Mr Arthur Davis, of Mewes and Davis of Old Burlington Street, was selected. This British-American design partnership worked in the closest secrecy, as the company were determined that no hint of the interior decoration of the ship should leak out. Some conception of what the directors were aiming at can be seen in this letter to Morris from one of them:

> When inexpert people like myself express a preference for period architecture, it is, I think, because one is afraid of the bizarre. If you tell a decorator one would like something modern in a room one feels it is dangerous, because he may feel it incumbent upon him to produce something striking and unrestful.
>
> If, on the other hand, modernism could mean simplification and the replacement of ornate decoration by pleasant and graceful colour schemes with new lighting effects and so forth, then it might prove to be what the travelling public really wants and might, at the same time, save the company a great deal of money.

Again the same director wrote later:

> I feel that a straight out-and-out period ship would be a disappointment, no matter how cleverly the unavoidable warfare waged between structural conditions and traditional proportions were waged. In a word we are, I hope, seeking convenience, simplicity and, if it can be brought about, a glimpse of beauty in proportion, form, and colour. The ship is bound to be 'dated' no matter what happens, but how about doing it without any more pose or cant than is necessary.

The main layout of the rooms having been agreed upon, the committee set about the task of finding artists and craftsmen to carry out the work. Mr Morris inspected the work of a number of painters and sculptors in their studios and talked with them. He visited numbers of dealers' galleries and public art galleries to see their works. Eventually he drew up a list of artists, who were asked to submit designs for a variety of rooms. When they had sent their preliminary sketches these were considered to see if they would be too bizarre, too modern, or too individualistic, and not likely to fit into the overall conception. Eventually a team of thirty artists, sculptors, painters and interior decorators was recruited for the task.

But all was not to be plain sailing. The company clearly felt that it was sponsoring that so-often-sought liaison between Art and Industry. But it soon became obvious in some respects that Industry wanted to dictate to Art, and that Art did not relish that. One of those asked to work in the ship was the late Sir Stanley Spencer, celebrated for his allegorical religious paintings, and in 1959 elected a member of the Royal Academy.

He decided against doing any work for the ship after his first panel design had been rejected. He is reported to have said at the time, "They felt it did not fit in with the general decorative scheme. It represented a group of riveters straining against a metal plate in the process of riveting. Below other workmen lay on their backs using pneumatic drills. I only want to paint what I like and not what people want me to paint."

The landscape painter Bertram Nicolls was asked to do a number of pastoral scenes for the Long Gallery, which ran along the port side of the Promenade Deck immediately out of the Lounge. These were accepted, and it was often suggested that *Summer Landscape* would surely bring nostalgia to many an outward-bound Briton.

The late Tommy Earp, distinguished art critic of the *Daily Telegraph*, apparently had different ideas on the subject. When it was shown on exhibition at the Royal Society of British Artists he described it in this way: "The foreground is occupied by a purple green cow and a tree of similar colour. In the background is a little hamlet of mock medieval 'Ye Old English' style. It is astonishing, but perhaps it will harmonize with a rough Atlantic crossing."

At this time one of the best-known names in theatrical and film costume design was Doris Zinkeisen. Her name appeared in all the gossip columns and in the glossy magazines. She was always to be seen at first nights. She did the costumes for such productions as *Nymph Errant*, *Wild Violets*, Anna Neagle's film *Nell Gwyn*, and numerous Cochran revues. She had been appointed 'Personality Creator' to one film studio, with the object of seeing that their stars were well groomed. She had had her first painting hung in the Royal Academy when she was seventeen years of age.

The directors asked her to do the décor for the Verandah Grill. This was a light, airy room, 70 ft long by 29 ft wide, with a broad sweep of twenty-two windows, each 5 ft 9 in high, which could be thrown open, facing aft, high up on the Sun Deck. This was to be the centre of sophistication in the ship; it was to be the rendezvous for the smart set at lunch time who did not want to go down to the main restaurant; it was to be the night club in the evening. It was one of the few rooms in the ship where wood-panelling and decoration was not a special feature. Years later, Doris Zinkeisen spoke of her work:

"They – you know the mysterious 'they' of companies – came to me and said they thought it was just the sort of room for me to design; it would suit my style and so on. You know, in their rather heavy way they wanted something light-hearted and gay.

"Well, you know, the idea appealed to me, so I agreed. But I told them that I must be able to design the whole place, curtains, chairs, carpets, and not just the murals. It had to be all or nothing.

"The first shock I got was when I asked if I could go down to the ship (or should it have been 'up' to the ship) and see the room. They were absolutely horrified. They gasped 'But there isn't anything there yet; just a mass of bare girders.'

"I asked how on earth I was supposed to work, and they were very sweet and made a most delightful model of the room."

She said that she decided to take, as her theme for the main mural, entertainment in all its phases and forms: theatre, circus, night club, ballet, with a representative from each, in a procession, carnival-gay, laughing and dancing along.

"I gave them their next shock when I said I wanted an all-black carpet. They were horrified, throwing up their hands. I gather they had in mind one of those awful pattern things you see in any hotel.

"I pointed out that black was the easiest colour for them to cut pieces out of when they were worn and replace." She chuckled and said, "That had never occurred to them. I decided to have curtains of deep-red velvet."

The main mural was thirty feet long.

"My own studio at that time was very small and simply would not take the canvas. I could not find one anywhere in London. About this time I took my family out of London and rented a big house in the country. This had a very large drawing-room. I cleared everything out of it and turned it into a studio. Even then I could only get the canvas in by putting it from one corner to the other. Later, when I returned to London, it was still not finished and I still had no studio.

"The directors of a gallery in Bond Street lent me their big gallery. The only trouble was that as I worked customers would come in and the directors would say, 'of course, you know Miss Zinkeisen is doing a mural for the new Cunarder. It's very secret but you can just have a peek.' This was infuriating, as I had to stop work and be introduced and so on, and I really wanted to get on. The whole thing took me about three months."

Zinkeisen then asked if she could go to Glasgow and put the finishing touches to the work as it hung in place.

"It was, my dear, absolute chaos. It was impossible, so impossible. There were workmen all over the place. I like to work in complete silence. You can just imagine what it was like.

"There was I, surrounded by hundreds of workmen, all very jolly and all passing remarks and wisecracks in their broad accents and even broader humour.

"There were wires all over the place, as they were doing electrical work. Then they discovered that the clock in the smoke room below could only be regulated from up there. So, if you please, they calmly cut a bit from my mural so that damned clock could be controlled. I can tell you I need a certain amount of controlling about that little lot.

"The next problem was that I had planned to have plain wall between the murals, with figures painted on them. To my horror, when I arrived I was stopped in my tracks to see that someone had painted huge oak leaves there. They were at least two feet across, all intertwining and hanging like spaghetti; all gold-encrusted and unbelievably ghastly.

"What was I to do? All round the place those workmen were silently watching. I said to the man who had done it that it would not blend with my scheme.

"He shrugged his shoulder and said, 'Oh, well, I thought it would be better this way.' Eventually he agreed with me. You should have seen those workmen when I told them to get the stuff off those walls. They were at them like tigers."

Zinkeisen recalls an amusing occasion when the captain was showing a friend around the unfinished vessel. When they reached her work they were obviously delighted: "They were like a couple of schoolboys seeing their first nude."

At each end of the long mural were theatre boxes, in one an elderly man and at the other a lady, upright, with a lorgnette, tiara and necklace.

When King Edward VIII was making a tour of the liner he paused before the mural, looked quietly at it for some time. He then saw the elderly lady, smiled, and said, "Oh dear, how like Mama."

Miss Zinkeisen said: "Quite unconsciously I had painted this figure to resemble Queen Mary. No one had noticed it until the King. Needless to say, after he had left, I altered it."

Her sister Anna was asked to do a series of decorations for the ballroom. She had four panels to do and chose, after much thought, the Four Seasons as her theme. They were "full of flowing lines and in pale colours, soft green and grey and then suddenly a bit of bright colour to startle. In some parts I left the canvas bare, in its original state as it blended with the whole," she said.

She spent six months working on the designs and painting them before they were sent up to the Clyde to be fitted in place in the ship.

She went up with her sister to put the finishing touches and, like her, was appalled at the noise.

"I had expected to find the liner virtually completed, except for the finishing touches here and there. But everywhere there was hammering, banging, drilling. I nearly sat down and wept. I couldn't see how I was ever going to get at my canvasses. I work in absolute quiet, otherwise you find yourself unable to do delicate brush work.

"Down the centre of the centre of the ballroom they had got some massive black pillars which were really terrible. I couldn't stand them and told them so and that they had better get them altered if they wanted the best result. They painted them over in a light colour, which was so much better.

"We were the only two women working in the ship at that time, and, of course those Clydeside men were always whistling after us. One day I overheard one of them say, 'Och, aye, they must be just a couple of polishers.' You see, we had our overalls on.

"We were given a cabin with a key in which to change and keep our things. Those men had a tremendous pride in building the ship, but they had no pride at all in helping themselves to anything that was left lying around. They pinched everything they could lay their hands on. It was winter-time and we had our fur coats. One day when we got back to the cabin and opened the wardrobe where we kept them they were covered with brown paper on which was written a notice that said, 'Even fur coats have legs,' which we took to be a warning."

The social centre of the liner was the air-conditioned main lounge, 26 ft high, running through three decks, 96 ft long, and 76 ft wide. It was a room of many purposes. In the morning it was used for organ recitals and relaxation; in the afternoon the gentle rattle of teacups would be heard after a recorded orchestral concert. But in the evenings after dinner, when the Wilton carpet and rugs had been rolled back, after the bingo or "horseracing", there was dancing until midnight to the ship's orchestra, playing on a fully equipped stage.

Originally the cinema performances were held in the lounge, which seated an audience of four hundred. Following World War II, however, a separate cinema was built as it was decided that the lounge was not really a suitable venue for screening films.

On Sunday morning, summoned there by recorded church bells, which sounded strangely odd in mid-Atlantic, passengers from all classes would form the congregation for an interdenominational service, always conducted by the Captain, with the staff captain reading the lesson.

The Catholic service would be held in the cinema on Sundays; but on other days Mass was celebrated in the drawing room, the lovely altar with the mural *The Madonna of the Tall Ships* being displayed by the opening of the doors at one end. By a special agreement with the Apostleship of the Sea and the Sisters of Saint Zita, everything was examined and maintained in good condition at the end of each voyage – whether in America or England. This service took special care of the furnishing of the altar linen and the maintenance of the sacred vessels. British designer Kenneth Shoesmith was responsible for the artistic work round the altar. Three altar frontals and five sets of priests' vestments were embroidered by disabled British ex-Servicemen. This was because of Queen Mary's special personal interest in the welfare of disabled ex-servicemen. Each piece was embroidered by one man working in his own home.

After church passengers walked in groups along the promenade deck, which then took on the air of a main street after Sunday church in any small township. It had a completely different atmosphere then than at any other time in the voyage.

There was a Scroll Room for Jewish worship. Many thousands of Jewish passengers worshipped in the liner's little synagogue over the years. The room was designed by the well-known Jewish architect Cecil Jacob Epril and consecrated in 1936 in a ceremony performed by the Very Reverend Dr Hertz, then Chief Rabbi of the British Empire. The very idea of the ship's synagogue had originated with the *Jewish Chronicle.*

The Cunard Company bore the entire expense of building and equipping it, with the exception of a few private gifts of ritual appurtenances. It is believed that this was the first synagogue to be established on board a liner in the history of shipping. Following the immediate success of it, the company decided to erect a Scroll Room in the *Queen Elizabeth.* Likewise *Queen Elizabeth 2* has a small synagogue, quietly situated on the forward section of Three Deck.

But it was over the decorations of this lounge that one of the bitterest artistic arguments in the history of interior decoration was fought. It concerned artist Duncan Grant, who had been commissioned to carry out the décor of this room. At that time Grant, son of an Army officer, cousin of Lytton Strachey, and one of what came to be know as the "original Bloomsbury set," was regarded by many as the finest landscape painter in England. He had turned to interior design, and was again hailed in many circles as the greatest decorator this country had produced.

He discussed the situation some years later:

"I was not only to paint some large murals to go over the fireplaces, but arrange for the carpets, curtains, textiles, all of which were to be chosen or designed by me.

"After my initial designs had been passed by the committee I worked on the actual designs for four months.

"I was then told that the committee objected to the scale of the figures on the panels. I consented to alter these, and, although it entailed considerable changes, I got a written assurance that I should not be asked to make any further alterations. I carried on, and from that time my work was seen constantly by the company's representative.

"When it was all ready I sent the panels to the ship to put the finishes touches to them when hanging. A few days later I received a visit from the company's man, who told me that the chairman had, on his own authority, turned down the panels, refusing to give any reason.

"From then on nothing went right. My carpet designs were rejected and my textiles were not required. The whole thing had taken me about a year. I sacrificed everything else for them. It was the first time I had been asked to do anything for a ship and naturally I had concentrated on them.

"I never saw Sir Percy Bates, and I never got any reason for the rejection of my work. The company simply said they were not suitable, paid my fee, and that was that."

It was hinted at the time that the company had suggested these paintings might go to the Tate Gallery. This inflamed part of the art world, who felt it rather odd that what was not good enough for the Cunard Company was good enough for the nation. The pictures were subsequently placed on exhibition, and at one time during the War, two of them were on display in the two windows of the National Gallery restaurant.

This matter is officially recorded in the minutes of the Shipbuilding Committee in these terms. "The Chairman reported that he and the majority of the directors and the company's architect, Mr Whipp, had inspected the paintings in position in the ship. Their view was unanimous that the paintings did not harmonize with the surrounding features and it was decided that other schemes should be considered for the space reserved."

Grant suggested that he was entitled to "substantial compensation for the damage to my reputation resulting from the cancellation of my contract," and maintained that the pictures remain his property. The chairman replied that the company had done no more than they were legally entitled to and he could not therefore discuss compensation.

The true story of what happened was that the chairman of the company walked into the main lounge to see the pictures hanging above the fireplaces, which were on either side of the ship. Sir Percy walked up to them, scowled , and walked away, saying, "Well you know what you can do with those." As he moved across the lounge one of his fellow-directors said hesitatingly, "Yes, sir?" A slight pause. "Give them to the blind school," and he stormed out.

Later Sir Percy Bates wrote to Mr Morris in New York:

> You will, I know, be sorry to hear that Duncan Grant's three paintings for the main lounge were a complete failure. We had two of the three in position in the ship last week and I took two separate parties of our directors, including Lord Essendon, to see them. All are unanimous that they could not remain in the ship. Apart from the fact that there will be a fearful howl from Grant and

his modern-art friends, we are faced with the troublesome problem of finding alternative decorations for the spaces in question, and the time is short.

We propose to revert to our original scheme of mirrors over the port and starboard fireplaces, and personally I am satisfied that these will look as nice, if not nicer, than any pictures would have done.

A letter, signed by fourteen prominent artists, was sent to the company protesting at the rejection of the pictures. Letters appeared in the newspapers. But the company remained silent, and Duncan Grant told us that one of the conditions under which he received his fee was that he was not to say anything to the Press.

Later, in an article in *The Listener*, Clive Bell on the general artistic scheme of the liner wrote:

> It is generally known that Duncan Grant, the best decorative artist in England and one of the best England has produced, was to have made lovely the central lounge. Had he done so the result must have been a landmark in the history of decorative art. It is known also that all competent judges who had seen his canvasses for the work considered them masterpieces. It goes without saying that the managers did not like them. But it is perhaps a little surprising that they should have refused to put them up.
>
> Frankly is it proper and seemly that on a matter of taste some ignorant businessman should be allowed to overrule the best official and unofficial opinion in England?

Raymond Mortimer, in *The Listener*, wrote of the panels when they were on show at Agnew's:

> For my part I think the mistake was not so much to reject the pictures as ever to commission them.
>
> A super-luxury transatlantic liner depends largely on the patronage of international film stars, financiers, and opera singers and their taste is presumably reflected in the international style of decoration which you find in the palatial hotels all over the world from Palm Beach to the Lido.
>
> I cannot think that such persons would take much notice of Mr Grant's panels, and it would obviously have been unwise not to give them what they prefer. There is certainly nothing alarming or 'modernistic' about the panels. They would, I think, present no difficulty to anyone with education enough to enjoy a Shell poster or the National Gallery.
>
> The colour is gay, the figures harmonious, and the subjects poetical. But they are possibly too English in character for the cosmopolitan purpose for which they were intended. The *Queen Mary* panels are radiant and fill the air with music.

While many of the newspapers praised the decoration of the ship in lavish phrases as setting a new standard in transatlantic travel, there were criticisms.

Clive Bell, in his article in *The Listener*, blamed Cunard's "businessmen" for what he considered a disappointing interior appearance:

The beauty of the ship, her graceful slenderness as one looks along her tapering and swelling hull from some point exactly in front of her bows, or as seen from the opposite bank, her precipitous side in splendour, is so satisfying that the seeker after beauty may be advised to go no farther.

Inside awaits disappointment. And yet nine tenths of the interior would have been well enough and something more than well, if only the people who settle these things could have left it alone. The ship is lined with wood, as a ship should be; lined with veneers of every texture and colour, ordered as often as not with considerable taste. But the good wood surface has been broken up and disfigured with what businessmen call 'art'.

He described the whole style as "teddy bear," and says:

The managers, having voted recklessly for decoration, have been overtaken by terror lest they should be accused of a taste for art. To escape this deadly impeachment they have decided to make a joke of it.

Eric Wadsworth, who painted two works for the smoke-room (which Cunard described as "typical of an English club or country house") has given his own commentary on one of the works, *The Sea*.

The shells are symbolic of organic life and are therefore the biggest objects in the picture, just as the *Queen Mary*, the largest object in life, becomes the smallest in the picture. The ark afloat is the symbol of buoyancy, while the sextant and masthead lights are symbols of orientation; the chains stand for security, and the anchor for faith. That funny thing in the foreground is a brush used for cleaning the boiler tubes and that's cleanliness. That pink ribbon round the column is what the *Queen Mary* is to win back. I made it pink because I thought we had enough blue. I did it all just to please myself.

The artist's initials, E.W., are shown by the International Code flags flying from the flag-pole.

The *Architect and Building News* reported on the décor in these terms:

For the public there is only one imaginative criterion by which the quality of a great liner is assured and that is the degree to which land conditions are reproduced afloat.

The entire romance of a ship design resides in the sensational contrast between the cold, frightening inhumanity of the steel hull cutting its way through the ocean and the cosy, intimate warmth of the interior, in which all the minutes of ordinary life are reproduced. A contemporary describing the public rooms of the *Queen Mary*, hits off these contrasts. "Here we have the rhythm of the people, and the warmth of the soft lighting, yet without the rain lashing the decks, and the grey rollers of the Atlantic may be merely a deeper showdown than the sullen clouds."

That is what people like to think about. There are two architects; the ship architect for the hull and the deck and the hotel architect for the inside.

The standard of finish and craftsmanship from beginning to end is beyond all criticism. The pictures and sculpture are varied in kind and quality and not all of them fit happily into their setting. The general effect is one of mild but expensive vulgarity.

The lounge, in maple burr and makone, carpeted in green and grey and offset with a great deal of gold is too reminiscent of Oxford-Street furniture shops. [This is not surprising, as an Oxford-Street firm had done the decoration!]

The dining-room certainly does achieve an atmosphere of richness unequalled by any London hotel.

It is the largest room ever built in a vessel and its architecture would do excellently for an important church. The soft lighting and grey, gold and bronze colour scheme lap the diners in a lavish haze of luxury.

This dining-saloon is still structurally preserved in its original state. It is enormous: 118 ft wide, covering the whole width of the ship and nearly half an acre in space. There is here, too, the largest decorative panel in the liner, 28 ft high and 14 ft wide, by Philip Connard, on the general theme of *England*. The bottom panel is cut out to make a doorway. High up above the tables, along the sides of the room, are Bainbridge Copnall's magnificent wood carvings.

Off the dining-room the private dining-rooms were decorated by well-known artists, including Dame Laura Knight and Vanessa Bell. This saloon, which could seat all the first-class passengers at one sitting, extends through three decks, and the hull of the first Cunarder and three of the ships of Columbus's fleet could be fitted into it and the foyer. It is, in fact, the largest room built in a ship.

Following World War II, a cocktail bar was created by one entrance.

One of the most striking features of the room was the large decorative map, 24 ft by 15 ft, by Macdonald Gill, complete with moving crystal models of the *Queen Mary* and the *Queen Elizabeth*, showing their relative positions in the Atlantic.

Originally the map showed the two tracks of the *Queen Mary*, as there was then no sister ship. It was after the War, during the refitting of the liner, that the *Queen Elizabeth* was added.

The mechanism which caused the model ships to move on this map was itself a testimony to the ingenuity of the ship's design team. A small motor would keep the models moving at a steady, slow rate as the ship progressed across the Atlantic, whilst slight adjustments could be made to accommodate speed variations caused by bad weather, etc. The entire mechanism was housed behind the map and could be accessed via panelling outside the room.

This map still occupies the whole of the wall facing what was the location of the captain's table. There was one post-war captain, who was very popular, who would refuse to come down to meals in the restaurant if the models were not operating and showing their exact positions. On one voyage there was considerable difficulty in getting it to operate efficiently. The captain was not in the dining-room for three days.

The design schemes for the cabins and state-rooms presented more problems. A number of models were made, and selected firms were invited to submit schemes for the design and layout of furniture, colour charts and decoration for wall surfaces.

The company could not make up its mind on the type of décor and put forward five ideas for wall surfaces, ranging from veneered dado with fabric above to complete fabric walls or plain painted surfaces. The idea that a cabin might be decorated with fabric produced some bitter criticism from Sir Ashley Sparkes, resident director in America.

He wrote to Sir Percy Bates:

> May I record, without the slightest wish or intention of giving offence, my absolute horror at finding that there is an intention of covering the walls of literally hundreds of this fine ship's rooms with what is called 'fabric.' Our fleet suffers now under a terrific handicap from this method of decoration and treatment, and I warn you most solemnly in completing this grand new vessel that is to cost millions of pounds that the travelling public will not stand much longer this form of decoration.
>
> They are becoming educated in simplicity and they are also becoming thoroughly "bitten" by a "pest-and-germ" complex and there is no comfort for any one with that complex to go into a cabin with fabric-covered walls with the knowledge that someone, God knows who, has just finished occupying that room.
>
> I have been in this room for nine weeks. If the walls were covered with row upon row of the impossible little Noah's ark trees that occur in some of our cabins I should by this time be completely potty.

B V Morris had made some inquiries on his own on this subject. He wrote:

> I inquired from two lady clients of mine, who travel annually to France. I asked them to let me know what they thought was desirable from the point of view of American women accustomed to luxury.
>
> They were strong for the inclusion of a number of de-luxe suites (as distinguished from merely cabins communicating through with accommodation for servants).
>
> With respect to fabrics, they were positive in their statement that fabrics gave the impression of stuffiness and that it held tobacco smoke more than wood or paint. The first question they ask themselves is, Who was their predecessor, and they have a feeling that the atmosphere of a previous occupant can be more easily eliminated where a room is either painted or veneered. My wife holds the same views. There is one advantage of fabric, however. It tends towards quietness by the absorption of sound.

Eventually some cabins were fitted with fabric, but in the main they were painted or wood-lined.

In those lean years when work on the actual hull construction was at a standstill the planners still continued their own labours on decorations.

In their desire to explore every artistic avenue in the creation of the interior, they searched Europe for ideas. They looked at the ornate and historic decorations of Europe; the marble and furniture at Chantilly; at Versailles; the balustrading at Fontainebleau; the doorways of Pisa Cathedral; the frieze of the Roman Theatre at Arles; the wood panelling and carving at the Vocchio Palace; and the temple of Diana at Nîmes were among the work inspected.

In 1935 Mr Leach visited the Exhibition of British Art in Industry at Burlington House and reported that the display of fabrics, ceramics and glass might prove a useful source of ideas, but that there was nothing to be learned from the decorations, furniture and carpets.

From the forests of the world came mysterious woods, woods with exotic names. The forests were combed and searched for beautiful wood, and the art of the craftsmen created much of this into delicate veneers. Many of these woods were collected and used for the first time ever, mingling grandeur with simplicity.

Indeed, the *Queen Mary* was to become almost legendary for her beautiful wood panelling. Cunard was very proud of the magnificent displays of marquetry formed from the various types of wood used throughout the vessel, and rightly so. In 1936 they actually published a booklet for their passengers entitled *Ship of Beautiful Woods*, which detailed the 56 different kinds of timber employed.

There were traditional English woods, oak and elm, yew and ash. There were silken avodire from West Africa, deep yellow angelon from South America; padouk from Burma and the Andaman Islands; Brazilian peroba and satinwood from Ceylon; thuya, a rich, deep red wood, used in the roof of Cordoba Cathedral, was carried from North Africa; while from the west coast of the same continent came zebrano. As modern shipping developed throughout the following years, international safety regulations would place more and more restrictions on the use of some materials in the construction of passenger liners and cruise ships. By the 1970s the use of untreated woods was outlawed in shipboard interior design, such were the risks of fire.

Many other materials were also used, some for the first time in a ship such as Quartgate and Malt-maple. Onyx quarried in North Africa and synthetic mother-of-pearl were used with great effect.

There were two personal links with Queen Mary herself. Looking towards the main staircase at the head of the first landing was the marble plaque, carried out by Lady Hilton Young, set in a panel of special walnut burr. Immediately beneath it was her personal standard, which she presented to the liner in May 1936, and which was placed in a glass panel. It was of silk, and measured 3 ft by 1.5 ft. It was of the same design as the large standard which was flown at Buckingham Palace when the Queen was in residence alone. Nowadays, it resides onboard *Queen Elizabeth 2.*

The Duke of Windsor, in his personal memoirs, has recorded this: "She [the *Queen Mary*] was to sail on her maiden voyage to New York on May 26, the birthday of Queen Mary, who the day before in my presence had presented the vessel with a silken replica of her own Standard."

It is a curious feature of ships and shipping that all vessels, regardless of size, age or type, after some years of service are refitted, refurbished and, more often than not, redecorated. This is not only for the express purpose of renewing ageing paint, carpet and wallpaper, but it also helps to maintain a freshness of character. On most occasions, this is a success; however, mistakes have been made from time to time.

Much later in her illustrious career, the *Queen Mary* was to add warm weather cruises to the Canary Islands to her already busy itinerary. This would be in the early 1960s, a difficult time when the air-travel industry posed a serious threat to transatlantic shipping.

In order to enhance the European flavour of these voyages (particularly the Spanish aspect), the Second Class Lounge became the Flamenco Room. The original artwork was covered with posters depicting bullfights, and to the pillars were attached trellises. This was not a popular change and it was generally felt that it detracted from the stately atmosphere perpetuated elsewhere on the ship. The room reverted to its original design when the ship was moved to California in 1967.

One of the men who encouraged Sir Percy through all the problems and difficulties of building the *Queen Mary* was his great friend Rudyard Kipling. As a reward for this Kipling was asked to devise a Latin motto for the *Queen Mary* medal.

After some time he submitted a text, and Sir Percy, ever a cautions man, gave it to the Master of the Mint to have it vetted by the best Latin scholars in the Civil Service.

In due course the Master reported that Whitehall admitted the appropriateness of the text but considered the Latin indifferent. It recommended a simpler phrase, *Maria Regina mari me commisit* (*Queen Mary* committed me to the sea), and this was the motto eventually selected.

Sir Percy wrote to Kipling to explain the situation. The following day he received this postcard: "Do you suppose I was ass enough to try to compose a Latin motto of my own? Tell your Whitehall pundits they'll find it in Horace's Odes."

8

A "Queen" Sails

At the traditional English afternoon tea-time on Wednesday May 27, 1936 the *Queen Mary* was gently and delicately pulled, pushed and tugged away from the quayside and out of her berth at Southampton.

As the strains of *Rule Britannia*, played by the band of the Royal Marines, floated across the water as a farewell tribute she turned her great, sleek black bows towards the open sea. Amid the hullabaloo of shouting, cheering, screaming, laughing thousands, and the roar of aeroplane engines overhead, and the hoot-tooting of the whistle of every vessel in the port, the band changed to the nostalgic notes of *Auld Lang Syne*.

The four thousand visitors, friends of passengers who had been allowed on board, had somehow been gathered up by stewards and officers and shepherded ashore.

"Long as a street and lofty as a tower," she sailed majestically and calmly away down Southampton Water, followed by an armada of tugs, paddle steamers, motor launches, yachts, and even rowing-boats struggling to keep up with the procession. It was at that moment, on a dull grey overcast afternoon, when the last mooring ropes had been cast off and she had eased away from the quay, that the liner really came to life and began her career. This was the beginning of her maiden voyage. It was fitting that this great liner sailed on the birthday of the Queen whose name she carries.

The press and radio-stations of the world ensured that those who stayed at home should not lack for any description of life in what even the dignified London *Times* continually referred to as "The Big Ship."

The British Broadcasting Corporation had sent a team of reporters and commentators to the quayside and to make the voyage. Twenty-eight microphone points had been installed in the ship from the bridge to the engine-rooms for programmes from her at sea. There were to be relays from her in mid-Atlantic of life on board. Two major American companies had sent their own teams of commentators. There were more than one hundred reporters on board charged with filing the vast descriptive stories, superlatives not objected to, on every aspect of the ship's life and progress.

Five special trains had carried the 1,849 passengers from London to Southampton, and the passenger list read like the pages of a social register.

On this day, before he embarked, Sir Percy Bates, the chairman of the company, sat down and wrote in his own handwriting a letter to another man, who had fought vigorously alongside him when work on the construction of the ship had stopped.

He wrote to David Kirkwood, Clydeside MP:

> On the *Queen Mary*'s sailing day it seems appropriate that I should write a line to you to express my appreciation of your faith and help in this great work. This is only your due.
> I sail in her to-day a thankful and a hopeful man.

Eighteen special excursion trains had carried tens of thousands of sightseers to see the liner sail. And this was on a Derby Day. The Ocean Dock and all the surrounding vantage points were black with masses of people.

Standing high on the bridge wing, eighty feet above the dock-side, and jutting out over the ship's side, stood a shy 5 ft 8 in Yorkshireman. His hands thrust deep down in the jacket pockets of his uniform, Captain Sir Edgar Britten, Commodore of the line, watched patiently as the scurrying, bustling tiny figures left his ship. He was anxious to get under way. The captain of the *Queen* had to be a social host as well as a sailor. He always disliked the social side of his work and was always happiest when on the bridge. For him this was a proud day. Sadly, however, within a few short months he was to collapse in his cabin on another sailing day and die in Southampton Hospital.

Perhaps his mind, just for a moment, went back to an evening a week before, when he had attended the first of five gala dinners at the Trocadero Restaurant in London. There he had sat, with his wife and daughter, at a "captain's table," in a restaurant transformed to represent the liner. The corridor entrance from Shaftesbury Avenue had been pictorially arranged to represent Southampton Docks, and a wall two feet thick had been cut through so that guests could use a regulation gangway to "go aboard."

In the restaurant itself there was a captain's bridge and a five-tier deck, built to scale. Searchlights, bells, navigation lights, house flags of the company and *Queen Mary* lifeboats completed the setting, with the roar of a whistle adding local colour. Guests sat in deck-chairs and were served by waiters dressed as stewards. Sir Edgar had autographed all the menus.

After a cabaret the guests danced in the rays of a searchlight in a salon which took the form of a raft moored to the ship, and the orchestra played from the lifeboats. This was typical of the spirit and age of the *Queen Mary*, for she had so captured the imagination of the nation.

For three days before she sailed fifteen thousand people had flocked to the port to pay five shillings a head to tour her. Three hundred French excursionists had crossed the Channel from Le Havre to see her. The £3,750 collected was given to seamen's charities. The company had had to restrict admission to a "ticket-only" basis.

The climax of the pre-voyage excitement had been the visit to the liner by King Edward VIII with his mother, Queen Mary, and other members of the Royal Family. All work in the ship in preparation for the voyage was stopped and all but a handful of the crew were sent ashore, so that the royal visitors could tour uninterrupted. The King flew from Fort Belvedere in his red and white private aircraft, landed at Eastleigh, and drove through cheering crowds to the dock.

Wearing a flannel suit and a straw hat, he walked along the dockside with Sir Edgar Britten, who showed him various features of the liner's design.

He waited until the arrival of the royal coaches which had been coupled on to the *Bournemouth Belle* express and stepped forward to greet his mother. With her were the Duke and Duchess of York, Princess Elizabeth, Princess Margaret, the Duke and Duchess of Kent, and the Duchess of Gloucester. One can immediately grasp the great sense of pageantry and ceremony which surrounded an occasion of this kind; an atmosphere which exists only rarely today. This ship was to be an ambassador abroad, a true emissary for her home land. It was only fitting that the most senior statesmen and women should bestow their blessing on such a noble seagoing lady.

This was Queen Mary's first visit to the ship since she had named and launched her, the first liner to be 'christened' by a Queen of England, two years before. For the King it was his second visit since the naming.

Queen Mary, still in mourning for her husband, King George V, who had died earlier that year, was told all the amazing, fantastic figures and statistics of the liner, including the fact that there were thirty-five public rooms, lounges, smoke-rooms, saloons, restaurants, cocktail bars, libraries, children's playroom.

When she had last seen the ship it was merely an empty shell, a skeleton. Now, she said, the decorations surpassed anything she had ever imagined they would be. After visiting the swimming pool, the Turkish baths, and the first-class accommodation and restaurant, she insisted on going to the kitchens. Here Queen Mary spoke to M. Riccault, the chef, in his native French and discussed with him the details of his staff and equipment.

Here the royal party saw their own lunch being prepared, and the King, noticing the steaks were being charcoal grilled, remarked, "We are going to get something good to eat. That is the best way to cook steak." The royal guests had lunch in the main restaurant, perfumed with the fragrance of sweet peas, carnations, roses and lilies of the valley. The lunch menu was lobster, fillets of beef, poussin, iced hot-house peaches and selected wines.

After lunch Princess Elizabeth and Princess Margaret visited the children's playroom, sliding down the chute, as did the King, and later they saw a Mickey Mouse film in the cinema, Princess Elizabeth herself pressing the control button to start the projector. Little could the young princess have imagined that some thirty-one years later, in 1967, she would perform the launching and christening ceremony for a superliner in her own name, *Queen Elizabeth 2*. The King wandered away from the party to have another look at the Doris Zinkeisen mural in the Verandah Grill.

Every nook and cranny of the liner was visited by the royal guests. Lifeboats were swung for them, and Queen Mary was told that each of the motor lifeboats could carry more passengers than the total complement of the first Cunarder, the *Britannia*.

The Duke and Duchess of York, Princess Elizabeth, and the Duke of Kent descended into the engine-rooms, and after ninety minutes had to be recalled and brought to the 'surface,' as Queen Mary was waiting for her afternoon tea. The King signed a portrait of himself for the ship, and Queen Mary's final comment was, "I am delighted with the ship. She is even more beautiful than I had expected to find her."

Now, on sailing day, the captain had received a radio message:

"All good wishes to you for a successful maiden voyage." It was signed, "Edward R.I."

Down below, out of sight, in the "brave new world" of the engine-rooms, sparkling and glisteningly new, Chief Engineer Llewellyn Roberts stood on the control platform and made a final check. His massive turbines had been turned over steadily for some hours, waiting, tuned, for the order to start. Young Bobby Johnston, a junior engineer, was at his post. He had been with the liner since the fitting out at Clydebank; his father had helped to build her ... and one day he would be chief engineer.

On B Deck Miss Turner, freckled, auburn-haired, stood at the ship's 700-line telephone switchboard (the largest ever installed in a liner), of which she was supervisor, and watched as her operators plugged in passengers still eagerly experimenting with the thrill of picking up the white telephone in their cabin and calling their fellow-passengers. For her this was the first time at sea, and she had already taken tablets to prevent sea-sickness.

She was not to know that, within twenty-four hours, her operators would be working harder than any land-based switchboard. In the radio-room on the sun deck five radio-operators prepared to cope with traffic.

On the first day they dealt with 120 calls to South Africa, Australia and Canada alone, and one caller excitedly told any one who cared to listen that she had heard her dog barking at home in Australia. So many people sent messages to the ship that the press had great difficulty in getting their stories away – some never did arrive.

Mrs Kilburn, in her trim grey uniform, with starched white cuffs, settled her white cap on her neatly waved hair and picked her way calmly and efficiently along the still crowded alleyway. She was not quite sure whether this new uniform was practical. It had been tried out for three months on the *Berengaria*, but she still had some doubts about it.

Going to sea was nothing new to her; her family had served the Cunard Company for three generations. She herself had been a schoolmistress and a nurse before family tradition and her own wishes took her to sea. Now, in charge of the stewardesses, she moved along, and her blue-black eyes did not miss any detail of how her staff were at work, helping the still puzzled passengers to settle down. She had her own philosophy for this job. "A perpetual smiling face never yet cheered a sick woman. Smile when you want to, otherwise just be efficient."

Up in the main square of the ship, along the shipping centre, Mrs Beggs was putting the final touches to her "window display": Spanish dolls at ten guineas each, and a hundred and one other colourful and fancy goods, as well as the more utilitarian wares that the forgetful or needy passenger might require. Charles Carreck, the bookshop manager, set out his magazines.

In the beauty parlour Miss Graham prepared to begin bookings and appointments for "a wave at sea" and for manicures and for the women who wanted to recover from all the fuss and bother of sailing day. Here it was possible to have everything to soothe the tired female; from a permanent wave for fifty shillings to a five-shilling camomile shampoo or eyebrow arching for two and six, or a peroxide and olive-oil massage for four shillings.

By the swimming pool, opposite the restaurant, six decks down, Miss Dand, six foot three, and still beautifully tanned from her previous voyage on a winter cruise, looked at the tiled pool and wondered who would be first to plunge in.

These were just a few of the sixty-seven seagoing women in the liner; stewardesses, kiosk-girls, switchboard-operators, each wondering what the voyage had in store, though each probably guessed they would be far too busy to have much time for thought.

In the dining saloon a young waiter, R Scolby, put the finishing touches to his table, little dreaming that for almost the next twenty-three years this liner was to be his home.

Busying himself all over the ship, here, there, and everywhere, in his new uniform, was Mr Seymour-Bell. He was the only "civilian" to wear an officer's uniform with three rows of gold lace with blue velvet in between on the sleeve. He had been appointed as host, master of entertainment, and generally concerned with the passengers' comforts. Little did he think that, in another twenty years, he would find himself general manager of the company in New York. He probably would not have realized that he was the first of a highly respected and envied line of men who were to preside over all matters pertaining to leisure and public relations on Cunard ships over the following decades. Later, they would be titled cruise directors.

Perhaps the most excited among the passengers was nineteen-year-old Sydney Harvey, a printing apprentice, who was on his way to New York at the invitation of the American YMCA to represent Britain at an exhibition there.

The least concerned was Peter Sommerscales, aged thirteen months, travelling with his mother from Baghdad. He simply slept soundly through all the excitement.

Stewardesses were already busy unpacking for their women passengers and carefully hanging new evening dresses in wardrobes or taking them to be pressed. Court mourning for King George V had prevented the usual gaiety of the London season. For many women this was to be the social event of the year. They had rushed to the Mayfair salons with the verve and abandon and headaches with which, in normal times, they prepared for Ascot or Henley. Evening dresses in colours much brighter than the mourning permitted were stitched and sewn by the costumiers' seamstresses far into the night to meet the demand. Hartnells' said that blues and greens and yellows were the themes for many, both for day and evening wear.

While many passengers lined the rails to watch the fading shore line or tried to find their way about the maze of corridors a slender, nervous, bespectacled man was busy with his own work. This was Henry Hall, whose name was then linked with the BBC Dance Orchestra. One-time music-hall artiste, civil servant and classical pianist, he was now making the voyage at the request of the company as musical director.

Behind the directors' choice lay not only the fact that they wanted a top, "named" band leader. It was planned to do a number of broadcasts from the liner at sea, and Hall's technical knowledge would be a valuable asset. He had gathered around him ten of the top instrumentalists in the country, each man a star on his own instrument, with pianist Eddie Carrol as leader.

One step forward the company took was a decision to have, besides a doctor, a surgeon on board. Mr E R Butler was appointed. This was his first trip to sea, and even today he still recalls the fact that "it was essential to make a correct diagnosis at sea. There were certain types of passenger in those days who travelled with the intention of trying to make money out of the company. We had to take every precaution of ensuring that nothing was left to chance. One woman turned on the hot tap instead of the cold, put her hand under it, then sued the company in America, claiming that the hot water was too hot. She won."

Every passenger had received a document in antique black lettering from the company welcoming them aboard and wishing them an enjoyable trip. Each sentence began and ended in illuminated scrolls, with the great golden seal of the ship on a scarlet panel and each one personally signed by Sir Edgar Britten. Indeed, he had spent much of his pre-sailing time signing autographs both in the ship and on the quay.

At 3:15 passengers had paused in their bustle to hear a commentary on the Derby, which was won by the Aga Khan's Mahmoud.

For several days dockers and seamen had been loading and stowing massive quantities of food and wine into the liner's store rooms and refrigerators. They were crammed into every available corner around the ship's working alleyway – the crew's main street, which runs below the restaurant.

Each room began to look almost like a wholesalers' warehouse as sacks, crates, boxes and cartons were crammed into them. For the ship, a floating town of three thousand people, had to carry not only food and drink, but every conceivable house-keeping article from floor cloths to toothpicks.

Here are just some of the items they had loaded for that maiden voyage:

Fresh meats	50,000 lb
Poultry	20,000 lb
Fresh fish	17,000 lb
Bacon and ham	9,000 lb
Sausages	2,000 lb
Vegetables	50,000 lb
Fresh fruits	30,000 lb
Butter and lard	10,000 lb
Eggs	50,000
Ice cream	6,000 quarts
Wines	14,500 bottles
General stores	200,000 lb
Potatoes	50,000 lb
Nuts	600 lb
Flour	35,000 lb
Sugar	20,000 lb
Tea and coffee	4,000 lb
Biscuits	1,000 lb
Milk	2,000 gallons
Beer	20,000 bottles
Draught beer	6,000 gallons
Cigars	5,000
Cigarettes	25,000 packets

They had also carefully placed on the boat deck, by the kennels, some live hens. These were being shipped out by Frances Day. She said she did not think that she would be able to get fresh eggs every day in mid-

Atlantic unless she took her own supply! They had also stowed her Rolls-Royce in the ship's garage. She was taking it just so that she could drive it down Broadway.

The ship carried 3,500 bags of mail. Philatelists had seized the opportunity, and one firm alone posted thousands of empty envelopes superscribed "Per S.S. *Queen Mary*," with a picture of the liner on the front. Sixteen thousand envelopes would be returned for disposal to collectors.

Frantically the purser's staff tried to cope with the hundreds and thousands of letters and telegrams which had been delivered to the ship. There were more than six thousand parcels, and maids' and valets' rooms were turned into store-rooms for them while every one who could be spared tried to sort and deliver them. Even Sir Percy Bates, company chairman, lent a hand. Some were never delivered at all.

Many of the passengers got lost on their wanderings round the ship and plaintively asked stewards the way to their cabins.

Flowers sent as farewell bouquets were everywhere, and stewards ran out of suitable containers to put them in. In some cases they had to use every conceivable type of utensil as a flower vase, even to the extent of using a bedroom utensil usually kept discreetly in a bedside cabinet.

One stewardess said, "It was really complete chaos, but such friendly chaos. Everyone was so charming and delightful and completely caught up in the spirit of the voyage."

Another stewardess, in answer to a ring from a cabin, entered and was asked for afternoon tea. By the time she had got it she had forgotten which cabin it was. She knocked on the first one and said, "Did you ask for afternoon tea?" The delighted passengers replied, "No, but we will have some." This was repeated throughout the twenty cabins which she cared for, and she did not know which was the original one until she was told, "You have been rather a long time."

By 6:30 the liner had reached the end of the processional way and began to steam across the Channel to Cherbourg. She arrived there in late evening, received another tumultuous welcome, embarked more passengers, and sailed again in the early hours of the morning. She took on board £2,500,000 of gold bullion. A champagne firm sent a three-bottle case of their product to every passenger and it took practically the whole voyage to deliver them. A woman stowaway was discovered and put ashore, but this was part of a newspaper "stunt."

All the way across was one long round of parties, and the party spirit pervaded the whole liner, though a few passengers did manage to go to bed early. No one noticed that there ware no hand-rails along the very wide alleyways for the passengers to hold on to if the ship rolled. No one thought she would roll.

There was dancing: there was 'horse-racing' along the promenade deck. One enterprising bookmaker had even applied to the company for permission to operate in the liner. Women flocked to the shops, buying jumpers, ornaments, and men purchased white-flannel trousers, then all the fashion, and light clothing. Austin Reed's designed a special *Queen Mary* tie, woven in black silk with stripes in the Cunard White Star colours and a narrow line of royal purple. It was only possible to buy this at their two shops on board, and it sold for 4s. 6d.

During the voyage across the Atlantic a second stowaway was discovered.. He was forty-one-year-old Frank Gardner, an unemployed builder's labourer from Cardiff. He was found in the port engine-room and said he had walked on board before sailing posing as a greaser. He was put to work in the kitchens. At New York he was removed by the immigration authorities to Ellis Island and re-embarked to be returned to England when the liner sailed.

Mrs C N Pillman won the first-ever auction pool in the ship, with 747 miles for the ship's noon-to-noon run. The pool totalled £833.

For dinner that first evening M Riccault, the chef, had prepared a special meal:

> *Honeydew melon glacé,*
> *Croûtes-au-pot au perles*
> *Tranche de Turbotin Poche Normande*
> *Poularde braisée, Belle Mère*
> *Haricots verts au beurre*
> *Pommes Garfield*
> *Salade française*
> *Fraises Chantilly*
> *Petits-fours*
> *Dessert*
> *Café*

When this menu was published in some of the newspapers a number of indignant people wrote in to say, "Seeing that the *Queen Mary* is an all-British boat, built and partly subsidized by English money, would it be out of place to have the menus in the good old English language?"

So many passengers wanted to have meals in the Verandah Grill that the *maître d'hôtel* had to make a rule that they could not reserve a table for the whole voyage, but for one meal only.

But while all this spirit of gaiety ran through the upper decks, while deck stewards in their new uniforms of brown jackets and red cuffs and facings served afternoon tea, deep down in the engine room there was no relaxation. In mid-Channel something had gone wrong. Word was passed immediately to Sir Percy Bates and to Mr (later Sir) Stephen Piggott of John Brown's.

Discussions were held as to what could be the cause of the trouble. There was a suggestion that perhaps the liner should be held at Cherbourg to make a complete examination of the engines. At the French port a preliminary investigation showed that a small piece of metal was lodged under the valve in the feed-heating bleed steam system. There was too, a warning of further trouble, with the port outer high-pressure turbine. Here it was discovered that pieces of blade shrouding were missing, and one blade was fractured in the first row on the impulse blading. Piggott thought this was due to overspeeding during her trials.

When the ship reached New York a further inspection was made which confirmed the original suspicions. It was learnt that a similar condition, to a greater or lesser degree, had developed in the first row of blading of each of the four high-pressure turbines. In fact, Piggott later reported that the damage was far worse than they had at first thought.

Constantly on the prowl throughout the ship during the voyage Sir Percy Bates studied the reaction of her to various tests which were carried out, mainly during the night. These included a number of speed changes and manoeuvrability tests. He watched also particularly for vibration, which was very pronounced, especially at the stern.

The whole world watched and waited to see if the new ship would win back the Blue Riband from the French liner *Normandie*. Each day her progress was reported by the radio and newspapers. Each day a progress-report conference was held.

Although on the third day she steamed 766 miles at 30.64 knots, there was to be no record. On Sunday afternoon she ran into fog, which was creeping down off the Grand Banks, and for eleven hours, steamed at reduced speed. When she was in the vicinity of the spot where the *Titanic* sank, a wreath was quietly and without ceremony dropped overboard into the waters of the North Atlantic.

Henry Hall had written for the voyage a special signature tune *Somewhere at Sea*, which was sung by Frances Day and became something of a hit. "As far as I know," Henry said, "this was the first time a liner had a special signature tune written for it."

Frances Day frequently sang with the band, and Larry Adler did virtuoso and novelty pieces on his harmonica.

Henry Hall knew that in the four days of the voyage he was to make fourteen radio broadcasts to England, America and Europe. As the liner sailed he was still discussing his plans. As the listening times in some of the countries were so different from ship times, it meant careful planning and playing at all sorts of odd times. On one occasion it was necessary to stop a film for fifteen minutes in the middle so that they could do their performance. "Actually," he said, "we just pumped out the stuff, and in some cases I fear that the passengers probably got a little tired of music."

As the ship neared New York she received a musical welcome from a number of top-ranking bands in America. As each one played its welcome, Henry Hall's orchestra played their signature tune back in response. For an hour one day Henry Hall and Larry Adler took over the bar, and every tip they collected was donated to seamen's charities.

At three minutes past nine on June 1 the *Queen Mary* reached the Ambrose Light, having crossed in 4 days, 5 hours, 46 minutes, at an average speed of 29.133 knots – 42 minutes behind the *Normandie* record.

In the pilot boat the men were playing cards and drinking coffee as she moved restlessly at her base in Sandy Hook. No one could tell which of them would take over the *Queen* when she arrived, for they worked in strict rotation, taking each ship as she came up. In fact, when the liner arrived and made a signal requesting a pilot, the next duty pilot, Gustav Svenson, was still in his off-duty clothes. He changed hurriedly and climbed into the dory which ferried him across, and began his long climb up the great black side of the liner, watched by passengers lining the rails. He went immediately up to the bridge, and the ship once more got under way to begin her triumphant entry into New York Harbour.

Above her, planes from the 29th Division Air Squadron of the United States base at Staten Island dived and circled; three Eastern Airlines planes under the command of Captain Eddie Rickenbacker first sighted the *Queen Mary* when she was a hundred miles away. One plane circled low and dropped flowers on to the liner's decks.

New York was sweltering and steaming in a heat wave, with temperatures high up in the eighties.

Coastguard cutters circled the ship like an escort of motorcycle policemen to keep the fleet of welcoming vessels clear of her. *God Save the King* was played from one pleasure steamer by fifteen girls dressed in white trousers and black hussar hats.

From another ship floated the music of the pipes. Destroyers, fire boats with their hoses spraying into the air, yachts, ferryboats, pleasure steamers, brought forth a flotilla of welcome.

Every inch on both sides of the river was packed with people, or, as the correspondent of *The Times* put it, "a herbaceous border of humanity." In fact, *The Times* really waxed lyrical, and in one phrase referred to the aircraft as "on tilted wings, like driven grouse coming off the hillside, swirled dizzily and fell suddenly astern." Or again, "from Broadway office windows a gentle blizzard of torn paper appeared in the great canyons between the buildings, bursting on the hot summer air as suddenly and decoratively as a flight of pigeons."

Slowly but surely the great liner eased her way up the river and, precisely on time, at 4.00 pm was pushed into her pier by the powerful Moran tugs; as one writer put it, "both warps curled outward and downward and yoked the proud ship to the city which had given her an unforgettable welcome."

But all was not over. Everyone from the ship was fêted, wined and dined. Celebration dinners were held on the ship. Each night a banquet, which ended at 9.30, was held in the dining room. Then a further fourteen hundred people visited the liner, wandering all over. To meet their thirst nine extra bars were installed on the Promenade Deck.

Sir Edgar Britten broadcast to the American nation:

We had our most sanguine expectations realized so far as the behaviour of the ship was concerned. By that I mean that she handled well at various speeds during the passage and behaved herself as a lady worthy of presentation to the travelling public of America.

Two thousand telegrams were delivered to the ship, but it was completely and utterly impossible to distribute them to passengers and they were returned to post offices and cable offices.

Sir Percy Bates said in one speech:

The *Queen Mary* is a ship of peace. Although our mail contract with the Government obliges us, if asked, to put in stiffening for guns, in the case of this ship no such instructions from the Government were received. In fact, there is no stiffening for guns of any kind. I think that this knowledge will give a satisfaction to you as intending to show that in building this ship we had no other object than the promotion of peaceful intercourse between the largest aggregation of civilized humanity separated by over three thousand miles of water.

The ship was invaded by souvenir hunters, who took everything they could lay their hands on. Ashtrays, plates, spoons, knives, forks, salt cellars, potted plants, brass nameplates, all disappeared in vast quantities. One woman was stopped in the act of taking down one of the paintings.

Six thousand people a day visited her, paying one dollar each for seaman's charities. Special buses ran from all over New York bringing sightseers. One firm made paperweight medallions of the liner, with eight pretty girls to sell them to visitors. Incredibly, only four were sold. Everyone was too busy helping themselves to "real" souvenirs.

Meanwhile, work went on refuelling and restoring the ship, and at 3.30 pm on the Friday she sailed for home. The captain took with him thirty thousand letters he had received, fan mail from all over America.

On the journey back, the second steward revealed that by means of a pedometer he had discovered he had walked twenty-eight miles in one day around the liner, supervising the stewards working under him. The waiter serving the table farthest away from the kitchens, using the same pedometer, established he had walked fifteen miles a day.

On arrival back at Southampton, Sir Percy Bates said:

We have had no bad weather at all. I really want just a bout of bad weather for this ship so as to shake her together. She is a very economical ship and she is an easy ship to handle. All we require for this schedule is 28.5 knots, and I think we have got a ship which will do that, and perhaps more. We have done 28.5 knots with a margin, but I do not know how much margin. Some day we may try to find out what this vessel can do, but records mean risks, and I am not for taking any risks. I am certainly not in any racing mood.

During the maiden voyage, there appeared in the liner's newspaper, the *Ocean Times*, a notice inviting all Rotarians to meet the manager's representative outside the Purser's Office. Seymour-Bell, who had had a good deal to do with Rotary in his days as an executive ashore, organized the meeting. This was the first of many thousands of such meetings to take place on Cunard ships throughout the years – "get togethers" of men of various trades and professions to exchange ideas and introductions for the good of the community. In more recent years the meetings have also included members of other beneficiary organisations; for example the Lions and Kiwanis. Furthermore, soon after the meeting described above, there would begin regular gatherings of Masonic brethren who happened to be travelling. In those days, these meetings were something of a major event on the ship's voyage calendar. Today they sadly pale into the shadows, eclipsed by the sophisticated large-scale entertainment programme offered on modern ships, particularly *Queen Elizabeth 2*.

Two comments from American passengers on that homeward voyage summed up the general feeling.

Dr Nicholas Butler of Columbia University said, "I require three things of a crossing: first, security; second, comfort; and third, speed. The *Queen Mary* has them all. She is the most luxurious liner I have ever travelled in."

Mr Jules S Bache, the well-known New York banker and a transatlantic traveller since 1872, said, "You have here the perfect ship."

9

The Blue Riband

In order to win the Blue Riband award, it is necessary for a ship to achieve the fastest crossing in both directions across the Atlantic Ocean. The official start and finish posts for this challenge are the Bishop's Rock, off the Scilly Isles, and at the Western end, the Ambrose Light Tower.

Two blasts on her whistle in salute to a solitary British fishing boat as the *Queen Mary* steamed past Bishop Rock at 8.12 on the evening of August 30, 1936 signified that she had won back for Britain the Blue Riband of the North Atlantic. She had beaten the record for the round-voyage which the French superliner *Normandie* had set up the previous year.

At that moment of time, unmarked on a chart, a moment which was merely a passing second in life, she had crossed the Atlantic in three minutes under four days; her official time being 3 days, 23 hours, 57 minutes from Ambrose Light, at an average speed of 30.63 knots for the 2938 miles steamed. The *Normandie*'s best time for that voyage was 4 days, 3 hours, 28 minutes, at a speed of 30.31 knots.

No announcements were made in the liner, and, indeed, many passengers did not even know that she had beaten the record, a record for which the British people had waited so hopefully ever since her maiden voyage. Others immediately organized last-minute "record" parties, which went on far into the night as she steamed up the Channel. Many people gathered on the cliff tops at Land's End in the hope of catching a glimpse of her as she passed, but mist came down and she was not visible.

Calmly, almost stoically, a Cunard spokesman at Southampton said, "We are not doing anything special to welcome the liner in the way of celebration. It is all in the day's work to us."

The record-breaking run had begun when she sailed from Southampton earlier in the month after a late arrival due to fog. It was very soon clear that she was to attempt a fast passage, and the world watched and waited for news of her progress.

On the first day she made her fastest run of 472 miles, at an average speed of 29.5 knots. The second day, at a speed of 30.4 knots, she steamed 760 miles, and it was clear she was doing well. So long as the weather held she stood a splendid chance of a record westbound run.

Although later held up by head winds, mists and fog, she reached Ambrose Light in 4 days, 0 hours, 27 minutes, at an average speed of 30.14 knots, in comparison with her French rival's 4 days, 3 hours, 2 minutes, at a speed of 29.98 knots.

Sir Edgar Britten said in New York, "I know that the British nation will share my own pleasure that this great ship on which so much thought and money have been expended has justified the expectations of her creators."

From Malta, where he was on a cruising holiday, the King sent this message, "Sincere congratulations on *Queen Mary*'s fine record."

Then she turned round and began her homeward bound voyage. As soon as news of her record was announced crowds began to gather at Southampton and in the Isle of Wight to see her arrival in her home port.

Up Southampton Water she steamed, followed by a vast armada of paddle-steamers, yachts and boats of every description, while steamers gave her a siren welcome. Huge crowds gathered at her berth to welcome the record-breaker home. She docked at 12.40 in the afternoon amid what were described as "scenes of tremendous enthusiasm."

Sir Edgar Britten said, "I believe we have a great deal in reserve. We have not been unduly pressing for speed on this last crossing." Chief Engineer Llewellyn Roberts, recalled form leave for the voyage, said, "I think we should all be surprised if we really opened her out."

The King, who had now joined the yacht *Nahlin*, which he had chartered from Lady Yule for his Mediterranean holiday with a small party of friends, including a woman whose name was beginning to be connected with him, Mrs Simpson, sent this message: "Heartiest congratulations on completing the record." This and his previous message were posted in the officers' and crew's quarters.

Few people knew that the whole voyage had been carefully calculated; each day's run mapped out, not to break the record, but to give the designers and builders of the engines of her sister ship, No. 552 (the *Queen Elizabeth*), fundamental and factual information which they required. This had been no haphazard speed attempt. It was scientifically devised fact-finding voyage and nothing else. The company was certainly not interested in the Blue Riband Trophy and very soon made this clear.

It was Mr H K Hales, then Member of Parliament for Hanley, who had originated the trophy. The rules under which it was presented were administered by an international committee of which the Duke of Sutherland was chairman. These laid down that the trophy would be awarded for the fastest two-way crossing, provided it stood unchallenged for three months.

As the liner was docking at Southampton after this voyage Sir Percy Bates in Liverpool was receiving from the representatives of the Liverpool Underwriters' Association and the London Institute of Underwriters a rose bowl for use on the captain's table. He said that he did not approve of a cup being connected with the Blue Riband of the Atlantic.

"I feel that we are proud of this honour without a prize. I would sooner the honour without a prize."

He stressed that it had always been the company's policy never to indulge in speed for speed's sake.

> While we have let out the *Queen Mary* during this voyage we had an object in what we were doing. We are at the moment engaged in consideration of the details of the *Queen Mary*'s sister ship. To help us to a proper consideration of the details of the machinery and the propellers the round voyage such as *Queen Mary* has run this last fortnight was of the greatest assistance.
>
> Accordingly, before the ship started on the last voyage I took counsel with the builders and our own technical experts, and the figures which we have obtained as a result of this voyage will be of the greatest assistance in considering No. 552 in the next few weeks.

The company refused to accept the trophy.

The *Normandie* did not allow the British liner to hold the record unchallenged. In 1937 she swept back to her position as holder of the Blue Riband with a westbound voyage of 3 days, 23 hours, 36 minutes, at a speed of 30.59 knots, and returned in 3 days, 22 hours, 7 minutes, at 31.2 knots.

Although the public heralded the new liner and Sir Percy Bates had said in public that he was quite satisfied with her, she was far from the perfect ship designed on paper and tested so thoroughly in the experimental tanks as a model. The vibration in the *Queen Mary* was no new problem in big-ship design. The French liner *Normandie* had a similar problem.

There are two ways in which the vibration can be cured. One is to change the pitch of the propeller or the revolutions of the engine; and the other is by stiffening the structure. In January 1937 steps were taken to combat vibration by stiffening.

The ship's framework was stiffened with a number of additional steel stanchions, 18 inches in circumference, extending from the sun deck to the lower decks and built into the hull. This was an immense task, and necessitated the complete stripping and dismantling of many staterooms and public rooms, including the lounge and smoking-room. All the oak panelling had to be taken down and the rooms stripped down to the steel work.

In several sections existing stanchions were reinforced by twelve-by-fourteen-inch steel channel-beams running across the ship. Similar beams were run the full length of the liner on both sides of the promenade deck. The bilge keels on either side of the ship were widened by several inches.

At the same time, despite those one thousand tests which had been carried out in an effort to ensure that the propeller design was correct, all was not well. The original design was found, in practice, to reach the design revolutions without absorbing the designed power. This did not help the vibration at the after end of the ship.

It was quite clear on the voyage down to Southampton from the Clyde that the propeller design was faulty and that the art of designing was far from being as scientifically accurate as had then been thought. Eight propellers had been ordered – four working and four for reserve – to John Brown's design. The order or construction was divided between J. Stone and Co. of Deptford and the Manganese Bronze and Brass Company of Millwall. They were, at the time, the largest solid propellers ever cast and the heaviest manganese-bronze casting in the world. They were four-bladed and 20 ft in diameter, and each weighed 30 tons. The *Mauretania's* propellers had weighed 18.5 tons and were 16 ft 9 in in diameter, while those of the *Bremen* were 18 tons and 16 ft 5 in in diameter.

At Stone's the molten metal was carried from the furnaces by overhead travelling cranes in huge ladles carrying 20 tons each. Each casting took eight days to cool off before being removed from the casting pit. Each propeller was subjected to severe tests on a balancing machine.

They were taken by eight-wheel adjustable lorries to the Surrey Commercial Docks in London (at night time because of the size of the load), and shipped to the Clyde.

The manganese-bronze propellers required fourteen days to cool down before they were taken from the moulds, each of which took eight weeks to prepare.

Mr S McAlister, the propeller-design expert at Stone's, was called in to see what he could do about the propeller design. He had made a careful study of propellers, with especial reference to vibration and was regarded as one of the world's experts.

"It was clear when the liner was brought down from the Clyde to the Southampton Graving Dock that the pitch of the working propellers was wrong and that the revolutions were too high to absorb the rate of power. In the dry dock the spare propellers were fitted and used as working propellers."

In the meantime, Stone's had designed their new Heliston propeller which had been fitted to the *Aquitania*, giving her either a 2.5 knot speed increase with no additional fuel consumption, or a reduction in running costs of £10,000 a year if she ran at her original speed and saved the cost of reduced amount of fuel due to increased efficiency.

"Sir Percy Bates said to me that if we could guarantee to give the *Queen Mary* an additional three knots in her speed (ship owners are greedy, you know) we could fit them to her. I said the best I could guarantee would be half a knot. But if he could guarantee from God that the weather in the North Atlantic would always be good, then we would guarantee a higher speed increase. He failed ... and so did we.

"I had investigated the propeller situation for the *Queen Mary* mathematically and studied three possible designs, for pitch, erosion and diameter.

"I then set to work and in ten days designed a new propeller which I felt was suitable for the liner. I did everything that the text-books said was wrong; reduced the pitch, the area and the diameter. I knew I was right and stuck to it. There comes a stage, with all design work, when all the text-book knowledge and the known experience can take you no further. You are on your own then and you have to make up your mind and stick to it. You just have to have faith in your ability."

Two of the new propellers were fitted after the ship had been in operation six months and placed in the outside positions. Close watch was kept on them and on performance and vibration during the next few trips. It was noticeable that the shaking was considerably reduced.

Sir Percy Bates made a trip in the liner with Mr McAlister.

"On one 24-hour run we ran on our two propellers and everything was "rigged" including the day's run. Vibration had virtually disappeared, and we got an order for four propellers. I myself sat in the shaft tunnel and there was no movement there at all. The original propellers gave 28 knots at 173 revolutions a minute, while the new ones gave a working speed of 28.5 knots at 173.5 revolutions. Running costs could be cut down by about £15,000 a year."

In the June overhaul the inner propellers were replaced by the new design, as it was felt this was justified after the running experience gained by the two in the outer positions.

Every one was so delighted with the original design of the ship that no one had thought for a moment that she would roll in those long Atlantic swells. They thought she was too strongly built for the sea to affect her. So no hand-rails had been fitted along the alleyways, which were much wider than those usually found in a liner, and much of the furniture in the dining-saloons and lounges had not been "anchored" to the floor. All went well for the first few voyages during the summer months. But in October of that first year she began to roll – suddenly and unexpectedly. A member of the crew, a stewardess, has described it: "It was in the middle of the night and she suddenly started to go and she went, so slowly, down and down and down and down. I was thrown out of my bunk and thought that she was never coming back. I remember thinking to myself even as she went down, 'This is the end. She can never come back from this angle.'

"Slowly she righted herself and then began a horrible corkscrew motion that went on and on even after the sea had become calm. She just didn't seem to be able to stop it."

Kay Stammers, the tennis star, was among the passengers on that trip and she said the liner rolled and rolled so much that some passengers became hysterical. Many were injured and treated in hospital. The liner had run into a 55 mph gale and was 3.5 hours late docking at Southampton. Speed had been reduced at times to 14 knots.

On the following voyage a small "army" of joiners and carpenters was embarked and began the task of fitting the hand-rails to the corridors and anchoring the furniture. They still had not finished when the liner reached New York.

Questions were asked in the House of Commons about the voyage, and the Government spokesman replied that "the owners have taken steps to ensure that the difficulties encountered during the recent rough weather should not recur."

It was in this month of October, on the 28th, two hours before the liner was due to sail for New York, that Captain Sir Edgar Britten was found unconscious in his cabin. His personal steward found him there, lying on the floor in his pyjamas. It was thought that he had got out of bed to dress before the morning crew inspection and had collapsed. He was taken off the ship to a Southampton nursing-home on a stretcher and died five hours later when the liner was in mid-Channel on her way to Cherbourg. He was sixty-one years of age, and due to retire early the following summer. Captain R V Peel, hastily summoned from his Southampton home, took over the liner for the voyage.

Later the body of the first master of this great ship was taken out to sea and buried in the Channel. Many of his friends said that the immense strain of commanding such a ship had taken its toll. He had always said he disliked "the entertaining which I have to do as captain of the *Queen*."

Smoke, too, had proved another problem. Once again all that the designers had done on paper and in their funnel tests had failed to provide the ideal solution. On the trials the after decks were covered in grit from the funnels, and during the first voyages the company paid out a lot of money in compensation to passengers for damage to clothes. Smoke-washing devices were eventually fitted into the funnels, which eliminated this difficulty.

During the overhaul new quarters were built for the engineer officers, who had complained of the location of their original ones deep in the ship. The new quarters were built above the first-class smoke-room and by the Verandah Grill, and had a direct lift to the engine-room and were complete with their own kitchens, pantries, bathrooms and ward-room.

One other fault of the liner, which could not be eliminated and which at times was a source of irritation to passengers, was her draught. She drew 38 ft, 10.5 in of water when fully loaded, and because of this and the depth of the water at Southampton she sometimes had to anchor off Cowes for the tide for several hours to get up the Ocean Terminal. One passenger whom this always irritated was Lord Beaverbrook, who eventually adopted the policy of leaving the liner at Cherbourg and flying to Southampton.

Colonel Denis Bates, the late chairman of the company, said, in referring to her displacement, "Carrying capacity is a compromise between conflicting requirements. It has to be as big as possible, but space per passenger has to be attractive, and if dimensions become excessive the added displacement increases engine power and fuel requirements for the same speed, again adding to displacement, and a stage is reached when draught, which affects also the power needed, limits the freedom of operation in ports.

"At 39 ft for the *Queen Mary* the limitations are severe, but at the time it was the best possible compromise."

After all these alterations and improvements the liner was once again ready to make a challenge for the fastest crossing. She and the *Normandie* on several occasions beat each other by a few minutes. But in August 1938 the *Queen Mary* finally won the honours. She made the westbound voyage in 3 days, 21 hours, 48 minutes, at 30.99 knots, and returned in 3 days, 20 hours, 42 minutes, at 31.69 knots.

This honour she held until the post-war era when the *United States*, the American 'secret' liner (whose engine-room details for many years remained unreleased), subsidized by the US Government, swept across at speeds of 35 knots. It is well known that she was capable of much higher speeds.

In July 1952, when then 53,000 ton *United States* had recaptured the Blue Riband, it was said that in Le Havre she was berthed immediately astern of HMS *Indomitable*. Jack Frost was standing on the flight deck eyeing her critically. An American sailor shouted across some remark about the Blue Riband.

Jack replied: "When you get to Southampton don't get too close to the *Queen Mary*. You might get hoisted inboard!"

10

Called Up

On August 30, 1939, the *Queen Mary* sailed from Southampton for New York, leaving an England where hopes of peace were dwindling. She carried a record number of 2,332 passengers, mostly Americans hurrying home from a Europe which had for so long been threatened with war. Many of those passengers had scurried around at the last minute, frantically changing their travel arrangements and bringing forward their return journey by weeks or even months, in an attempt to flee a Britain which was rapidly descending into the ravages of war. The situation was even worse for those who had first to make the journey from the continent, across the English Channel, in order to board the *Queen*. One passenger, Janet Aschaffenburg, remembers the turmoil:

"In 1938, I crossed the ocean for the first time on the *Normandie* and we were due, my aunt and I, to come back on the *Queen Mary* at a later date, than we were forced to come back. So we had to scramble around to change our departure. We left under cover of darkness on the boat train from Paris to Cherbourg and it was touch and go whether or not we would be able to sail or not. The ship was in complete darkness. Every inch of space was taken not only by Americans, but by foreigners who were scrambling to get to the United States."

On the morning of the *Queen Mary*'s departure, one newspaper carried the headline: "Americans Go Home!" and another: "Americans leave immediately." The *Queen Mary* was filled to capacity. Every berth was taken, every cabin full. Even the public rooms were packed with people who had been unable to buy a "real" bed. Some slept on the floor, some in cots, others in the armchairs and on the settees. The ship was crowded with thousands of nervous, frightened souls, all desperate to get to the United States.

On September 3, that mild September morning when Neville Chamberlain mournfully broadcast to the British people, gathered round their radio sets, that the country was at war, the liner was more than halfway across the Atlantic. She reached New York and lay at her berth in that then neutral port in the harbour on the Hudson River all through September, while the authorities puzzled over how she could best be used. The majority of her crew were shipped home, and her peacetime colours were replaced by a characterless wartime grey.

With her immense size, for she was then the largest and fastest passenger liner afloat, and a tempting target for any German submarine commander, the authorities were anxious not to sail her without fully examining her capabilities in wartime and without assessing what protective measures would have to be taken for her safety. Certainly while the War's opening phases were being fought out there was not much use to which she could be put. On October 10 the Admiralty instructed the Cunard Company that they were not to sail the liner for time being. Actually, earlier in April 1939, unknown to her passengers, the eleven hundred men and women of her crew had been trained in air-raid-precaution work while she crossed the Atlantic. By the end of the third voyage the whole complement had received instructions and were well versed in gas-mask drill, decontamination, how to deal with casualties, and all the other air-raid-precaution essentials.

All throughout that winter of the "Phoney War" she lay in New York, with searchlights playing on her as a precaution. One member of the Houses of Parliament suggested in 1940 that she should be sold to the then-neutral Americans, as she appeared to be completely unsuitable for any wartime use.

Eventually there was a great and pressing need for tonnage on the Atlantic route, but the authorities were not prepared to risk the liner, because U-boats were beginning to take a mounting toll of British shipping.

In October 1939 it was reported that elaborate precautions had been taken to strengthen the guard on her. This followed a warning from the United States Intelligence Department that an attempt might be made to damage her within the next few days. It was thought that Nazi agents in America would attempt to blow her up or set fire to her.

Late in the evening of March 1, 1940, a telephone rang in the company's headquarters in Liverpool. It was the Ministry of Shipping saying that the *Queen Mary* was needed for Government service. The liner had received her "calling up" papers. Throughout those first days of March, painters gave her a further coat of dull-grey paint, while sand suckers were at work removing the silt which had accumulated under the keel in the past seven months.

It was in New York on March 7, 1940 that the *Queen Mary* first met her sister, the grey-painted *Queen Elizabeth*, when she arrived there after her secret dash across the Atlantic from the Clyde, still unfinished.

The two would lay side by side for two weeks, accompanied by their French counterpart, the beautiful *Normandie*.

Early in the afternoon of March 19, 470 British seamen arrived onboard, confirming the public's suspicions that the liner was to move and to be used as a troop transport. Those crew members had been transferred from another Cunard ship, the *Antonia*. Passers-by noticed that some of the ship's lifeboats were being tested.

On March 21 the *Queen Mary* slipped down the Hudson River away from New York; her work as a Government transporter had begun. She would not meet the *Queen Elizabeth* again until a year later, when both would be in Sydney, Australia. The *Normandie* would meet a different fate; in the midst of refitting as a troop transport, she caught fire on February 9, 1942. The thousands of tons of water poured onto her superstructure to extinguish the fire caused her to capsize in her berth and she remained in that position, humiliated and undignified, until salvaged in an operation that would take some fifteen months and $5,000,000.

The *Queen Mary* took a southerly route and maintained her usual peacetime speed of around 28 knots, as she hugged the coast of South America until turning right across the South Atlantic and on to South Africa.

On April 29 it was reported from Cape Town, South Africa, that when residents had awoken at dawn one morning earlier in the month they had seen what King George V had described as "the stateliest ship in being," steaming into Table Bay escorted by low-flying bombers. From the South African port, after bunkering, she set course for Sydney, again averaging more than 28 knots.

She reached the Australian port on April 17 and immediately was prepared for war service. Her interior was completely stripped and much of her luxurious fittings and furnishings were subject to a stringent inventory and sent up country for storage. Others items had already been taken ashore in New York. In the astonishingly short time of fourteen days the Cockatoo Docks and Engineering Company prepared her as a troopship. Wooden-tiered bunks were erected in cabins and hammock racks and hooks fixed on the bulkheads in public rooms; sanitary equipment was augmented, and stores loaded for thirty-two days. Her passenger capacity was increased from just over 2,000 to 5,500 and a new certificate issued accordingly.

The company had sent out a team of experts to supervise this work of changing the character of the liner. These were invaluable and were headed by Frank H Dawson, who later was to become general manager of the company.

The *Queen Mary* embarked 5,000 Australian troops and at 7.00 am on May 5[†] she weighed anchor and departed for England. She set sail

---

† Some sources determine the date of the convoy's departure as May 4. By local time in Sydney, Australia (ten hours ahead of British Summer Time), however, the departure time was 7.00 am on May 5.

with five other great ships – Cunard's *Aquitania* and *Mauretania*, Canadian Pacific's *Empress of Britain* and *Empress of Japan* and the Royal Mail Line's *Andes*. "Convoy US3" was completed the next day by the addition of a seventh ship: the *Empress of Canada*. But even as the *Queen Mary* sailed in those strange waters of the East, travelling in waters where no one had ever dreamed she would sail, with the added complication that she was not equipped for tropical climates, the war situation was changing.

The convoy called at Freemantle on May 10, and sailed again on May 12 at 12.30 pm. They were bound for Trincomalee, Ceylon when on May 16 they received orders to alter course for Cape Town. From there, they were routed for the United Kingdom with a call at Freetown for oil.

Surprisingly perhaps, and despite her new role as a troop carrier, the *Queen Mary* still carried liquor. In fact many of her fine wine stewards were still onboard during this voyage. The soldiers were able to enjoy an occasional drink (mostly beer); the officers lived in comparative luxury, enjoying their meals in magnificent dining areas complete with passenger-standard trimmings and full service.

The *Queen Mary* reached the Clyde on June 16, 1940 and safely disembarked her precious human cargo. The Australian troops were eventually stationed at Colchester. There was no such journey south for the *Queen* herself, however. The prospect of docking at Southampton was considered far too dangerous by this time. She, like her running mate the *Queen Elizabeth,* would be sitting ducks for enemy aircraft.

France had fallen. Britain after Dunkirk, still living under the threat of a German invasion, was desperately short of men and materials. But at the same time the war leaders knew that the key theatre was to become the Mediterranean. The role of the *Queen* was immediately switched. She became one of the monsters who were to rush troops who could be spared from the task of defending England to bolster up the sadly depleted force in the Middle East. She embarked five thousand British troops in the Clyde and sailed to make a rendezvous with other transports in one of the greatest convoys ever to leave British shores, heading for the Middle East. Other ships in that historic fleet included the *Empress of Britain* (Canadian Pacific), *Franconia* (Cunard), *Andes* (Royal Mail Line), *Stratheden* and *Strathaird* (P & O), the *Orion*, the *Otranto* and the *Ormonde* (Orient Line), *Monarch of Bermuda* (Furness Line), the *Batory* (Gdynia-America Line), the *Aska* (British India Line) and the *Kanimbla*, an Australian armed merchant cruiser. This incredible convoy comprised some 30,000 passengers onboard £25,000,000 worth of seagoing hardware.

For the next few months the *Queen Mary* was to be a multipurpose troopship, being switched here and there. Though there was a virtual surplus of large shipping at this time in this trade in these waters, the authorities would not yet risk her on the North Atlantic, where the toll of shipping sunk by submarines was steadily increasing.

All ships require maintenance whether at war or peace, and it was decided to drydock the *Queen Mary* during late summer 1940. After calling in at Cape Town once more and then at Trincomalee, Ceylon she arrived in Singapore. It was here that she would be drydocked, at the only facility big enough to take her. Designed to accommodate the largest capital ships in the Royal Navy, it was too small to take the 1,020 feet of the *Queen Mary* comfortably, though on August 5, she was eventually squeezed in with just inches to spare. A 41-day refit and overhaul commenced immediately, during which all routine cleaning, maintenance and painting was carried out, together with several modifications, included the installation of a new minesweeping paravane system. She left the Singapore drydock somewhat earlier than planned and raced back to Sydney in a state of emergency, prompted by the Italian invasion of Egypt, which had triggered a major risk to the security of the Suez Canal.

All through 1941 she made Sydney her base, and it was there in April of that year that once again she met her sister. Although the Australians were rightly proud of their harbour in Sydney, in the event of a gale blowing up there was safe anchorage for only one of the *Queens*, and so while one was there the other went to Hobart in Tasmania.

At Sydney voyage repairs were carried out and boiler cleaning took place. Twelve water-tube boilers were cleaned at a time, steam being kept on the other twelve in case a southerly gale should suddenly come up. Here too, armoured protection was fitted over the skylights above the engine room.

All through that year the *Queen Mary* ferried troops to the Middle East, sometimes taking Italian prisoners of war back to Australia.

These voyages in the East were always tense. Many of the troops understandably found the enforced confined space of a troopship very claustrophobic. The situation was heightened by the continuous state of alert, brought about by the ever present threat of attack from German submarines and surface craft. The ship was not dry in those days, and beer was sold to the men. This undoubtedly prompted much of the trouble that occurred and on one occasion the naval commander of the convoy made a recommendation that the ship should be dry, as there had been so many outbreaks of violence and fighting.

Lovers of animals, they smuggled all types of pets onboard. On one occasion a ship's officer walking along the working alleyway got the shock of his life to see a young wallaby come hopping towards him. Stunned, he saw it disappear somewhere in the maze of the liner and never did find out what happened to it.

Tom Webster, the cartoonist, had sketched a series of famous sportsmen as a decoration for the gymnasium. Some enterprising soldier felt that this "shipboard Hall of Fame" was no place for Don Bradman and cut out his picture. It was later discovered in a new location – proudly enhancing the wall of an Australian school, though this did not come to light until the post-war refitting of the vessel as a passenger liner, when the covering boards were removed.

At times there was fierce fighting among the crew. Included in the crew at that time were representatives of two well-known Liverpool gangs, the Kellys and the Sweeneys. In Liverpool, these gangs had their own territory, vigorously and jealously guarded, where no member of the other gang would set foot, unless out on a raid. This policy of territory was transferred to the ship by these gang members and there were many fights. Secret drinking was the main cause of the quarrels and, on more than one occasion, the target for their wrath (when they were not fighting among themselves) was the cook! He had been at sea all his working life and always, when he turned in at night time, slept with a large and heavy file under his pillow. More than once he had to use it.

The ship's company, especially when in the Indian Ocean, was liable to errupt. She had never been designed for these areas, and conditions were indescribably hot, tempers were frayed and gang warfare broke out. One gang's favourite "weapon" was to raid the firemen's galley and throw boiling water over their rivals. The attackers would then be cooled down by having the fireman's hose played on them. An alternative punishment was salt-water showers.

At the same time there was a large number of roughnecks among the crew, who were always complaining about the food and conditions. On one occasion, a body of these men marched into the kitchens, seized one of the cooks and put him into his own oven, which was heated.

Those responsible were rounded up and, full of their own importance, were put into the lounge. They soon changed their attitude when a detachment of the Royal Marines came onboard from the cruiser *Cornwall*, which was escorting the liner. These, with all the discipline and pomp and ceremony of the fine corps, almost as if they were at their home depot, marched onboard with fixed bayonets. The offenders' jaws dropped and, with the aid of a few bayonet jabs, they were taken onboard the cruiser and put ashore at Cape Town. From there they were shipped home to Glasgow.

In May 1940 Bombadier Leslie Gabriel of Hobart, Tasmania, travelled in the *Queen Mary* with 4,999 other "passengers" from Sydney to Greenock. He vowed that one day he would sail in the liner as a fare-paying passenger and, in 1959, he achieved his wish. After a business trip to America, he embarked the ship in New York and met Captain Andrew McKellar, the master, who had been the first officer onboard during his previous voyage in 1940.

The captain showed him a polished wooden plaque with silver mounting which the Australians had presented to the ship at the end of their 43-day voyage. Gabriel told the Captain that he and his colleagues contributed sixpence each to the cost of the plaque but never really knew whether one was bought or what happened to it. The captain told him that it held an honoured position in the captain's cabin. He had a photograph of it taken, and Gabriel took it with him to show the members of his Old Comrades' Association at home.

Earlier in 1941, it had been decided that she should again go to Singapore for drydocking and cleaning. But the landings of the Japanese in North Malaya and the startling progress they made down the mainland towards Singapore caused the naval authorities to have second thoughts and, twelve days after the attack on Pearl Harbour, she was ordered to return to New York.

She arrived in New York on January 12, 1942 and was soon after transferred to drydock in Boston, where she was subjected to a thirteen-day refit programme. It was during this refit that her troop-carrying capacity was increased to 8,500. She was fitted with an enormous number of extra standee bunks, placed in every possible location. The standee bunk was an American invention. A simple device, it consisted of a tubular steel frame which supported strips of strong canvas. Depending on the height of the ceiling several bunks could be installed above one another. Stowage was easy: they had provision for being lifted up and hinged against the wall, thereby providing extra working and living space when not occupied by sleeping troops. Furthermore, they could be tiered so that far greater numbers of men could fill the same space utilized by hammocks. In some cases they were erected six high, with just enough room for a man to squeeze into his standee, with the man above him practically resting on top of him. The standees were installed all over the ship; in the cocktail bar, the bottom half of the boarded-over swimming pool, in the cabins; in every conceivable nook and cranny, leaving only a few rooms for eating.

Enough standees were erected to enable 8,000 men to sleep in them. But the realistic Army authorities pointed out that a man does not sleep twenty-four hours a day, and that each berth could be used twice, so that, in effect, each bunk had two occupants. In some cases they had three occupants in the twenty-four hours in eight-hour shifts.

One slept during the night time, leaving it in the morning, while his fellow-occupant slept in the day time. In this way 15,000 men could be carried. One third of the troops slept on the decks, and there was a nightly rotation so that each man slept inside two nights and outside two nights. During this major Boston refit, extra toilets and showers were added too.

All through 1941 there had been complaints about the inadequacy of the liner's anti-aircraft defences. These were described by one officer commanding troops as "inadequate, with an insufficiency of arms for training and an inadequate supply of weapons."

She was mostly defended by a number of Vickers and Lewis guns, as if she had been some small tramp steamer, and for other defence had only one 4-inch gun. Frequently even the Admiralty complained about her lack of defensive armament. During this 1942 refit she was fitted with ten 40-mm cannons, twenty-four 20-mm cannons, six 3-inch guns and four 2-inch anti-aircraft rocket launchers which were fitted next to the aft funnel.

Just as land-based radar had played such a vital role in the defence of Britain during the early days of the War and had played such an important part in the Battle of Britain, so, too, it provided an important link in the defence of the great liner. Even when Britain had very few marine radar sets the *Queen Mary* had one fitted in 1942. This was to prove invaluable.

To protect her from magnetic and acoustic mines, she was equipped with degaussing equipment. This consisted of heavy copper strips suspended in a rubber channel around the exterior of her hull, and also with equipment which sent out sound waves to explode mines at a distance.

On February 18, the *Queen Mary* set sail for Australia via Rio de Janeiro and Cape Town; she was carrying 8,398 troops who were desperately needed to augment the defences of the Australian mainland against the steadily advancing, seemingly invincible, troops of the Imperial Japanese Army.

Captain (later Commodore Sir) James Bisset took over in command of the vessel on his first voyage with American troops. He boarded her off Key West and took over from Captain Townley, who was retiring. Bisset should have relieved Townley at Trinidad, but the authorities said there were too many submarines in the vicinity, and the ship had been diverted.

Captain Bisset was the most senior master with the Cunard Company at the time. Not known for his love of social activities with passengers or crew, he preferred to keep himself to himself for much of the time. He did however, command enormous respect from his crew and fellow officers. John Mace, a Quartermaster at the time remembers that, "His reputation was wonderful as a tough and gruff sailor. He was [around] 68 or 70 years old and he was a captain who had sailed on sailing ships. He was a very super person [but] not a social captain at all."

She took a circuitous route through the Caribbean and out to the open sea by way of the Anegada Passage doing 30 knots and zig-zagging. The *Queen Mary* travelled without surface escort but was guarded during daylight by three American planes until she was clear of land. The Anegada Passage was calm and narrow. Half an hour after the *Queen Mary* sped through it the radio room picked up an SOS from a steamer that had been attacked by a German submarine only ten miles astern. The remainder of the voyage was uneventful.

It was during this journey down towards Rio that there was much concern regarding reports of the imminent placement of several long-range U-boats in the Western Atlantic and the Caribbean. This concern would prove to be completely justified.

She arrived at Rio de Janeiro on March 6 to take on oil fuel. At Sao Paulo, John Hubner, a United States Foreign Department official, had discovered a radio transmitter, imported by a German firm and held for delivery to a purchaser whose address was non-existent. Hubner got the police to watch the store shed throughout the day and night, and their patience was rewarded when one evening a young German called to collect the package and was arrested.

Taken to headquarters for interrogation, he eventually disclosed the names of his confederates and the location of a secret radio station in the hills above Rio. Hubner flew down to Rio and with the police raided the station, operated by a Nazi organization, just as a message was being sent, giving the time of sailing and the course of the *Queen Mary*. A message was sent in time to the liner and she changed her course. It was thought that the spies had been radioing to the newly arrived U-boats operating in the area so that they could intercept the ship.

At the same time another spy ring was operating in the country for the Italians. This was eventually broken up late in September of the same year. The Argentine police announced that an Italian count, an officer in an airline, had confessed to providing information for secret radio transmission to Rome about the passage of the *Queen Mary*. The police said that the seizure, together with that of several others who were rounded up, had broken up a big Italian espionage ring similar to the group operating for Germany, which was smashed several months before.

President Eisenhower, in his book *Crusade in Europe,* described the incident in these terms:

> The transport of personnel without heavy equipment did not involve elaborate arrangements when fast ships were available. These vessels depended solely on their speed for safety against the submarine. The British gave us the use of some of the fastest and largest passenger ships afloat. Among these was the *Queen Mary*.
>
> One day we despatched her, without escort, from an Eastern port in the United States to Australia, loaded with 14,000 American troops. It would have been only bad luck of the worst kind if a submarine had got close enough to attack her successfully. Moreover, we believed that even if one torpedo should strike her she would probably have enough remaining speed to escape from any submarine of the type then possessed by the Germans. However, such probabilities could provide no assurance that she would get through.
>
> On that trip the *Queen Mary* had put into a Brazilian port for fuel. We were horrified to intercept a radio message from an Italian in Rio who reported her presence to the Italian Government and upon her departure actually gave the direction upon which she set out to sea. For the next week we lived in terror, fearing that the Axis might be able to plant across her path such a nest of submarines in the South Atlantic as to make it impossible for her to evade them completely. I do not remember whether General Marshall knew of this incident at the time, but it was the type of thing that we kept from him when

possible. There was no use burdening his mind with the worries that we were forced to carry to bed with us. He had enough of his own.

Another type of drama befell the *Queen Mary* during her crossing from Rio to Cape Town. Over 1,000 miles from land, a fire broke out in a corridor on Deck B. It is thought that this blaze was caused by faulty wiring. The prompt action of soldiers and crewmen resulted in the total control of the fire – despite the fact that smoke rose as far up as the bridge – and the conflagration was soon extinguished.

On April 6, 1942, she sailed from Sydney, bound for New York. It was on this return Voyage to New York, when two hundred miles off Bermuda, that the liner passed five lifeboats with survivors from a sunken merchant vessel. The boats were taking advantage of a fine day and moderately northerly wind. They were under sail and navigating towards Bermuda. Commodore Bisset, warned of one or possibly two submarines in the area, determined to continue his way, despite his natural inclination to rescue the seamen. Signalling with his morse lamp, he told the lifeboats he would report their position. Upon arrival in New York he was thanked by the Navy and told that the lifeboats had been picked up by an American ship the following day.

Some time later the *Queen Mary*'s purser, Charles Johnson, received a note from his wife telling him that their son had been in one of the boats. The lad, she said, was annoyed, to say the least, to see his father's ship speed by, leaving him and his companions in the lurch, and was said to have commented: "There goes the big bastard!"

On her arrival in New York on May 7 at the end of the round voyage she was ordered to the Clyde with American troops. Her ship's company thought that at last they would have some leave and stay in an English port. But early in 1942 Rommel had counter-attacked, and in a campaign of seventeen days had pushed and driven the British back and later, launching another drive, had pushed towards Alexandria. Only the exhaustion of his forces and supplies seemed to save the situation.

The British desperately needed reinforcements; men, tanks and war materials of every kind and of a quality to match the superior weapons of the Germans. It was a question of who could re-equip first, the British or the Germans. Ships were collected and it was once again the size and capabilities of the *Queen Mary* which played a vital role. It is probably true that the liner played a bigger part than any other single ship in saving the situation.

Within a few short months she would carry new armies of men, hundreds of American tanks, and vast supplies of war material that were to help to make the victory of El Alamein possible and, with that turn in the fortunes of the Allies, ultimate victory possible.

It was on the night of May 10/11, 1942 that the *Queen Mary* embarked 9,880 troops for her first military trip across the Atlantic. Any of her

The beautiful, stately boardroom in Cunard's Liverpool headquarters. It was here that many historic discussions took place and where several momentous decisions were made, including that to go ahead and build no. 534. *Liverpool University Archives*

Sir Percy Bates at his desk.
Liverpool University Archives

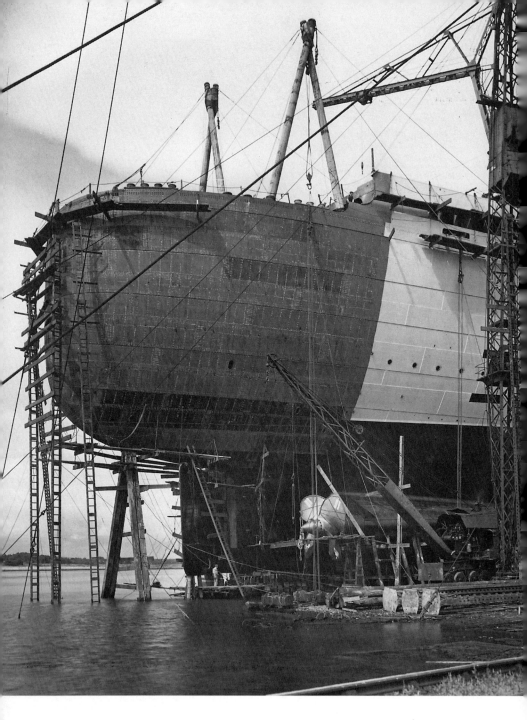

The huge stern of 534 hangs over the end of the launching ways, awaiting a coat of paint and dwarfing a shipyard worker standing beneath. The unpainted section clearly reveals the incredible number of heavy gauge steel panels required to build the hull, all of them painstakingly riveted together. The blades of the propellers are rimmed with protective material. *Liverpool University Archives*

At the very aft of the ship, skilled workmen labour at the propeller bossing. One of them sits atop the end of the gigantic stern frame. The rudder alone, in the background, is evidence of the enormous number of rivets used in the vessel's construction.

Liverpool University Archives

A shipyard execut[ive]
stands under the h[ull]
during the latter p[art]
of construction,
probably
mesmerised by the
sheer size of the
structure. The hea[vy]
timber poles are
securely jammed
into position by th[e]
numerous wooden
wedges on the
ground.
Liverpool Univers[ity]
Archi[ve]

Underneath the hu[ll]
thousands of tons [of]
drag chains lie,
waiting for the day
when they will be
put to use, tugging
and pulling the hug[e]
metal hull to stop i[n]
the River Clyde.
Liverpool Univers[ity]
Archi[ve]

The device which supported the bows and kept the hull steady during the critical stages of the launch the launching cradle. The picture is a perfect study of the juxtaposition of timber and steel.   *Liverpool University Archives*

Waterborne and almost clear of the launching ways, the *Queen Mary* is still draped with cables and chains which gradually bring her to a halt in the Clyde. A small steamer looks on, (right).   *Liverpool University Archives*

The fitting-out process was a lengthy one and involved intricate co-ordination between the shipyard and hundreds of smaller companies around the country. Here, the brand new *Queen Mary* is seen against the industrial landscape of John Brown's and the town of Clydebank.   *Liverpool University Archives*

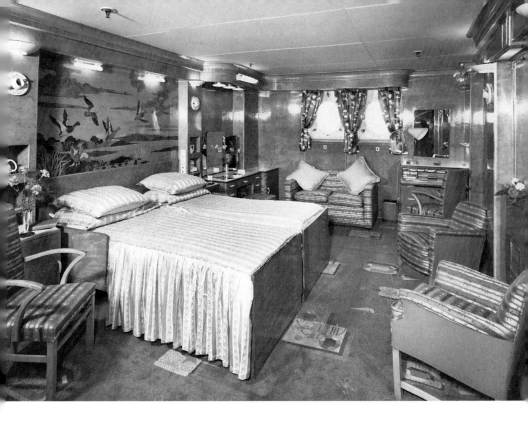

Stately, comfortable: a First Class stateroom. *Liverpool University Archives*

The contrast between classes was obvious. Though comfortable, this Tourist Class cabin had none of the trimmings to be found in the First Class staterooms.

Liverpool University Archives

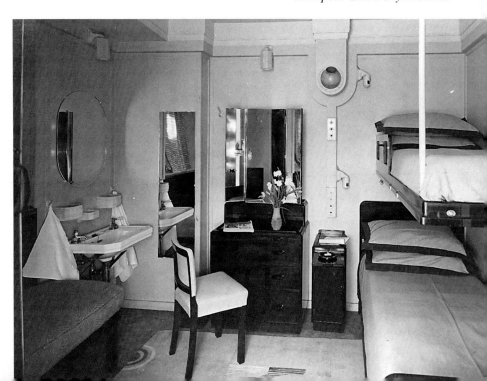

The vast expanse that was the First Class Restaurant. The map at the end of the room has become legendary. Two crystal models of the *Queen Mary* and the *Queen Elizabeth* would move across the map as the voyage progressed, indicating the exact location of each ship. *Liverpool University Archives*

The First Class Lounge was one of the most comfortable and luxurious public areas ever put to sea. It was also one of the largest. Note the beautiful trumpet type lighting fixtures placed around the room and the heavy marble fireplace at the far end. *Liverpool University Archives*

The most talked-about room at sea; the fabulous Veranda Grill. Situated high up in the aft end of the ship, this beautiful extra-tariff restaurant was everybody's favourite evening haunt. Note the mast housing passing up through the room, just behind the grand piano.

Liverpool University Archives

A favourite location of many passengers, the Observation Bar or the O.B. This room is, as its name suggests, situated at the very forward end of the ship, overlooking the forecastle. A fine example of art deco at sea.

Liverpool University Archives

One innovation was the addition of a Tourist Class cocktail bar, situated on Main Deck. Featuring much use of Formica, inlaid metal and glass, the room was regarded as strikingly modern at the time.

Cunard Line Ltd

Long before the digital age, all telephone calls had to pass through a telephone operator. The switchboard would be manned continuously night and day.

Liverpool University Archives

Ship owners were still eager to convince the public of the enormous size of their vessels. One sure way to do this was to publish comparison illustrations, showing the ships in unlikely and absurd situations. This classic picture depicts the *Queen Mary* as she would appear if placed across Trafalgar Square, London.   *Liverpool University Archives*

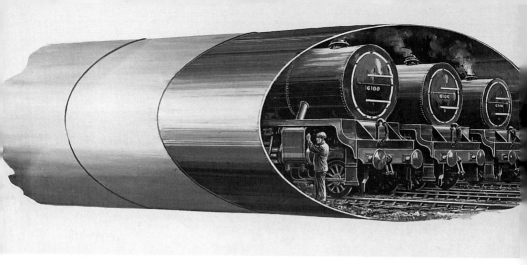

In this comparison picture, the enormous size of the *Queen Mary*'s funnels is conveyed by demonstrating that three locomotive engines could fit inside one stack.

Liverpool University Archives

The first Cunader *Britannia* rests inside the First Class Restaurant. She is neatly flanked by Columbus' entire fleet - the *Nina, Pinta* and *Santa Maria*. It is apparent that this picture is still at the drawing board stage and far from completion. It is, in fact, one of several comparisons that were never used for commercial purposes.

Liverpool University Archives

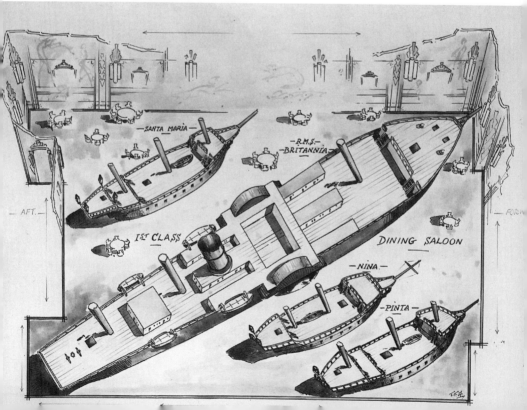

Seemingly, not a single inch of the forecastle is left unoccupied in this wartime view. All the troops are wearing lifejackets. Whilst this was of course a sensible precaution, it restricted the men's movement and took up extra room.

Liverpool University Archives

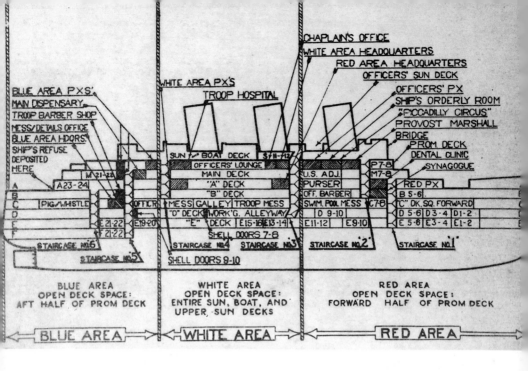

Troops, officers and crew were strictly zoned within the three main colour-coded areas, Blue, White and Red. Traffic systems were set up, ensuring that congestion was kept to a minimum.

Liverpool University Archives

The First Class dining room on the *Queen Mary*, converted into a mess hall. It was here that thousands of meals would be served each day, in record time.

Imperial War Museum A25924

The swimming pool converted into a messdeck, compete with bunks and cabins.
Imperial War Museum A25931

The *Queen Mary* under way in the North Atlantic. The Grey Ghost as she was known, steams across the dark waters of the Atlantic carrying thousands of troops en route between continents. Her speed and the use of zig zag courses, saved the huge ship from enemy attack.
Imperial War Museum A11325

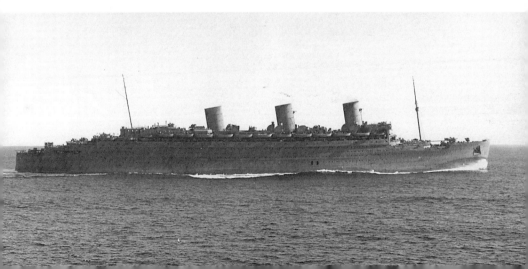

The *Queen Mary*'s bow following the collision with the *Curacao*. The impact caused the steel to buckle in on itself otherwise she was unharmed. The degaussing strip is visible, running around the grey-painted hull.   *Liverpool University Archives*

One can only guess at the thoughts in this young girl's mind as she holds her baby close and gazes across the ocean through one of the *Queen Mary*'s windows. Thousands of young women would cross the ocean on this voyage of discovery.
Liverpool University Archives

March 28, 1946. GI Brides and their children en route to their new homes. Left to right Maureen Novick and son Gary; Philomene Berry and daughter Valerie; Marjorie Nese and son Michael; Mary King and son Adrian; Betty Kilpatrick and daughter Denise; Vera Kinkle and son Barry.   *Liverpool University Archives*

The *Queen Mary* rests in the drydock during overhaul, her bows festooned with
scaffolding and walkways. The anchors have been lowered from the pipes and painting
and restoration work has started. *Liverpool University Archives*

As the sun glints down across the black steel panels with their thousands of rivets, cleaning and maintenance work progresses in the King George V drydock. Dockyard personnel working on the propellers perch on planks supported by wooden ladders. Lights, for night work have been slung over the ship's stern rails.

Liverpool University Archives

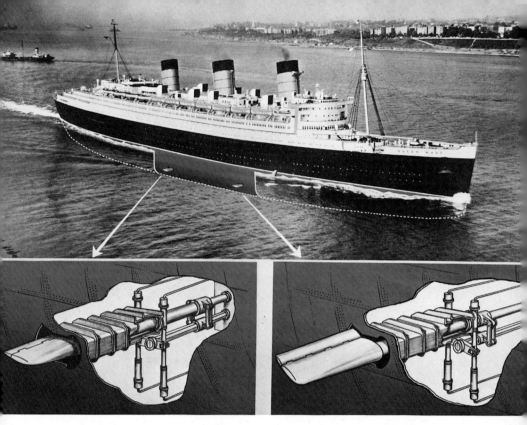

The addition of stabilizers was of tremendous marketing value to Cunard, though their installation was not easy and required much rearrangement of existing machinery. They were literally squeezed in.   *Liverpool University Archives*

In her years as a liner, the *Queen Mary*'s engine and boiler rooms had been filled with machinery of every kind.
Liverpool University Archives

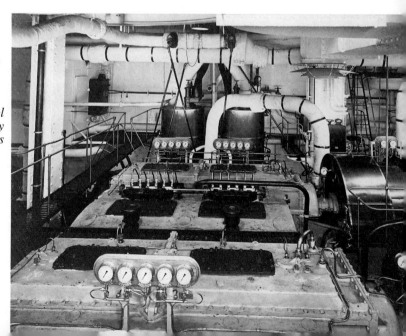

Now, in Long Beach these massive areas inside the ship are empty, gutted and strangely eerie.
RMS Foundation, Queen Mary *Archives*

Despite the numerous political wranglings and arguments, work actually did steadily progress through the first few years in Long Beach. In this gutted boiler room, an escalator has been installed, together with a new staircase. Rough iron decking has been covered with quality flooring
RMS Foundation, Queen Mary *Archives*

The long streamlined structure of the world's most loved ship rests at last in Long Beach Harbour. She would soon become the subject of never ending management and power struggles.   *RMS Foundation,* Queen Mary *Archives*

The giant promenade decks, where thousands of passengers would stroll away the hours during the heyday of transatlantic travel

On the opposite side of the ship, part of the old Promenade Deck has been converted to the Promenade Cafe.

Looking aft, the massive funnels still present an imposing sight. Note that these are not the *Queen Mary*'s original stacks these replacements were installed following the Long Beach refit. Two London telephone boxes rest on the deck, at the bottom of the picture.

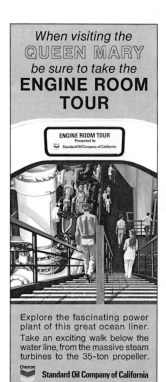

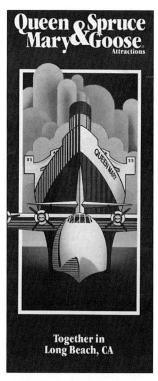

Over the years, numerous tours and promotions have been offered onboard the *Queen Mary*, with varying degrees of success.

RMS Foundation, Queen Mary Archives

crew looking forward to shore leave in Britain were disappointed. Upon arrival in Gourock, another 9,357 troops were embarked and the ship sailed almost immediately to Suez, via Cape Town. John Mace remembers the conditions well:

"the ship was not designed for high temperatures. It was not a warm weather ship, so we had a few people who died onboard. Some of the boys died because we were passing [through] the tropics. The conditions onboard were very hot onboard and some people succumbed to heat exhaustion."

Despite the appalling conditions, the operation went smoothly and after 24 hours the ship was loaded up with German prisoners-of-war, Polish guards and an assortment of allied military personnel. She then turned and sped back to New York via the Cape and Rio.

From October 14 to November 2 she was drydocked again in Boston to facilitate repairs following a tragic collision with a naval cruiser, the *Curacoa*. This incident would be the only disaster of her otherwise unblemished wartime career. Following the drydocking, she went to New York until, on December 8, she sailed once again for Britain carrying 10,389 soldiers and arriving in Gourock on December 14, her last visit there during 1942. It was then that she began her last voyage to the Mediterranean and Australian waters. This has been recorded as the 'Long Voyage'.

This odyssey lasted four months, and she called in West, South and East Africa, Egypt, Arabia, British East Indies and Australia, steaming forty thousand miles and carrying thirty thousand troops. During this voyage there was a great deal of trouble and disturbance with the crew, who were getting very restless, particularly towards the end. Messages were sent to the Ministry warning the authorities that unless the ship returned to a home port fairly soon there would be serious trouble.

After her return from this voyage she began to undertake the journey for which she had been built – the North Atlantic run, although her terminal port here was Gourock in the Clyde. She was to make a total of twenty-eight round trips on this route, with occasional calls at Halifax, before victory had been won in Europe.

In New York, where the *Queen* tied up at the quayside, there was always the possibility of sabotage. A strong guard totalling some 750 military police was placed on her and all along the quay and at the entrances when she was there. The commanding officer of this guard said to them: "You begin today guarding a ship so vital to the United Nations that if it meant choosing between your safety and that of the vessel I would necessarily sacrifice every man in this company."

Four officers and 135 men were placed onboard and were on duty for six hours at a time. It took four and a half hours for duty officers to check this guard and that on the quayside.

There were numerous alarms. On one occasion beer bottle tops were found stuck in the nozzles of the fire hoses. On another occasion when the lifeboats were lowered into the water to test them, a number of them began to sink. It was found that holes had been bored in the bottom of them.

Some of the most important and far-reaching British decisions regarding the conduct and course of the War were made in the liner as she ploughed her way across the Atlantic. On three occasions Winston Churchill travelled in her to America and Canada, accompanied by the Chiefs of Staff Committee and an assorted collection of other experts in many fields, as well as a large secretariat. Various ministers would travel with the Prime Minister according to the subjects to be discussed with the Americans, as well as planners, administrative staff, intelligence and staff officers, representatives from the three Services, cipher clerks, detectives and a guard of Royal Marines, who also acted as orderlies. In fact, the liner became a veritable floating Whitehall. Winston Churchill's wife accompanied him, as well as his daughter Mary.

It was while lying in bed in his stateroom on "M" Deck that Churchill heard for the first time the whole overall detailed plan for the Allied invasion of Europe. It was one morning when Brigadier K G McLean and two other officers from the planning staff of General Morgan came to his cabin at his request and, after setting up a large-scale map of the beaches and the coastline explained, as Churchill put it, "in a tense and cogent tale the plans which had been prepared for the cross-Channel descent upon France." They explained to him the whole plan, with exact detail about number of troops, aircraft, ships and tonnage.

Each time the Prime Minister travelled, structural alterations had to be made within the ship. In the first place, the whole of the accommodation occupied by his suite had to be sealed off from the rest of the liner. Offices had to be provided for his staff, map-rooms set up, as well as a conference room and eating quarters for the entourage.

Furniture had to be taken out of store so that the cabins and staterooms could be restored to something like their former sate of comfort. The suite became a "kingdom" of its own, with its entrances carefully guarded by the Marines and with laws of its own. The ship, then ferrying American troops, was always dry. When Churchill first heard of this he pulled what was described at the time as "a very glum face". So it was decided that his accommodation should have its own licensing laws and that alcohol could be served.

On one occasion when a steward was moving round pouring out tumblers of water before going round with the champagne, Churchill said, "Stop pouring all that water out. It is too depressing a sight."

It was at the end of April 1943, just after the Tunisian offensive, that the Prime Minister decided it was time he and President Roosevelt had a personal conference. He was anxious to discuss Sicily, Burma and the grave shipping position with him.

He had just recovered from pneumonia and his doctors refused to allow him to fly in a bomber. The *Queen Mary* had reached Gourock on

April 22, at the end of the Long Voyage, which had lasted four months. She was then preparing to sail to New York with five thousand German prisoners onboard.

The point was raised by the security authorities whether it was advisable for the Prime Minister to sail with so many of the enemy, and it was at one time mooted that the prisoners should be transferred to another ship. No one would make a decision so that the matter, in the end, was referred to Churchill himself who replied, "I could not see what harm they could do us under due control and without weapons, so I gave instructions that they should come along."

All the arrangements were made, including the building up by the security forces of innumerable "cover" stories to hide the identity of their important passenger. A number of notices were put up in Dutch and the security men allowed it to be circulated that Queen Wilhelmina and her suite were going to America. In the alleyways, ramps were built to give the impression that perhaps Roosevelt was returning in the liner. Various other stories were spread about for, as Churchill said, "the more stories, the more safety."

But all the carefully laid plans were endangered when, at the last moment, it was discovered that the ship was bug-ridden. This had happened when moving troops on the Suez-Australian run, and it was said that the vermin came from the baggage and equipment of the Australian Division, which had been in store in Egypt and also from the coolies who had loaded the ship there. Whatever the source, the authorities were determined that the Prime Minister should not sail with the ship in such a condition.

To have her properly treated now would necessitate her going into dry dock, and the Ministry of Sea Transport officials were anxious to avoid this, as it would mean losing a round voyage, with the resultant heavy loss of troop capacity. It was decided that if the Prime Minister could postpone his trip, a gassing process could be used in the Clyde, which, it was claimed, should give the passengers relative immunity. The process would take around a week.

The security forces were alarmed at the delay, as they felt that each day the voyage was postponed increased the chance of information leaking out as to the identity of the passengers. Lord Alanbrooke, in his diaries, said, "The main danger rested in the German embassy in Dublin. They would soon be aware of the journey and might use their wireless to inform Germany, who would then be in a position to station submarines to try and intercept the *Queen Mary*.... However, the risk did not appear to be much."

Actually, Alanbrooke tried to get the Prime Minister to postpone the date of his departure, as the Chiefs of Staff were not ready for discussions with the American authorities. He was told they could utilise the time during the voyage to make their final plans and that they would leave on Sunday.

In the interim period security was discussed with the Prime Minister and the Chiefs of Staff. Churchill was told that an aircraft carrier would provide escort in the areas where there was danger of air attack. Cruisers had been detailed to provide protection on sections of the journey, beginning off the coast of Northern Ireland. On May 5 Alanbrooke embarked. The party were taken by special train from the station near Olympia. He recorded at the time:

> We arrived at Greenock at 3.40 pm and transferred to a launch which took us out to the *Queen Mary*. The height of her was most impressive as we drew alongside and when we got onboard it was a job to find one's way about.... They have done marvels in a short time, and the cabin I am in must be almost up to pre-war standard. A very large double room very well fitted with sitting room, two bathrooms, and masses of cupboards and armchairs.

His diaries were written in a number of small leather lock-up books bought at a Salisbury bookshop, out of remaindered stock from the *Queen Mary*. The party was in no way immune from the stringent safety precautions and the following day all had to attend boat drill.

> Tonight we go through the worst part of the run, and there are several submarines spread out on our course, but they are mainly on their way to and from the ports of Biscay and Northern Convoy routes. Escaped reasonably early and in bed by midnight. We had taken a southerly course towards Cape Finisterre so as to cross Submarine Piccadilly, the route linking their operating areas with their reporting base, at right angles.

On this voyage Lord and Lady Beveridge accompanied the Prime Minister. It was their honeymoon trip. At the first meal they attended with the Prime Minister Lady Beveridge appeared very badly bitten by bugs, while there was not a mark on Lord Beveridge. The eagle eye of Churchill spotted this, and with a twinkle in his eye, he remarked in a stage whisper, "What's the matter Beveridge – are you sleeping apart?"

When the ship arrived in New York, American newspaper men asked Lady Beveridge whether, during the trip, she had been frightened of submarine attack. "Submarine attack?" she replied. "You should have seen the attack of the bugs. They were the most frightening thing." This gave the journalists an opportunity to produce a banner headline reading "BUGS WORSE THAN SUBMARINES."

The next time Churchill travelled in the liner was to the Quebec Conference in August 1943. This journey was to Halifax, Nova Scotia. The Prime Minister arrived onboard after lunch. This time, in view of the importance of the mission, which was to make the final plans for the Allied assault on the mainland of France, the strictest secrecy was maintained.

Churchill was taken out from Gourock to the Tail o' the Bank in the tug *Romsey*, (which was later moved to Southampton). Having put him onboard however, the tug did not return to the pier, but was sent up one of the lochs and the crew kept there incommunicado until news was received that the *Queen Mary* had docked safely in Halifax. Only then did they return to Gourock.

As Churchill himself was to write later:

> The *Queen Mary* drove on through the waves, and we lived in the utmost comfort onboard her with a diet of pre-war times. As usual on these voyages, we worked all day long. Our large cipher staff, with attendant cruisers to despatch outgoing messages, kept us in touch from hour to hour. Each day I studied with the Chiefs of Staff the various aspects of the problems we were to discuss with our American friends. The most important of these was, of course, "Overlord."

His wife travelled with him on this trip with his daughter Mary, a subaltern in an anti-aircraft battery as his aide-de-camp. There were more than two hundred staff besides the fifty Royal Marines.

He also took with him, at very short notice, the young Brigadier Wingate, the brilliant Chindit leader, for discussion on Wingate's idea of long-range jungle groups in Burma. The Brigadier had been flown home from Burma and had met the Prime Minister at 10 Downing Street.

Earlier that year his long-range penetration group had made its operation in Arakan. After dinner at Downing Street Churchill had decided that the Chiefs of Staff should hear of his ideas and plans for this type of operation.

> I decided at once to take him with me on the voyage. I told him that our train would leave at ten. It was then nearly nine. Wingate had arrived just as he was after three days' flight from the actual front and with no clothes but what he stood up in. He was, of course, quite ready to go, but expressed regret that he would not be able to see his wife.

She was in Aberdeen and on her way to London by the night express. The Prime Minister gave instructions and at 11.15 pm that night she was taken off the train at Edinburgh and the following morning the couple met, and she travelled in the liner with her husband.

One morning during the voyage Wingate was summoned to Churchill's cabin to explain his plans for an increased, improved Long Range Penetration Force. Churchill had before him a copy of Wingate's report to the Chiefs of Staff Committee, and they discussed it at length.

On another day when the Chiefs of Staff were discussing the whole campaign in the Far East, Wingate was called in to explain his views. He wore a battle dress of naval cut with no badges of rank and no ribbons except his triple DSO, the last bar for which he had been awarded while on his way to England. Some of his fellow passengers, while admiring the greatness of the distinction, commented adversely on the oddity of the uniform. Apparently this was all he could obtain on the ship to fit him. The two hundred and fifty people travelling to "Quadrant" and Quebec had been on this trip before and consequently made something of a "set" or a group, from which the Wingates naturally felt apart. This was remarked upon and a Major-General, noted for jollity, was urged to make friends with the strange couple and bring them into the shipboard convivialities. The General found his efforts quite fruitless, and was somewhat daunted by the stern, concentrated spirit which met him.

Wing Commander Guy Gibson, fresh from leading the attack which had destroyed the Mohne and Eder Dams, was also in the party. Three officers sent by General Morgan, Chief of Staff to the Allied Supreme Commander (who had not yet been chosen), were there too. They were responsible for the Allied landing plans.

The Prime Minister was listed in the secret passenger list merely as "Colonel Warden", his wartime pseudonym. As the liner forged her way on her evasive course across the ocean, making wide sweeps to port and starboard in accordance with the anti-submarine strategy so imperative for so large a vessel on such a momentous journey, within the first-class cabins the great task of preparing for D-Day went on.

One member of the staff who worked during that voyage later recalled:

As soon as we boarded the *Queen Mary* lying in the silent waters of the Clyde, with her camouflage of blue-grey to tone with the sea, we knew for the first time what our destination was.

We immediately set to work preparing minutes and other documents. Relentlessly the pressure of work fell upon us, hour after hour, as with the needs to put back the clocks, so the working hours multiplied until we fell exhausted in our beds when our chiefs cried a halt - usually when Churchill himself had retired in the early hours of the morning.

The luxury of our cabins and the excellence of the food took us out of the austerity of war-wrecked London into a new world of graceful living.

The need for secrecy naturally extended to communication methods. Despite the fact that the Prime Minister was onboard, radio messages were hardly ever sent from the liner. Churchill's numerous messages were flashed by morse lamp to a nearby cruiser, which would then dash to a new location, maybe 100 miles away, and only then transmit the message by radio.

There is a short anecdote – perhaps of doubtful authenticity but nevertheless typical of this liner – concerning her arrival at Halifax. A small pilot boat was trying to get alongside the massive ship. It made several attempts but each time missed her. One of the officers on the bridge of the *Queen Mary* then leant over the edge of the bridge and shouted, "You stay where you are. We will come alongside you."

At the end of the voyage the Prime Minister wrote to Captain Bisset:

A second time this fine ship while under your command has conveyed myself and a highly important mission across the Atlantic.

I can only repeat what I wrote to Captain Illingworth on the last voyage that all arrangements have been admirable, and the efficiency with which they have been carried out had contributed not only to the comfort and convenience of the passengers, but to the output of work which they have been doing and have been able to continue to do without interruption since leaving England. Will you please convey my thanks to all officers and ship's company.

Yours Sincerely
WINSTON S. CHURCHILL

The Prime Minister's final wartime journey on the liner was to the Second Quebec Conference in 1944. Shortly before he was due to sail he had arrived back in England from a visit to Italy with a temperature of 104 degrees and a minor attack of pneumonia. Despite this the doctors declared him fit to travel. So he made the journey to Quebec for the talks which had been called to determine what role Britain could play in the final assault in the Far East, particularly in respect of the use to be made of the Royal Navy in the campaign in Burma, as well as to plan the final stages of the war in Europe.

The ship intercepted a radio signal on September 7 from a German submarine, reporting having seen the liner. One wonders what impact this made in German Naval headquarters and whether they could have taken more determined steps to attack the liner if they had known who was onboard.

Admiral of the Fleet, Viscount Cunningham, who was also travelling on the ship recalls that Churchill sent for Commodore Bisset and tried to persuade him to alter course into cooler weather. "As this would have taken us over the Newfoundland Banks and have caused a deviation from the track laid down by the Admiralty, Bisset very rightly objected."

The *Queen Mary* reached Halifax on the morning of September 10, and after lunch the party left by special train for Quebec. At the end of the conference, Alanbrooke, Cunningham and Portal were invited on a fishing trip to the Oriskany Lake. After the second day Cunningham had to leave to rejoin the liner for a journey home with the Prime Minister. Alanbrooke and Portal, who were flying to England, spent another two days in the wilds.

After one night in Quebec, I [Cunningham] flew to New York with some others and embarked in the *Queen Mary* that evening, September 19. We left the jetty at 7.30 the next morning and the Prime Minister and his party came onboard at the quarantine anchorage. Escorted by three American destroyers, we sailed soon afterwards. I lunched that day with the Prime Minister, Lord Leathers, the Minister of War Transport, and General Ismay. Mr Churchill seemed very well and in high spirits and now thoroughly converted to the use of the British Fleet in the Pacific. That is why I mention this particular meal, of soft-shelled crab, and large beefsteaks, because the Prime Minister told Lord Leathers that the Fleet train for the Pacific must be done on a handsome scale. If we needed thirty or even forty ships we must have them. Lord Leathers became somewhat pensive.

We had hoped to save a day by landing at Fishguard, But there was a heavy sea running and we had to push on to Greenock, where we arrived at 5.30 pm on September 25 and travelled by the night train from Glasgow to London.

11

G.I. Ferry

Early in 1942, the Prime Minister decided it was time to make a journey to the USA, now that America was at war after Pearl Harbour. He was anxious to have a personal talk with President Roosevelt and discuss with him the whole future concept of the War. He took with him a large team of advisers and the talks covered a multitude of crucial issues.

When the main discussions had finished the Prime Minister asked the President to move three of four United State divisions to Northern Ireland. He felt that this move would demonstrate to the world in general, and Hitler in particular, that the Americans really meant business in Europe as well as the Far East and that they were anxious for their troops to reach the fighting fronts as soon as was possible. The troops would be men in training who could complete that training just as well in Ulster as in America, and, at the same time, their arrival would allow trained British troops to be relieved and sent to the Middle East, where they were needed desperately. Finally, the presence of four American divisions would be an added deterrent to the German plans for the invasion of the British Isles.

The American War Secretary, Henry L Stimson, and all his advisers were delighted at the prospect of sending the divisions to Ulster. It coincided with their desire to invade Europe at the earliest possible moment. They readily agreed to the request and decided to send the four divisions, one armoured.

Churchill offered them the *Queen Mary* and *Queen Elizabeth* to move the troops. The shipping position was desperate, and the Americans were anxious to pack as many men as possible into the *Queen Mary*.

Hitler was said to be already offering high rewards to any commander who could sink the *Queen Mary*: the Iron Cross with oak leaves, financial rewards, and a hero's welcome home to the Fatherland. Indeed, too, it would be striking a mortal blow at the Allies' plans if the great ship could be sunk or even damaged badly; not only from the practical point of view but also for propaganda.

Sir Winston Churchill, in his book *The Second World War*, writes of the problem as early as January 1942; he was in America when the decision to use the ships was made. This is indicative of how even the war leaders were worried over the problem of how many troops should be carried:

> One evening General Marshall came to see me and put a hard question. He had agreed to send nearly 30,000 American soldiers to Northern Ireland. We had, or course, placed the two *Queens*, the only two 80,000-ton ships in the world, at his disposal for this purpose.
>
> General Marshall asked me how many men we ought to put on board, observing the boat, rafts, and other means of flotation could only be provided for about 8,000. If this were disregarded they could carry about 16,000.

As Churchill says, "A hard question." He goes on:

> I gave the following answer: "I can only tell you what WE should do. You must judge for yourselves the risks you will run. If it were a direct part of an actual operation we should put all on board they could carry. If it were only a question of moving troops in a reasonable time we should not go beyond the limits of the lifeboats, rafts, etc. It is for you to decide!

To this apparently enigmatic reply Churchill recalled:

> He received this in silence and our conversation turned to other matters.... In their first voyages these ships carried the lesser number, but later on they were filled to the brim. As it happened, Fortune stood our friend.

There were sufficient lifeboats to take 3,785 people and, it was claimed, sufficient rafts to support every one on board. In June 1942 she was carrying 10,000, but the Americans asked for this to be increased, and it was raised to 15,000 for the summer months.

One problem to be faced was the difference between crossing the North Atlantic in winter and in summer.

On September 2, 1942, talks were held at the offices of the Ministry. Captain J G Bisset (later Sir James Bisset, master of the *Queen Mary*), told the meeting that on a recent voyage he had carried 15,000 troops in the liner. He observed that when the ship was zigzagging, in addition to her roll, due to helm movement, she had a disconcerting movement of his large human cargo. "But," he said, "this occurred to such an extent that I was concerned about the ship's stability." There was no sign of this extraordinary movement when he had carried only 11,000 troops on previous voyages.

He pointed out that in these conditions occasions would possibly arise when the master would have to decide whether to proceed or heave to: "With all his other responsibilities I do not think he should be put in such a position." He added that standee berths, while suitable for a fine-weather voyage, were unsuitable for Atlantic crossings in the winter, as the men would be liable to fall out of them when the ship was rolling heavily. Commodore Irving, of the *Queen Elizabeth*, was of the opinion that in bad weather and with so many men on board, many broken limbs would result as with the fluid movement of the men the ship was liable to heel over as much as 30 degrees, and the crowded state on board would certainly lead to accidents. If the weather continued rough the master would have to decide whether to heave to or continue the voyage with the possible result of further injuries; this would be putting a strain on the medical staff, which they would be unable to cope with, even if no accidents occurred to any of the medical staff. Further, the messing would become a difficult problem, as the long delays would certainly occur in getting the men to their mess desks. "At present each meal takes five hours to complete all ranks."

After further discussions it was agreed that in the winter months not more than 10,000 should be carried. Furthermore, at this time of the year, only the lower standee berths should be used. None of the standee berths on the promenade deck would be suitable in winter conditions, as no heat could be provided for them, and the temperature might drop to 30 degrees.

On March 4 the following year, 1943, another meeting was held to discuss the situation for the summer months. The seamen were still opposed to carrying 15,000 men. Captain B H Davies, marine superintendent of Cunard, said the ships were now carrying additional top weight as they had been fitted with a control tower. This tended to have an effect on their behaviour and added to the risk of serious accidents among the troops, particularly in heavy gales, "which can be as bad in the summer months as in the winter."

He added that with 15,000 men on board there would be an excessive strain on the ship's personnel, particularly the catering department, as the troops would have to be messed in six sittings at each of two daily meals. With the quick turn-round in this country, the crew would be hard at it in port, and he did not think the crew would be able to stand up to the strain if the ships were continuously on the ferry service. Captain Fall, master then of the *Queen Mary*, said it took a few days for both crew and troops to settle down, which added considerably to the difficulties of the five-day North Atlantic voyages. "When my ship carried 15,000 last summer we had good weather. I would not have liked to have had that number in bad weather.

"The increasing number of U-boats in the North Atlantic is making matters much more serious. We are frequently having to take violent avoiding action when we get alarms, and, I can tell you, that at such times, with the large numbers on board, the handling of the ship is a very difficult matter."

Despite the captain's objections, the meeting eventually agreed that "a safe number for each ship would be 15,000, including ratings and permanent staff, which totalled nearly 200, but excluding the ship's crew." This would relieve the strain on the crews somewhat. This information, together with the seamen's warnings of the possible dangers, was conveyed to the Americans. General Lee, who was responsible for the build-up of forces and equipment in Europe, wrote to Lord Leathers, the Minister of War Transport:

> I believe we should accept 15,000 as the maximum capacity of the *Queens* during the summer months, May to September inclusive. The element of risk due to sudden heel, which you mention, must I believe, be taken in view of the difficulties in meeting present shipping commitments. The Americans are fully aware of the implication of increasing the numbers each trip and their decision, whatever it may be, will be taken with their eyes open.

It was not until June 1943 that the *Queen Mary*, referred to always by a code number, began a regular ferry service and returned to doing the work for which she had been originally built – voyaging to and fro across the Atlantic. On June 1, 1943 she sailed from New York to Gourock in the Clyde after a nineteen-day stay in New York.

She reached the Clyde in June 6, turned round, and sailed again four days later. This was to be her pattern of life until the War in Europe had ended, during which time she made twenty-eight round voyages. These four-day turn-rounds are incredible when one recalls that it took thirty-six hours normally to turn the liner round in peace-time with some 2,500 passengers to deal with.

The whole success of the movement of these large numbers of men depended entirely on the internal organization of the ship. For the earlier voyages the permanent military staff on board was two officers, two warrant officers, four other ranks, a pay master and his clerk. Now a combined permanent staff was set up.

The ship's commandant was to be a British Army colonel, with a major as his staff-officer; an American colonel would be second-in-command as well as O.C. United States forces on board. The total staff was to be eighty. This included senior medical officer, medical officer, nursing sisters, orderlies, intelligence officer, Provost-Marshal, chaplain, paymaster, baggage officer, clerical staff, as well as warrant officers and sergeants to operate the orderly room. This was really the permanent staff of a town hall, with powers to run what was, in effect, a small township in transit.

The commandant and adjutant had their offices on the starboard side of the promenade deck at No. 3 staircase; the American headquarters were on the main deck, directly below. The Midland Bank on A deck square became the headquarters of the forward area, while the starboard promenade deck on Piccadilly Circus (the shopping mall) housed the offices of the amidship section. Aft on C deck was located the headquarters of that area. Police headquarters were set up in the Austin Reed shop, and the ship's hospital on the Promenade Deck aft of the officer's main lounge, and in Cabin 45, on Main Deck, the American Red Cross operated. There were eight P.X.'s and canteens on A deck, the main deck and the promenade deck. The Verandah Grill was the anti-aircraft Control Centre.

Whole areas of the huge ship were restructured and converted to strange usage. The swimming pools were, for example, converted not only for sleeping quarters but also for military business. As Renee Partheons, a US sergeant, remembers: "We set up our orderly room in what was once the swimming pool. It was our main place to report for our duties while onboard the ship"

The American authorities also laid down a scale of tipping. For a five–ten day trip the bedroom steward should get one dollar from a single officer and 1.50 dollars from a family and the same for the table steward. The British rates recommended were: for the cabin steward, by an officer of the rank of major and above, 5s single or 7s 6d married, with 4s 6d and 6s 6d for the table steward; for captains and below the rate was 4s 6d and 5s for cabin and table stewards from single and married men.

One of the miracles of wartime shipping was the embarkation procedure used on both the *Queen Mary* and *Queen Elizabeth*. The taking on of over 15,000 servicemen was an extraordinary feat and required much planning and supervision. To begin with, a large number of the military personnel due to make the voyage would board the ship as an advance party to survey the liner and note the various zones and areas forming this vast military township. In a military camp in New Jersey, vast sections of the ships had been "rebuilt" on land, in order that thousands of military personnel could practice the embarkation procedure. These practice runs were even filmed and then analysed afterwards. This proved to be invaluable with the result that virtually everyone knew what to expect during embarkation and where to go once onboard. These monstrous embarkation sessions would, amazingly, take only a few hours and would usually be carried out through the night, between 7.00 pm and 1.00 am.

Many of the personnel would arrive in the city by train, alighting in Hoboken. They would then have to board a ferry which would transport them from the Jersey shore across to the *Queen*'s pier in Manhattan.

Care was taken to ensure that the personnel who would be occupying the lower decks were embarked first; this would prevent too much congestion and cross-traffic up and down staircases. A simple security measure was employed to make sure that intruders were not let past checkpoints: the guard checking the boarding roster would confirm the last name of the embarking soldier. In return the soldier himself would have to offer his first name. If the two names matched as per the list, the man would be permitted to embark; if not, questions were asked.

The following morning, a series of musters, emergency drills and instructional sessions would take place for all the men. During these they would be versed in such subjects as air-raids, blackouts and abandon ship methods. In fact, boat drill and ARP drills were carried out each day of the voyage, sometimes twice a day.

It was obvious from the start that one of the biggest problems was having 15,000 men wandering about all over the ship, with none of them knowing their way around. So she was divided into three sections, each with a distinctive colour. Forward from the bows after the main stairway, excluding the sun deck, was RED area, with a Royal Navy commander in charge. Midship from the main stairway aft to the cabin smoke-room stairway and including all the sun deck was WHITE area, with a lieutenant-colonel Canadian Army in charge. Aft from the cabin smoke-room to the stern of the ship was BLUE area, with an RAF wing commander in charge.

Immediately the American troops set foot in the ship at New York they were given a metal disc corresponding to the colour of the area to which they had been assigned and designating the parts of the ship they were to use and the number of their mess sitting. That was their area for the trip, and strict regulations were laid down that this was where they would stay during the trip. The identification tag was worn over the heart on the outer garment at all times. Military police had instructions to check continually that there were no 'wrong colours' in their section. If a GI were to cross, accidentally or otherwise, into the wrong colour zone, he would be "captured" by one of the military police and assigned a special duty, usually in the form of some menial task assisting the Cunard crew in the kitchens or stores.

The correct dress for the voyage was laid down: "Enlisted men will wear fatigues unless specifically stated otherwise; officers will wear shirts and ties [and] blouses, if available, during the evening meal."

In normal conditions, with a reasonably calm sea, there were six sittings for each of the two meals, the first at 6.30 am. Each sitting was scheduled to last three-quarters of an hour, and the number of times on which the sixth sitting was more than ten minutes late could be counted on the fingers. Enlisted men ate in the first-class dining-saloon – stripped of its finery – and in the entrance to the swimming pool. The men were allowed to eat as much as they wanted and to take with them, as they left the dining-room, cold meats or sandwiches to last through the rest of the day. Not that the food available constituted a gourmet selection. A typical breakfast would consist of boiled eggs, cereal, bread and jam, coffee or tea. Dinner could comprise thick soup, meat and potatoes.

As for all activities in the ship, there were rules and regulations for eating: a soldier had to attend the sitting corresponding with the number on his identification tag. He was not admitted to the mess unless he was wearing it.

When going to mess each man takes with him his field mess kit. The mess lines are formed by the compartment officers five minutes before the scheduled sittings – no later. These lines are held in the corridors adjacent to the main staircase, but do not proceed down until told to do so by the Military Police control officers. When the troops do descend they do so under the M.P. control, two lines on the starboard side and two lines on the port side.

Once inside troops proceed WITH MAXIMUM SPEED to seats as directed by the messing officers and stewards. Tables must be filled to rated capacities, otherwise no seats are left for the last men to enter the mess hall. Once seated the troops remain seated, and their food is brought from the galley by K.P.'s

As soon as a soldier has finished his meal he gets up from his seat, empties his garbage into the garbage pan at the end of the table, and proceeds to the aft end of the mess hall, taking his mess kit with him. The troops exit in six lines, two through each of the three exits. Troops leaving the mess hall through the centre doors are routed by M.P.'s to mess-kit washers on A and B decks; those leaving through the side exits are routed to mess-kit washers on D deck.

At the washers the mess kits are washed first in hot, salt-water spray, then a bath of hot, soapy salt-water, and finally in a clear, salt-water rinse. The soap used in the salt-water wash is a non-lathering type, therefore few suds are visible. In washing their mess-kits, troops must use the minimum time necessary and at all times MUST KEEP MOVING. After leaving the mess-kit washers troops immediately return to their quarters, seeking directions from the M.P.'s as to the best available route.

Officers too, on joining the ship, were given a card indicating the number of their mess sitting; the officers' mess hall was on C deck aft by the No. 5 staircase in the tourist-class dining-room. If the actual feeding of these men was a problem, the preparation of the food was even more of a headache.

Work in the kitchens went on throughout the twenty-four hours of the day from the time she left New York until she returned. On the voyage to England much of the food was being prepared for the return voyage. It was said that it was necessary for the slicing of the ham to begin feeding the machines as soon as the liner sailed, and that it took nearly the whole voyage to slice enough for the round trip. Something like 30,000 eggs would be boiled for one morning's breakfast. At the same time bad weather sometimes prevented the serving of meals, and on one Christmas Day, all the troops were given dry bread and cold meat. The daily consumption was astonishing: 240 gallons of milk, 14,000 loaves of bread, 880 lb of butter, 80 bags of flour and so on. In one single voyage no less than 124,000 lbs of potatoes would be consumed, 29,000 lb of fresh fruit, 155,000 lb of meat and poultry. Throughout the ship, a "chain" of kiosks sold cigarettes, soft drinks and sweets. Chewing gum, however, was banned from the liner on account of the fact that it had previously been the cause of innumerable hours extra work for the ship's crew members.

In the narrow "streets" of the liner a one-way-traffic system was operated. The starboard passageways were used by personnel walking forward, while the port alleyways were reserved for traffic moving towards the stern. A notice was issued to the troops:

TRAFFIC
During emergencies or emergency drills all traffic will be UP or DOWN depending on the signal or alarm sounded. Otherwise all traffic on stairs will keep to the right. Traffic on #3 Staircase will be Starboard Side UP and Port Side DOWN.

In order to run this floating military city, a strict duty rota was devised, a duty rota which encompassed every possible area of discipline, service and security. Despite the size of the vessel, the requirements were simple:

Mess orderlies	340	
Police	1,200	
Mess hall cleaners	60	
Store carriers	40	
AA gun parties	300	
Potato peelers	70	(3 times a day)
Stairway cleaners	300	(twice a day)
Spare men	200	

Any attempt to detail these requirements from drafts or units was doomed to failure. The details were simply done by quarters. If a man slept in B.125 for example, he was automatically a mess orderly and if he had a bunk forward he might suddenly find himself a policeman for five days. In all more than 2,200 men and 74 NCO's had to be at work supplementing the permanent staff on each trip.

Discipline was strict for all, including officers. Guards were given specific instructions that they were to make no distinction between anyone breaking the regulations.

One strict regulation for example, was that every man should carry his lifejacket at all times and the authorities adopted a simple method of dealing with those who felt it unnecessary to do so. Anyone caught without one was made to surrender his shoes.

An eyewitness recalled one such example: "The finest incident I saw in any of my trips was the sight of an American Admiral stopped by a GI and ordered to remove his shoes because he had no lifebelt. I can see the great man now, padding obediently away in his socks over the wet decks and returning meekly with the belt."

Standing Orders were clear and to the point.

All orders will be issued in the spirit that this ship is engaged in a combined operation of war, requiring a full loyalty, obedience, and co-operation from all personnel on board.

There was one regulation which must have been extremely difficult, if not impossible, to enforce:

Gambling, profane or obscene language, and all unnecessary noises are prohibited.

Despite the warnings, gambling was rife. Mandel Siegall was a regular Private First Class in 1945. As he remembers:

"There was nothing to do. We played cards – those that liked to play craps, played craps. We got up on the deck for a little fresh air and exercise."

Chester Hall was a Sergeant in the 82nd Airborne Division. He sailed westwards on December 28, 1945. He recalls such a gambling incident:

"One of the duties I had as First Sergeant was to assign people to clean up the recreation hall each day. The fellas who I had assigned came down one night and I saw them counting out all this money. It turned out that a couple of professional gamblers got them to hold a craps table for them up in the hall. They were paying them $50 a day to hold the table for them. Before they got off the ship, they hired two more guys to be bodyguards at $5.00 a day because they had so much money."

The games included such favourites as poker, blackjack, craps and even hearts. Of all of the games, it was this last one that held the greatest fascination for the troops. On many voyages a hearts game would last from sailing time to when the ship tied up in New York or dropped anchor in the Clyde; sometimes 24 hours a day, as when one player dropped out, another would quickly take his place. Hundreds, if not thousands, of dollars were lost and won.

Other regulations included such items as:

INTOXICANTS ARE PROHIBITED. THIS IS A DRY SHIP.
The washing of laundry is prohibited.
Personnel will not climb in the ship's rigging, sit on the railings, liferafts, or climb into the lifeboats. With both feet on deck you cannot fall overboard. IT WILL BE IMPOSSIBLE TO STOP THE SHIP FOR RECOVERY PURPOSES.
The ship will be very crowded. The exigencies of the times demand it. Officers and men should not view this trip as a vacation; it will be anything but that.
Radio sets, electric razors, electric phonographs and flashlights, electric irons, knives useable as weapons, and cameras are forbidden. (No exceptions.)
As long as the ship floats, your best place is on board. Have your lifejacket properly adjusted. It will support you for a very long time. There are ample ladders, scramble nets, and knotted ropes to allow everyone to enter the water without jumping, and go for a raft.
Smoking is prohibited in cabins, troops' compartments and corridors at all times.

As one member of the permanent staff said, "It was exactly like putting a load of feathers into a bag. They eventually settled down, but things are a bit difficult and out of hand until they do."

Each day, there were usually two film shows for the troops. Often too, concerts were performed by the troops, for the troops. The ship was also supplied with record players, cards and puzzles. Boredom was nevertheless a major enemy. One staff member said that he saw *Pride and Prejudice* 120 times.

The Americans carved their initials, nicknames, names and home-towns on every inch of the wood rail around the 750-foot promenade deck. At one time it was stated that these would be left intact when the liner was reconditioned after the war years; or it was proposed to preserve a small portion of them as a memento of the historic numbers carried. But this was never done, and at her first reconditioning they were planed and rubbed away. A small section was sent to the American Army as a memento.

During the voyage every man was handed a *Short Guide to Great Britain* prepared by the Special Service Division of the United States Army and published by the War and Navy Departments in Washington. This was aimed at getting the men acquainted with the British, their country, and their ways.

Among "Some important 'Do's and Don'ts'" are listed:

> You are higher paid than the British "Tommy". Don't rub it in. Play fair with him. He can be a pal in need.
>
> If you are invited to eat with a family don't eat too much. Otherwise you may eat up their weekly rations.

Referring to the differences in phrases and colloquialisms, the booklet issued this warning:

> It isn't a good idea to say "bloody" in mixed company in Britain – it is one of their swear words. To say "I look like a bum", is offensive to their ears, for to the British this means that you look like your own backside.

It pointed out to the American GI's that the British are tough.

> Don't be misled by the British tendency to be soft-spoken and polite. If they need to be they can be plenty tough. The English language didn't spread across the oceans and over the mountains and jungles and swamps of the world because these people were panty-waists.

On the subject of Indoor Amusements appeared this sentence: "The British are beer-drinkers – and they can hold it."

A clearly written, easily understandable pamphlet, it was filled with good advice to the troops. Pointing out that a British woman officer or non-commissioned officer often gave orders to a man private, the booklet said, "The men obey smartly and know it is no shame." The British women had proved themselves in the war. "They have won the right to the utmost respect. When you see a girl in khaki or Air Force blue with a bit of ribbon on her tunic, remember she didn't get it for knitting more socks than anyone else in Ipswich."

Despite the fact that Standing Orders made it clear that the ship was British, despite the fact that she flew the British flag, the majority of Americans believed she was an American ship. Nothing could convince them otherwise.

The Captain used to give a broadcast telling them that the ship was British and that her service as a troop transport for the American Army was part of Britain's "Reverse Lease-Lend" programme. But as one naval captain who made many voyages on the liner put it, "I am convinced that even this did not make much impression. The GIs still insisted that this was British propaganda and that she was American. Only the Americans, they thought, could build such a liner."

Perhaps the greatest enemy of the troops who sailed in the *Queen Mary* during those war years was seasickness. Conditions were quite appalling. Long before the advent of sophisticated stabilizers, the liner rolled very badly and, unlike her French counterpart the *Normandie*, she was slow to right herself. Even during her earlier civilian voyages she had caused alarm and fear to many peacetime passengers who really thought that the ship was about to capsize. It was a characteristic of her design which would eventually be cured in 1958 with the installation of Denny Brown stabilizers. During the War years, however, the problem was very much in existence and was further exaggerated by the incredible number of human beings on board and the resultant crowding in virtually every area of the ship. Lewis Gwentert was a Captain in the Air Corps of the U.S. Army, assigned to meteorological duties. He was transferring to Britain in November 1943. He recalls: "November, December and January were the rough times of the year and many people got sick. Many fellas missed their meals. I'm not kidding you, people would turn green on that ship."

Nor did "Mal de Mer" have any respect for rank. Gwentert was an officer, in quarters far superior to the enlisted men. However, he remembers: "We had a stateroom and the bunks were five high. The higher you got, the better off you were in case someone got sick. It wouldn't get on top of you."

George Neil was a lieutenant with the 7th Corps Headquarters. He sailed in 1943 and described the awful conditions with clarity:

> I was lucky. The previous voyage, Winston Churchill had come over and we occupied what was his library; a stateroom which had sixteen lieutenants stacked four deep. It was palatial conditions compared to the enlisted people. I was in charge of the forwardmost compartment of the ship. It was the bottom compartment and it had approximately 400 people from an aircraft battalion. The seas were about twenty or thirty feet. The ship rolled from side to side at tremendous angles, but up at the [beam] of the ship where my compartment was it would rise and fall 40 ft and all of those poor soldiers were sick. Now I don't get seasick but when you go into a compartment

that's got 400 sick people, it's hard not to be sick yourself. They could not go topside because of the roll of the ship – if somebody got swept overboard, they were gone. When I'd go down in my compartment it was just terrible down there. There was no way to get air down there to clear up all of that stench. They mopped and swept and so forth, but we took this upchuck out of there in great big 32 gallon cans.

Fear too, was an serious adversary. Many of the men could not understand why the *Queen Mary*, like her younger sister, was sailing without escort and out of convoy. This frightened them and, together with a feeling of dreadful claustrophobia, drove them to the upper decks. They felt that they would have a better chance of survival if the ship were struck by a torpedo.

That fear was not limited to foreign attack. Quite often, the dreadful weather was, by itself, enough to alarm the most hardy military man. The *Mary* was a vessel of mighty strength, capable of withstanding the most dramatic of sea conditions. When the sea became rough she would twist and turn through amazing angles; often the propellers themselves would be thrown clear of the water and, still spinning, would shake and shudder the entire aft end like a grotesque earth tremor. As the stern fell back into the sea, the bow would rise thirty, forty, maybe fifty feet, creating a dizzy upwards levitation for anyone unlucky enough to be in the very forward section. As the stem crashed back into the swirling, churning ocean, so those who had been lifted up towards the heavens would experience a near weightless plummet back toward the surf.

Personal hygiene was a difficult matter. Since there were 15,000 troops on board the ship, there were clearly not enough showers for everyone to bath every day. Some men would not be able to take a shower or bath for the entire trip. George Neil recalls conditions clearly:

"There was a shower but the water was strictly rationed of course and you were only permitted to take one bath during the crossing. I don't believe the enlisted men ever got a bath. In other words they only got to take a sponge bath. That's all."

Apart from all the problems of plotting an operational convoy route for the great liner, and this route was changed every voyage according to the moon's phases, there was the difficulty of deciding on a terminal port in Britain. This had to provide a safe anchorage for the ship in any weather, a safe anchorage from sea and air attack, and at the same time be capable of handling large numbers of men quickly. Once landed there had to be facilities for speedily transporting them by rail to their various destinations.

It was decided therefore that the Firth of Clyde offered the best selection. Here was a large natural harbour, where sometimes more than one hundred ships could anchor, protected from the air by powerful anti-aircraft defences and from the sea by anti-submarine nets and patrols.

Greenock would probably have been the ideal choice. Prince's Pier there had long been used for embarking and disembarking transatlantic travellers. But this was part of the naval base and was fully occupied. So Gourock was chosen.

James Bird, of the Cunard Company, later their manager at Cobh, was the liaison officer between ship and shore. Working in close co-operation with the naval authorities, with Army and RAF Movement Control, and with the railway staffs, road transport services, Customs, pilots and tug masters, police, WVS, ships' chandlers, ship-repair yards, dockers and victuallers, to mention but a few, he was the link between the men who ferried the troops across the ocean, the various agencies which made that ferrying possible, and the necessary services for sending the troops to their destinations.

From his little hut, while the *Queen Mary* was at her anchorage at the Tail o' the Bank, at a deep-water spot known as the Hole, and where she had plenty of room to swing, he would be in touch by telephone with his company's offices in Glasgow, Liverpool, London and Southampton, passing company, as opposed to Service, instructions to the master and transmitting requests from him and his ship's company to all concerned. Not the least of his tasks was to ensure that a tender daily took out to the anchorage a small army of cleaners to the liner while she was free of troops.

For the ferrying of the crew, as well as troops, there were pleasure steamers, *King George V* and *King Edward VII*, the tender *Rowena* from Belfast, and the Alexandra Towing Company's fast tug-tender *Romsey*, which was sunk in the Clyde during the War, raised again, and which then continued to act as tug to the *Queen Mary* in her peacetime career and a tender to foreign-flag liners using Southampton.

The stores were taken out by Dutch *schoots*, or small coasters; in fact, there were so many of them that the stretch of water between Gourock and Greenock were they were moored when not ferrying was soon dubbed "Rotterdam Bay."

From that tiny railway station of Gourock went troop trains to all parts of Britain. All were cleared from the liner in thirty-six hours.

Westbound, the liner carried a variety of passengers, including a number of Service personnel, Ministry officials going for talks with their American counterparts, as well as diplomats and business and industrial leaders with official permission to travel, and usually some three to five thousand German prisoners-of-war bound for Canada.

In the main these caused little trouble, although some remained arrogant. On the voyage from Gourock in September 1943 General Gotthard Granitz complained to the Commanding Officer of Troops, Colonel C J Hocking, that the treatment of German officers, especially of generals, was not good. He demanded more politeness, which was the right of exalted ranks, and said that the meals were not correct according to the Geneva Convention. His twin-bedded cabin was without any curtains or privacy, so that the guards could overhear conversations and watch them dressing. "The kitchen staff and stewards refer to us in derogatory terms and contempt, and nothing is done by the American escort to prevent this," he said. He added that the generals were jostled and crowded in the corridors.

Colonel Hocking remarked in his report that these complaints were "frivolous," and that it was quite unnecessary for any court of inquiry to be held. He pointed out, with typical British understatement, that the ship was crowded and that Allied officers got jostled in the corridors too, and that they did not have too much privacy either.

On one voyage a number of prisoners were found with matches, which were strictly forbidden. They were also equipped with knives, forks and spoons. Captain Bisset impounded these, as untold damage could be done to the ship's fittings by an ingenious man, apart from the fact that they had great potential as weapons.

An order was posted.

> Attention is drawn to the fact that in spite of the removal from troop sections of all loose metal articles likely to be used as weapons, the prisoners of war have an effective weapon always ready to hand in the shape of the supporting chains at the end of the standee bunk. Certain officers of the permanent staff have personal experiences of sanguinary fights from this type of weapon.

On the westbound trips with prisoners there would be occasional disappearances when the liner arrived in New York. The American authorities always counted the prisoners off, and on one occasion, one was missing. The whole day was spent in searching the liner from stem to stern without any trace of the missing man. Eventually the engineers, looking behind an inspection panel in a cabin, located him, curled up in a space where it had been thought impossible for a man to get, with enough food to last two or three days.

During these voyages, the *Queen Mary* carried around 800 to 900 British crew members, in addition to the troops. They were still managed and employed by the Cunard Company but were actually under military jurisdiction whilst onboard the ship. The coordination of the work schedule for these crew members was a complex and time-consuming business as they were rotated, relieved, transferred, replaced, sent home and brought back on board.

Once the invasion had started she began to carry westbound large numbers of wounded American soldiers. This meant the installation of yet more equipment and the carrying of more specializsed staff. At the start of each voyage a number of standee berths would be temporarily removed to accommodate stretcher cases.

The American Army medical staff was increased to eighty and the ship's organization had to be altered to meet the requirements of many different diets, often of more than 2,500 patients. Stewards were provided, too, to help feed those who were too badly wounded to manage for themselves. At New York fleets of ambulances met the ship and in a matter of hours the stretchers were disembarked and taken to Army Base Hospitals.

The permanent military medical staff consisted of a lieutenant-colonel as senior medical officer, and usually the surgical specialist, two medical officers, two nursing sisters, one warrant officer, and twenty-eight other ranks from the Royal Army Medical Corps as nursing orderlies and clerks. There was also an American officer who acted as a liaison officer between the British and the Americans.

This staff was totally inadequate to care for 15,000 men and was supplemented each voyage by the permanent staff combing through the "passengers" to enlist the help of all medical personnel from the Service who were making the voyage. Usually some thirty American medical officers and as many nurses as could be found, together with a sprinkling of Canadian or British officers, were recruited as temporary help.

The Cunard Company's ship's surgeon was Dr G A Goolden, who was ever ready with help and advice and co-operation for the Army medical staff. In fact, one senior medical officer paid this tribute to him:

"I shall never forget the friendship extended to me by Dr G A Goolden: his ready help and advice, his unfailing courtesy and cooperation helped beyond all measure in the success of the enterprise and in the smaller part of my job, the practice of my real profession."

This doctor recalled, "We had all the penicillin we needed for the treatment of all the cases where its use was indicated. This was a thrilling experience for me, for at that time in all British formations and at home it was regarded as experimental and was in very short supply.

"Many of the troops we carried had never seen the sea before and had no idea there was so much of it. It was not unusual to have to deal with hysterical outbursts, which varied from just bursting into tears to violent behaviour, because they believed they would never see land again and certainly not their homeland."

He said that even then in 1944 the 180-cot troop hospital had only a very makeshift operating theatre, a space for dressings, and for a few medical stores; "I had been posted from a hospital ship in the fitting-out of which I had been given a free hand in New York about a year previously and by comparison this seemed shoddy and poor in the extreme."

Actually this surgeon said that he did all his abdominal operations and major surgical cases in the ship's hospital through the kindness of Dr Goolden.

> This was an excellent but small hospital with a lovely little operating theatre with all modern equipment and conveniences and at that time thoroughly up-to-date. I nursed the patients post-operatively in this hospital too.

A few cabins had been set aside for the purpose of isolating and treating cases of venereal disease; and there was also an isolation hospital (very isolated). Each area had its own medical inspection and consulting room and at each gunsite there was a first-aid post. Staffed by the Americans were an elaborate dental department, a pathological laboratory and an X-ray room.

On joining the ship, I soon found myself involved in two major exercises; firstly to convert her into a hospital ship of 2,000 cots for the westbound trip from a troop carrier of 15,000 people on the eastbound voyage. This had to be accomplished in the four days turn-round at her terminal ports each trip.

Secondly having got this running smoothly, I had to hand over the medical services, lock, stock and barrel to the American Army.

Two real emergencies stand out in my memory.

On one occasion the ship's butcher, Mr Edwardson, was bashed about in his own department by a large chopping block that broke loose in a howling gale. He sustained multiple injuries which included a fractured femur of unusual severity. A big, heavy, powerful man, extracting him from his predicament was quite a task. In that same storm the forward gun turret and some of the superstructure were considerably bent and necessitated refit in the Bayonne naval dockyard in New York.

My other memorable surgical problem was extracting some steel filings embedded in the eye of one of the engineers without the aid of a magnet and in roughish sea.

The American poet Leonora Speyer described this period of the ship's life perfectly:

Bearing her load of lives, over and back
The great Queen passes, scorning the deep sea pack
Snarling below; in crimson, gold and rose
The skies salute, waves curtsey as she goes.

Still the great liner led a charmed life. German submarines were operating in all the areas where the *Queen Mary* went in the Alantic: off Freetown and Cape Town; off Florida and Trinidad; off Rio and South America. At one time the German pocket battleship *Leutzow* was out in the Atlantic with specific instructions to find the liner. But she was unsuccessful.

After the War Wilhelm Schulze, a former U-Boat commander, said that he missed the *Queen Mary* by half an hour.

In April 1944 there was a mysterious heavy explosion half a mile from the ship on the port side when she was off the Irish coast. This sent geysers of water 300 ft into the air. The ship steamed on. This is generally assumed to have been an acoustic mine, triggered off by the rumbling of such a massive ship at close quarters. An alternative suggestion is that it may have been torpedoes exploding too soon.

On June 2, 1945, President Truman in an eight-thousand-word message to Congress on the "problems, difficulties and dangers confronting the United States in finishing the war against Japan" said that the *Queen Mary* and the *Queen Elizabeth* and the *Aquitania* were to help. "The British are letting us have their three proudest passenger liners". But, with the dropping of the A-bomb and the final surrender of Japan, she was never called upon to sail in yet stranger waters.

In June 1945 the *Queen Mary*, still on war duty, but no longer on the secret list, made a gala entry into New York harbour. The liner, decorated with flags, but still painted dull grey, moved to her pier with thousands of returning American soldiers and sailors lining the rails. In their enthusiasm to see the symbol of everything for which they had been fighting those past years, thousands of soldiers rushed to the port side of the ship to see the Statue of Liberty. As Harold Parsons, a Captain in the U.S. Army put it: "The weather was fine and when we came into New York Harbour, everybody rushed over to the port side. [He thought] Boy! This thing's going to tip over!" Eleven other vessels had held down their whistles as she passed by, and patrol planes flew overhead.

The *New York Herald Tribune* described her arrival in these terms:

> The British liner *Queen Mary*, looking almost as big as Staten Island, and just as proud as a queen, even in her war-time drab gray, steamed up the harbour yesterday with the largest contingent of troops ever to arrive in New York in a single ship.
>
> For her passengers it was home. None of the thousands of brown-and-blue clad figures that covered every inch of her superstructure and waved wildly from all her 2,000 port-holes expressed it more eloquently than a blond nurse. Hers was one of the three winsome heads stuck through a port-hole built to accommodate only one head, and at Red Cross girls on Pier 90 she waved a flimsy black-silk unmentionable from Paris, shouting, "We won!"
>
> The ship got the welcome that the harbour had not seen since the days of greetings accorded to great liners making their first voyage to New York in peace-time!
>
> Along the highways that border the Narrows thousands of people lined the shore and hundreds of flags hung from apartment windows.
>
> Harbour craft of every description from flippant little tugs to vessels outward bound for Europe gave "the Mary," as the troops affectionately called her, their varied salutes.

For the rest of that year, she continued to sail under military juristiction carrying as many westbound as she had eastwards in the recent years of the war.

On August 13, 1945, she returned to the port of Southampton for the first time since she had sailed away on that late August day in 1939. She was, as was right and fitting, given a tremendous welcome.

It was Sir Percy Bates, the man who had dreamed of these ships and who loved them so much, who said, "I like to believe that the *Queen Mary* and the *Queen Elizabeth* had between them shortened the War in Europe by a whole year."

Lord Salter, who was UK representative on the Combined Shipping Adjustment Board in Washington during the vital stages of the War, said in 1960, "Sir Percy Bates, by his foresight, certainly shortened the War. But for the *Queen Mary* and the *Queen Elizabeth* bringing to Europe a division of US troops at a time, we could not have done D-day when we did, and London and the provincial cities must have been badly damaged by the V1's and V2's."

One of the men who played an important role in the preparation of the liner in New York and who did much to foster the good relations and spirit of co-operation so essential to the success of such a difficult combined operation was Seymour-Bell, who had been the first and only liaison officer in the *Queen Mary* on that maiden voyage. He had been mobilized as a Territorial Officer shortly before the outbreak of War, and in 1941 was sent to New York in civilian clothes to set up a British Army movements organization. He personally supervised the troop transport operation of the *Queen Mary* and other Cunarders. It was he who received the urgent secret message that the French liner *Normandie* had been set on fire and that he would have to prepare the *Queen Mary* for what was to become the Long Voyage. By 1960 he was working in New York as General Manager, and personally supervised every arrival and departure of the *Queen Mary*.

On April 16, 1946, Major-General Homer M Groninger, Port Commander of the New York Port of Embarkation from before Pearl Harbour until after VE Day, wrote to Brigadier (as he was then) Seymour-Bell, saying:

> [in] my position I saw the tremendous and necessary part that transportation played in the prosecution of the war to its victorious conclusion. One of the outstanding accomplishments of World War II was the movement across the oceans of the millions of men comprising our huge army, in which the ships of the British Ministry of War Transport contributed greatly.
>
> Superlative performance was rendered by the two *Queens*, which, because of their amazing capacity and speed were able to supplement other shipping to the extent of moving alone a sizeable percentage of the millions of U.S. troops sent to the British Isles to prepare for and later to support the invasion of the Continent.

As the end of the War there were many rumours, in America in particular, that large profits were made by the British Government and the Cunard Company by carrying American troops during the War. It was wildly suggested that the Government had charged the Americans more than a hundred million dollars for transporting the troops in the two *Queens*.

This was completely untrue.

The position was that, under the Master Agreement, which was executed in February 1942, to implement the Lend-Lease Act of 1941, both sides contributed vessels which were physically well adapted or suitably located to fulfil specific requirements in the command cause. The two *Queens* were used for the transport of American forces as part of the British contribution. No payment was ever made by the US Government for the use of these ships, nor was any debit made during the whole of this period.

After the termination of these arrangements, the services of the *Queens* were, for a short period until a specific ships' exchange agreement was made, brought into account for the purpose of the settlement under the Lend-Lease Act and Reciprocal Aid pipeline and offsetting arrangements. During this time the *Queen Elizabeth* was employed for about one month before she was withdrawn for reconditioning and the *Queen Mary* for two months. About 72,000 US personnel were carried during this period.

For this period alone and solely for book-keeping purposes, an arbitrary figure of £20 ($80.70) per man was used in calculating the US debit for the accounting arrangement.

No actual payment was ever made.

The traffic, even during the pipeline period, was mainly one way, and the whole cost of operating the ship both ways was met by the UK Government, who also had to pay the Cunard Company for the use of the ships. The payment to the company was extremely modest being at the rate of 7.5% of the original cost, based on 5% for depreciation and only 2.5%. for profit. Any inference that Cunard made large profits during the war in the operation of the two liners was entirely without foundation

In all her war-time service the *Queen Mary* never sighted a submarine or a torpedo and never suffered an air attack. Nor did she ever fire a gun "in anger."

12

Anatomy of a Disaster

It was October 2, 1942, at five minutes past two o'clock in the afternoon, forty miles to the north of Tory Island, off the coast of Donegal. The weather was fine and clear with a moderate breeze, but the cold waters of the grey North Atlantic were rough, and there was a considerable westerly swell running.

Six days out from New York, with her full winter complement of 10,000 American troops on board, the *Queen Mary* steamed on. She was on just another routine Atlantic ferry voyage. Steaming at her normal 28.5 knots, headed for the safe waters of the Clyde, she was just approaching the danger zone. This was where German submarines lurked, looking for a victim, and where enemy aircraft might be found overhead.

Following her normal routine, she had come this far unescorted since she left the swept channel off New York harbour. Now she had an anti-submarine escort of six destroyers, which were steaming hull down ahead of her, and an anti-aircraft cruiser steaming close by her to starboard.

The escort had made a rendezvous with the liner at nine o'clock that morning. This was, perhaps, a large escort for a convoy of just one ship. But that one ship happened to be one of the most valuable vessels in the British Merchant Navy at that time, and the Admiralty was not taking risks. The liner herself was powerfully armed against air attack, with forty anti-aircraft guns, six of which were dual-purpose. She had a special gunnery officer and a crew of some two hundred for operating the guns. While the British Admiralty and the American naval and military authorities trusted to her speed and manoeuvrability to get her safely across the vast tracts of the North Atlantic, they were doubly wary in this danger zone. Not only was she escorted for the sea, but until an hour ago she had been guarded from the air by a Flying Fortress, acting as watchdog until the naval escort arrived.

On the bridge of the liner as she ploughed through the heavy swell at more than thirty miles an hour, were thirty-four-year-old Stanley Joseph Wright, Junior First and Navigating Officer, and Junior Third Officer William Douglas Heighway, an Australian. At the wheel was Quartermaster John Leyden, who had taken over a few minutes before from John Lockhart, who had gone for a cup of tea. Around the bridge were two ordinary seamen as bridge-boys, a look-out and a signal rating. High up on the crow's nest on the foremast was another look-out.

The master, Captain Cyril Gordon Illingworth, was in his chart-room at the back of the bridge on the port side behind the wheelhouse. He was working out his estimated time of arrival in the Clyde, information required by the senior escort officer.

Only half an hour before, he had gone on to the bridge he had felt a sudden swerve in the ship's course. He had then told Mr Wright that the liner was to complete all the legs of the zigzag course she was then steering. Mr Wright had told him that he felt a little unhappy about the proximity of the escorting cruiser. The captain told him that she was used to escorting ships and "she will keep out of your way."

At the pre-convoy conference held in New York the American naval authorities had discussed the voyage with Captain Illingworth. They had handed him his sailing instructions which laid down the route he was to take (for the route was changed each voyage), and the speed he was to maintain throughout. They also laid down that he was to zigzag, but did not specify any particular method; that was left to his discretion. He was also told what ships he might expect to meet during the crossing, the known location of enemy submarines in the Atlantic, and the escort he would have.

At that moment the liner was steaming on the starboard leg of her zigzag course. In fact, in seven minutes' time she was due to turn fifty degrees to her port on the next leg. The zigzag was the method used to throw U-boats off the scent as to the actual course and to prevent their commanders from getting into a suitable position for attack. A special zigzag bell had been installed on the bridge, positioned above the helmsman's head. This bell operated electrically and would ring every ten minutes or so, signalling the helmsman to make the changes of course within the chosen zigzag pattern. As an example, on the first ring, the helmsman would steer thirty degrees to port, sending the ship thirty degrees off course. On the next ring some ten minutes later, he would steer sixty degrees to starboard bringing her to thirty degrees off the side of the true course. A third ring would signal another change, thirty degrees to port, bringing the ship back on true course. There were various zigzag patterns available for the captain to use. On this particular voyage the liner was following her normal practice of steaming on what the code books knew as Zigzag No. 8.

Zigzagging in that heavy swell, it was not easy for the helmsman to maintain the gigantic liner on her course every minute. She was apt to yaw if a particularly heavy sea or a gust of wind caught her, and the quartermaster at the wheel had to be alert to get her back on the correct course as soon as possible.

At precisely 2.09 pm Senior First Officer Noel James Robinson, who was being relieved by Mr Wright, returned to the bridge. His route from the dining room, aft on C Deck, to the starboard wing of the open bridge, was completely closed in, so until he actually stepped outside he had no idea of what was happening at sea. As he himself was to say later, "You might as well be a 100 miles from the sea when you are in that corridor." Even the wheelhouse was protected by concrete slabs with slits in.

As he stepped on to the bridge he met Mr Wright, who handed over to him, saying, "Same course, same speed. The captain wants me in the chart-room as soon as possible." He said nothing to him about the captain's order that all zigzagging legs should be fully completed. As Mr Robinson walked the fourteen final paces towards the open bridge, Mr Heighway approached him and told him of what the captain had said, adding that he had said the cruiser would keep out of the way.

When Mr Robinson had gone for his lunch the cruiser had been two miles away. He now looked to see where she was and noticed immediately that she was much closer; in fact, he estimated she was about 1,200 ft away, just one length of the liner.

The cruiser he was looking at was the *Curacoa*, 450 ft long, of 4,200 tons, about one-twentieth of the tonnage of the liner. She was armed with eight 4-inch guns and had top speed of somewhere about 25 knots. She was commanded by Captain John Wilfrid Boutwood, DSO, a regular naval officer, and had a total crew of 439 officers and ratings.

Captain Boutwood was the senior officer in charge of this escort force detailed to guard the *Queen Mary*. He had sent his anti-submarine destroyers ahead. His protective plan was for the *Queen Mary*, which was a faster ship, to pass him. He would then tuck himself astern of her to protect her from air attack until she was so far ahead of him that she would have caught up with the destroyers. These were the *Bulldog*, *Skate*, *Saladin*, *Bramham* and *Cowdray* and the Polish destroyer *Blyskawica*. Captain Boutwood had been in command of the *Curacoa* since June and had escorted the *Queen Mary* in similar circumstances on three occasions.

The *Curacoa* had been at sea for two days, having left port on the evening of September 30. She had met some heavy weather, and if the *Queen Mary* was having some difficulty in keeping station in that heavy swell, so too was the much lighter and smaller cruiser.

At five minutes past two Captain Boutwood was on the bridge and with him were Lieutenant Johnson, his navigating officer, Lieutenant

Manwell, Officer of the Watch, and the Principal Control Officer, Lieutenant Britton.

From time to time they glanced over at the liner and watched her ploughing on at speed. Only half an hour before, when the two ships had been close to one another, one of the officers had taken some photographs of her. One of his fellow officers had said to him, "Yes, don't miss that. Perhaps you won't get another opportunity of taking the *Queen Mary* like that."

How tragically prophetic those words were.

This, then, was the scene as the officers on the bridge of both ships went about their business. Only seven minutes to go before the liner changed course, yet those naval officers had not the slightest idea just what course the *Queen Mary* was following. They talked among themselves and thought that she was not following her correct zigzag. At the same time they never thought to ask her just what course she was steaming.

Onboard the *Queen Mary*, Mr Robinson surveyed the scene and felt then that perhaps the cruiser was coming just a little uncomfortably close. He gave an order to the quartermaster through the voice pipe, "Port a little," He then strolled casually along the open bridge the few paces to the open wheelhouse door to make sure the helmsman was putting the wheel over the right way. He even looked at the clock. It was then 2.10 pm.

On the *Curacoa*, Captain Boutwood and his officers discussed what they felt the liner was doing; whether she was yawing or actually turning to starboard. Then Boutwood ordered, "Starboard 15," to his helmsman, as he later said, "just to be on the safe side."

Robinson was sure that the cruiser would take some action to avoid any collision. The captain of the cruiser was equally sure that there was nothing to worry about. He felt that the liner would keep out of his way. He gave the order, as he said, "in a moment of no concern."

But still the two ships converged.

Third Officer Hewitt was watching from the outer bridge of the liner. He looked through a telescope to see if he could recognize any of the officers onboard the cruiser. He did not recognize any faces but he saw the danger. Even as he turned to warn his fellow officers, Mr Robinson was ordering "Hard a port." From that moment, when he realized the peril, Robinson had exactly two minutes in which to act. They were not enough.

Captain Boutwood had seen that the two ships were approaching each other "at a considerable and alarming rate" and had taken control of his ship. But he could not afterwards remember what orders he had given.

The *Queen Mary* caught the cruiser a glancing blow at an acute angle, eleven feet from her stern. The impact spun the smaller vessel round to an angle of ninety degrees, and the liner slashed right through and over her, cutting her in two like a knife through butter. It was like a steamroller crushing a bubble-car.

Just at that moment, in all the confusion, the zigzag clock on the *Queen Mary*'s bridge rang for the next alteration of course. It was exactly 2.12 pm.

Within seven minutes the two ships had converged, collided, and 338 experienced officers and men of the Royal Navy had lost their lives, drowned, trapped, chopped to pieces by the liners propellers, or smashed to pulp below decks as the *Queen Mary*'s bows carved the cruiser in two. The *Curacoa* heeled over on her beam ends, so that for just a fleeting moment, it seemed to the onlookers that she would go under immediately. But the forepart of the ship, about two-thirds of her, began slowly to right itself. The stern by this time was end up in the water, drifting away beyond the liner and sinking.

There was no hope. Sailors were diving, scrambling, jumping, into the cold stormy waters as fast as they could. Within five minutes the *Curacoa* had sunk.

American servicemen on the decks of the liner rushed to the rails, throwing lifebelts into the water, although many of them did not know what had happened. Down below in the engine-room the engineers, feeling a slight bump, thought the liner had lit a large wave.

Only the captain, one other officer, and 99 ratings were saved. The liner, her bow stoved in below the water-line, could not, dared not stop to pick up survivors. This was the rigid rule of the sea governing troop transporters during the war. If any one was to be saved it must be by the escorting destroyers.

The crippled liner summoned help from them, and the officers in charge of the destroyers in HMS *Bulldog* immediately despatched two H-class destroyers, *Bramham* and *Cowdray*, to pick up any survivors.

At 2.20 pm a secret message was radioed in code to the Commander-in-Chief, Western Approaches, at his headquarters in Liverpool, and passed on to the Admiralty in London. "HMS *Curacoa* rammed and sunk by Queen Mary in position 55.50 N. 08.38 W. *Queen Mary* damaged forward. Speed 10 knots."

At 2.44 pm the *Queen Mary* flashed a signal by lamp to *Bulldog*. "It would appear that *Curacoa* attempted to cross my bows when collision occurred. Am reducing speed to 10 knots to ascertain extent of damage and have ceased zigzag. Will keep informed."

Captain Illingworth immediately sent officers and carpenters forward to see how badly damaged the liner was. They found her stem buckled back so that in a way it had helped to close the hole; her stem was fractured. She was a sitting duck for any submarine commander lucky enough to have been there.

At 3.19 pm Captain Illingworth sent another signal: "After careful consideration can only conclude *Curacoa* put helm wrong way." He then set off limping home to the Clyde at 13 knots, hoping that his collision mats would hold.

They did hold and, when the *Queen Mary* reached the Clyde, startled seamen gazed in amazement at the hole in her bows and Clydeside was riddled with rumours. Temporary repairs were made and the liner sailed across to Boston. There in the dockyard she was repaired so that she could once again take her place on the Atlantic ferry.

It was suggested in some quarters that a look-out in the liner had raised the alarm of a suspected U-boat on the port bow and that the liner had wheeled to starboard and at the same time the cruiser had turned in across her bows to investigate. This story persisted for many years, but Captain Boutwood, in answer to the judge on the very first day of the hearing stated categorically that there was no submarine alarm at all.

The story of the collision was very carefully kept from the British public. One of the ship's crew, however, reported that, at home on leave in Dublin, he had switched on his wireless to hear the Germans gloatingly giving details of the collision.

It was not until May 18, 1945, when an Admiralty list of ships lost and not previously reported was published, that the story became known. For among the list was the name *Curacoa*.

Almost one month later, on June 12, 1945 at 10.30 am in the High Courts of Justice, in Number 10 Court of the Probate, Divorce and Admiralty Division, a group gathered to try and find out just what went wrong.

High up, almost as if he himself was on the bridge, sat Mr Justice Pilcher. With him he had two Trinity House masters, Captain G C H Noakes and Captain W E Crumplin, skilled, experienced seamen, who would guide him in the ways and rules of the sea and in the actions of seamen.

If the *Queen Mary* were found to be at blame at all, the relatives of the men who lost their lives in the cruiser would be able to claim compensation from Cunard for damages and loss of expectation of life. If, on the other hand, the whole of the blame were placed on the cruiser the families would be entitled only to a service pension and whatever compensation the Admiralty might award.

The Lords of the Admiralty claimed, among other things, that the collision was due to the *Queen Mary* deliberately turning to starboard at the crucial moment; that she failed to keep clear of the cruiser or to take any steps to avoid the collision. The Cunard Company claimed, on the other hand, that the navigation of the cruiser was negligent, and that she altered course to port improperly and had failed to keep clear of the liner.

The first witness was a sandy-haired naval officer, wearing two rows of medal ribbons on his tunic breast. This was Captain Boutwood. He had been in the Navy since 1917. He told of his plans for the defence of the *Queen Mary*. Then he was asked: "What was the first thing you noticed with regard to the *Queen Mary* which caused you any trouble?"

"I have described the *Queen Mary* coming ahead on my port quarter until she reached a position which satisfied me; and she, so far as I could see, was on a parallel course to me, with her stem practically abeam. It was just at this time that I myself and the other officers on the bridge had a feeling of doubt as to whether she was actually maintaining a perfectly steady course. It was natural at this time that we should all be observing her with the greatest interest.

"My officers, exchanging views with me, agree that we were not confident that her course was perfectly steady and remained in this state of doubt for what I would think was a longish period when judging such periods.

"Again I cannot bind myself to times, but I would estimate that for possibly something in the nature of a minute or a minute and a half we were in some doubt as to whether she was keeping a steady course, and I remember my navigating officer saying, 'I think she may be turning, or it is only a yaw?'"

So he continued, through his questions, telling his thoughts and those of his fellow-officers on the bridge. He spoke of giving the order "Starboard 15"– that is, fifteen degrees of rudder – in a moment of "no concern". He then told how he suddenly appreciated that the liner was "altering more and more to starboard, and fifteen seconds later I realized that a most alarming and dangerous situation was coming about and increasing.

"As soon as I appreciated a dangerous situation was developing, I myself went to a position to the gyro-compass, which indicated to myself and everybody else that I had taken control of the ship. From then onwards until the time of the crash I cannot say with any assurance of any order which I may have given. All I can say, and I am convinced of it in my own mind, is that from the moment of assuming command of the handling of the ship I did all I conceived was for the best possible to avoid a collision between the *Queen Mary* and the *Curacoa*."

"But you cannot remember now what you did?"

"I cannot now remember anything which I definitely said or did."

He described what happened after the collision.

"Did the *Curacoa* heel over as a result of the blow?"

"Yes, very much indeed. She heeled over to certainly her beam ends. I formed the opinion that she heeled over more than that, and for a moment I thought she would never recover. On the bridge we were hanging on."

"Then what did she do?"

"The fore part of the ship, which formed the major part, then righted to within not very many degrees from upright, and I formed an instant opinion that there was a chance to save the fore part.

"Very shortly after that, within perhaps a minute and a half or two minutes, I realized that there was no chance of saving any part of the ship, and in a very short time it was quite clear to me that the fore part must go down. The noise of escaping steam and other things was deafening. After I gave up hope of saving the ship I instructed the officers who were with me to go down and take charge of what ratings they could get hold of and to get the lifesaving equipment down for use.

"I did not myself actually give the order 'Abandon ship' because there was no hope of getting the order carried out in all that noise. But then I think I heard somebody below shouting 'Abandon ship,' and who ever gave that order was justified in giving it. My officers had gone below with the impression that that was to be done. I did nothing to countermand the order. The ratings got into the water, or a good many of them did, as quickly as they could, but within the space of five minutes the ship sank. I can say that because I referred to my watch."

"I think you were thrown into the water?"

"I was standing on a portion of the *Curacoa* until she finally dipped and then I dipped too."

"What did the *Queen Mary* do after the collision?"

"She steamed on."

"Was that the proper thing for her to do?"

"Yes."

Mr Hayward, KC, who appeared for the Cunard Company, rose and began his cross-examination. He began to ask Captain Boutwood why he had not inquired of the liner at what times she would alter course on her zigzag.

"You say you did not think it a wise course to ask her what her zigzag was? At a distance of half a mile in daylight a couple of expert signalmen could pass that information, without even using flags, like tick-tack men on a racecourse, could they not?"

"I agree that expert signalmen could get a good deal of signalling done without trouble."

"What do you mean when you say that you did not consider it wise to ask her for that information? Were you thinking of any security measures when you said that?"

"There were two or three considerations. The first was that I thought I had made it abundantly clear, and the master of the *Queen Mary* knew from his experience of my practice, that I would not zigzag. I had been careful to give him no hint that I intended to zigzag. I thought if I asked plainly what zigzag he was doing that might lead him to suppose that I was willing to conform to it. It was perfectly clear in my mind that he knew that I was not intending to conform to any zigzag. I expected rather that any ship properly handled, approaching me from astern, would never alter in such a manner as to endanger another ship, at least without making a sound signal. Furthermore, this is a much smaller point, I regret to say that in my opinion the signalmen in the *Queen Mary* were not very expert."

Mr Robinson, the Senior First Officer of the *Queen Mary*, was the first witness for the Cunard Company. He had held a Master's Certificate since January 1939, and had joined the company in April of that year. He joined the *Queen Mary* in August 1942 as Junior First Officer and was promoted Senior First in September, a month before the collision.

"At the time you gave the order to your wheel 'port a little' did you or did you not anticipate the danger of collision."

He replied, "No, definitely not."

"Had you at that time anticipated danger of collision what would your action have been?"

"Hard a port."

He also told the judge that in his opinion the engines would not have had time to pull the liner up appreciably even if he had put them astern shortly after assessing the situation.

The other officers on the bridge of the liner Mr Heighway, Junior Third, Mr Wright, Junior First and Mr Hewitt, Senior Third, also gave evidence, as did the two quartermasters.

Scientific evidence was also given on the possibility of interaction between the two vessels. For some time ship designers and naval architects had been working on this problem. In 1942, at the time of the collision, they knew that there was some such interaction between a larger and a smaller vessel in shallow waters. One occasion that seemed to serve as an omen of tragedy, was that involving the *Titanic*, when her propellers sucked the American liner *New York* away from the quayside in Southampton at the start of her maiden voyage in 1912. Another incident that was blamed on this phenomenon was the unlikely collision that occurred when, on a calm day in the Solent, the Navy cruiser HMS *Hawke* rammed into the White Star liner *Olympic*. The event was attributed to the "interaction" between the two moving vessels, though it was later revealed that the steering gear on HMS *Hawke* had jammed only seconds before impact.

During the inquiry a number of tests were carried out in the experimental tank at the National Physical Laboratory at Teddington. The judge and his assessors and counsel witnessed some of them.

So far, the scientists working on this problem had done some calculations on the theory and a number of tests had been made with models. But now for the first time experiments were made with self-propelled models, equipped with propellers and rudders. Perfect scale models of the two vessels were made, one fifty-sixth of full size. Sea and weather conditions at the time of the collision were reproduced. By delicate instruments carefully placed on the models the forces of interaction were measured.

These tests were naturally scientific, and the evidence of the witnesses very technical. It became established that both sides agreed that the forces of interaction were not practically perceptible until the vessels were eight hundred to one thousand feet apart and that at less than half this distance the forces were easily overcome by slight helm action. It was also agreed that on converging courses the effects were less marked than when on parallel courses.

Of critical importance was the testimony of Captain Cyril Gordon Illingworth, holder of an Extra Master's Certificate, in sail since 1907, and with the Cunard Company since 1910. He first took command of the *Queen Mary* in August 1942 while in the Clyde. "Captain Boutwood came to see me and mentioned zigzags. I told him he could always rely on my using No. 8 Zigzag whenever he was escorting me in the *Queen Mary.*"

At 1.30 on the day of the collision he was on the bridge and then went into his chart-room to work out the ship's position. He heard an order "hard a starboard" given. "I immediately walked out on to the bridge to find out why the ship should have had her helm put hard a starboard. I went to the port wing of the bridge and saw Mr Wright and said, "What's going on?"

"He said he was not quite sure he could clear the *Curacoa* if he completed that leg of the zigzag. I told him to carry on with the zigzag course. It was perfectly safe. I went down to my day cabin to get a sandwich and a cup of coffee."

This was one deck below the bridge. A signalman came in while he was there at 1.55 pm with a message from Captain Boutwood, asking for his expected time of arrival in the Clyde. He finished his lunch and then went up to his chartroom to "calculate it carefully." He said he did not send for Mr Wright. "He was passing my room on his way to his own cabin and I said, 'Come here and check these figures.'" He added he would never send for the senior officer when he was on watch, so he knew that Mr Wright had been relieved by Mr Robinson.

"When you were told you had run down the cruiser and had not been warned that there was any danger of collision I suppose you were very surprised?"

'I was very stricken, sir, I admit."

"You feel you ought to have been sent for?"

"That I cannot say, because it is impossible for me to visualize what the situation was at that moment. It all seemed to happen so quickly and so very unexpectedly that I really could not say."

At about ten past two Wright had said, "I think that is as near as we can get it, sir." Captain Illingworth said, "I think so, too. You seem to make it the same as me. Send for the signalman and make the signal."

Then he felt a bump. "I said, 'I wonder what that is. I wonder if we are being bombed!' We always expected to be bombed. We never were.

"I said to the quartermaster, who was steering, 'Was that a bomb?' and he said, 'No sir, we hit the cruiser.'"

On Tuesday, January 21, 1947, Mr Justice Pilcher delivered his considered judgement on the collision.

Right at the very start, in his very first sentence, he referred to a "disastrous collision ... and it is abundantly clear that the collision was one which never ought to have been permitted to occur."

"I conclude that after 1.40 pm the *Queen Mary* carried on with her zigzag and that Captain Boutwood's observation or his recollection are at fault when he says that during that period she did not do so."

He ruled that Captain Boutwood's order, "Starboard 15" had not been carried out. "It follows either that the wheel of the *Curacoa* was put to port at some later moment or that she was so affected by the forces of interaction that she sheered to port against her starboard rudder.

"Captain Boutwood was not prepared to say that he had not steadied the helm and possibly given port wheel at the last. On the facts as I have found them, to port the wheel at this stage was to court disaster. It is possible that in the stress of the moment Captain Boutwood took this action.

"I have little doubt that it was because the vessels were so close to each other and the situation so tense that the fatal order was given which resulted in the wheel being ported at a time, and in a situation, when there was no opportunity for proper reflection.

"Whether the wheel was put to port at the last and as a result of a panic order or as the result of a misinterpretation of some order given by the Captain will never be known. I am satisfied that the vessel was, in fact, put to port at the last and that the putting of the wheel to port was negligent and that it was this action which immediately brought about the collision."

He said it was clearly the duty of the cruiser to keep out of the way of the liner if there was any danger of collision. He criticized the bad look-out kept by the cruiser officers and their failure to signal the liner and ask her what she was doing if they thought she was not following the zigzag.

"I find it very difficult to believe that Mr Robinson is to blame for not taking earlier or more drastic helm action."

He found the liner free from blame, and that the collision was solely due to the negligence of the cruiser.

The Admiralty immediately lodged an appeal and on July 30, 1947 after a fourteen-day hearing, the Court of Appeal delivered its verdict. By a two to one majority it held that the *Queen Mary* was to blame one third and the cruiser two-thirds.

This time the Cunard company appealed to the House of Lords, and on February 8, 1949, six and a half years after the collision itself, its verdict upheld that of the Court of Appeal.

This began a spate of more legal cases when relatives of the men who lost their lives in the cruiser sued the company for damages and loss of expectancy of life. Two test cases were heard, one for a married man and one for a bachelor. Eventually a figure was agreed upon, and the company paid out on these figures.

The final verdict of the courts was to cause much comment among seamen. For the inter-relation of one warship escorting one merchant ship had never really been laid down before. No one had been able to say exactly what rule applied in these circumstances. Captain W H Coombs, President of the Merchant Navy Officers' Federation, wrote in his journal:

> Those on the bridge of the *Queen Mary* at the time of the collision will perhaps find some consolation in the thought that it had probably taken the efforts of the best legal brains engaged in the practice and administration of Admiralty law just about as many weeks as they had seconds in which to decide what was the correct action to be taken in the circumstances.
>
> A factor of great concern to Merchant Navy shipmasters and officers is the disturbing disclosure that it is not certain that contrary to what many have believed, it is NOT the absolute duty of the naval vessel to keep out of the way of her charge - i.e., the sheep may be blameworthy if it allows the sheep-dog to bite it.

One cannot help but speculate as to the likelihood of such a disaster, had the two vessels had the advantage of modern electronic radar and proximity warning devices. True, a radar was fitted to the *Queen Mary* in 1942, however radar was still in its infancy and this could hardly be compared to the high-tech wizardry in use on the bridges of modern ships.

Years later, Captain Peter Jackson (in command of *Queen Elizabeth 2* during the 1982 Falklands crisis, and formerly a junior officer onboard *Queen Mary*), described the navigational methods in use at the time:

> We did have something called the Decca Navigator, and that depended on certain shore stations, but the reception was not good and therefore it was treated with some suspicion by navigating officers. No, in those days, we all had sextants and we worked out the star, sun and moon sights. That was the way our navigation was done but when you crossed the Atlantic you frequently had to go across without sight of sun or anything because you'd have either pouring rain or thick fog.
>
> [They used] dead reckoning. You worked on the speed of the ship and the course that you thought you were steering. Usually you weren't far out and you could do the whole crossing on this dead reckoning situation.

The original trial judge, who had listened to the witnesses, heard their account and relived the very atmosphere of war-time convoy conditions at sea, had no hesitation in finding the *Queen Mary* completely blameless. The Appeal Court and the House of Lords, considering the matter perhaps a little more coldly and analytically in the light of pure legal argument, far removed from the atmosphere of war and from the witnesses, still held the cruiser two thirds to blame.

But despite this, it cost Cunard, who had virtually won the case, far more money than the Admiralty. For the Naval authorities were protected by the conditions of service, which limited their liability to the payment of Service pensions. On the other hand, the company had to meet all the common-law claims for loss of expectancy of life and for damages, towards which the Admiralty, sticking to the letter of the law, made no contribution.

13

Demobilization

The *Queen Mary*, as we have seen, ferried American troops from Europe back home.

In America, the moment the War was ended, there was a demand from all sides for a speedier demobilization programme. On August 23, only nine days after the capitulation of Japan, President Truman had to point out at his Press conference that there had already been considerable criticism of the programme.

Truman wrote:

> Prime Minister Attlee called my attention to the fact that many of their men had been on active service and away from their homes for five or more years, and that the demand for their early return, now that hostilities were over, had become loud and insistent. The Prime Minister also reminded me that the arrangement to loan the two *Queens* and the *Aquitania* had been conditioned solely on the urgency of redeploying American forces for the war against Japan. With the unexpected early termination of the Japanese war, Attlee pointed out, these conditions had ceased to exist....
>
> Our Chiefs of Staff had told the British that they regretted "that the necessity to return U.S. forces from Europe as expeditiously as possible required all lifts scheduled under present agreements to December, 1945, and that therefore they are unable to provide assistance in U.S. controlled troop shipping before the end of 1945."
>
> On the other hand I was impressed by Attlee's cable. "I shall speak with the utmost frankness," his message concluded. "While so many of our troops overseas are awaiting repatriation after nearly six years of war and of separation from their families, I cannot continue to justify to the British public the use of our three biggest ships in the American service. I am reluctant to suggest the return of the *Queens* and the *Aquitania*. I must, however, ask you most earnestly, Mr President, to provide us in the immediate future with an equivalent lift for these three ships."
>
> There could be no doubt that Attlee was right and I cabled him: "I have directed the Joint Chiefs of Staff to return to you the two *Queens* and the

Aquitania or to provide equivalent personnel lift, the details to be worked out with your staff representatives here."

On October 12, the Minister of War Transport, Mr Barnes, reported to the House of Commons:

> The *Queen Elizabeth* and the *Aquitania* will be used for the carriage of British troops. The *Queen Mary* is to remain at the disposal of the American authorities for the present, but the Americans are placing at our disposal a number of smaller ships.
>
> In total these smaller vessels will render an equivalent service which it is most convenient for us to have, as we shall be so enabled to move forces from areas where it would be wasteful and even impracticable to use such a large vessel as the *Queen Mary*.

On February 3, 1946, still in her 'war paint,' the liner sailed from Southampton in yet another role in her varied career. Already she had been transatlantic liner, troopship, hospital ship, floating "Whitehall," prison ship, and now she was to be a brides' ship. She was beginning the mass transportation of thousands of British girls who had married American soldiers during the War and taking them and their children to their new homes in a strange land.

In all she carried 30% of all brides who travelled to America under the United States Government scheme. In six voyages from February to May that year she transported 12,886 of these "new" Americans, plus 1,683 children and 2,085 infants.

Structural alterations had to be made once more in the passenger accommodation to fit her for this role as GI Bride ship. Hundreds of cots were put on board, special washing and ironing rooms were set aside, and nurseries staffed by American Red Cross nurses were made available in the cabin lounges. The late Bertie Camp, superintendent of furnishing at Southampton, designed a collapsible baby chair which could be fitted to dining room chairs, so that the mothers could have their youngsters at the table.

Towards the end of May she was switched to carrying Canadian brides, and took on each voyage (up to the end of September 1946) 2,100 dependants and children to Halifax, as well as 200 priority civilians for New York. There was generally a comradely spirit amongst the women. Joan Bates, a bride on her way to meet her husband in Ottawa, recalled how they would share the supervision of the children: "The mothers had to look after the children and those of us who did not have children were all volunteering to look after them if the mother needed help. They had assistance from the crew but mostly it was a case of helping each other."

As the *Queen Mary* was due to leave on her first "brides'" voyage a south-westerly gale, which had sprung up the day before, reached gale force on the Sunday and the master, the late Sir Gordon Illingworth, decided to delay the sailing for twenty-four hours. "This is a valuable ship with a very valuable freight – future citizens of the United States. The weather is much too bad." Boat drill was held in port, and the older children wore special lifebelts made for the occasion.

American immigration officials had been sent over to do their work while the liner was on her way. They decided to begin there and then, even though the liner was still in Southampton.

The women were under the discipline of the British Army ship's commandant, Colonel Beaufoy Lane, a former actor and journalist. A large, cheerful family man, who enjoyed every moment of life, while a strict disciplinarian, he had a "human" touch which was very popular with the families.

There were also twenty business and professional men on board, all travelling to the United States on Government business. Most of these were family men, and made themselves very useful helping with the children during the voyage, which was one of the roughest for many years.

There was the discovery of a stowaway. A twenty-year-old bride from Wandsworth was found hiding in a cabin occupied by four other women. Although she begged them not to give her away, they decided that by assisting her they would jeopardize their own position and be accused of collusion. They therefore told her to hide somewhere else. A stewardess later found her hiding in a linen locker, and she was handed over to the police, but the company decided not to charge her.

The children were all over the liner, running, playing, screaming and becoming very excited though, strangely enough, there were no injuries and none fell overboard. Captain Donald Sorrell was staff captain of the liner at the time, and at the end of the voyage the brides wrote him a letter of thanks for all he had done for them to make the journey pleasant. Chief Steward Edward Charlton, thinking he was helping the women to become acclimatized to the American coffee-drinking habit, served it twice daily outside meal times. The brides sent a deputation to Colonel Lane begging for tea instead.

Throughout those months whilst she was carrying the GI brides, and despite the frequently adverse weather conditions, the children would rarely fall victim to seasickness. The young mothers were not always as fortunate. Many would succumb to the lurching and rolling of the enormous liner; that grotesque leaning which would take seemingly ages to recover and right itself. There were other discomforts too. Food was still basic and bland following the war, as Joan Bates recalls simply: "canned peas and that kind of thing."

Because the ship was still strictly under military jurisdiction, entertainment was of course minimal, though enterprising. Apart from competitions and cinema shows there were occasionally informal shows or "concerts" by the ladies themselves. There were also daily lectures during which the American way of life was explained and girls going to the same area of America were put in touch with each other. In a way, these lectures fulfilled the same role as those delivered to the troops going to Europe at the beginning of the war. Then of course, there was also that time-honoured seagoing sport – bingo. As some of the young women who crossed at the time recall, there was no charge to play, and prizes were modest. But at least there was the diversion of the game itself.

On February 7 the liner received the news that the New York tugboat men were on strike. Captain Illingworth said he was prepared to dock the liner without the aid of tugs. Sol Bloom, of the Committee of Foreign Affairs in the House of Representatives, who was a passenger, wirelessed President Truman asking "on behalf of British wives and children of American servicemen on board the *Queen Mary*," that he, the President, should request tugboat strikers to permit the safe docking of the liner, to avoid undue danger and hazard to wives and babies of US servicemen, and permit them to continue with the arrangements made for them to reach their husbands and fathers without delay. He added, "Immediate action is necessary."

President Truman sent eight Army tugs to help the liner dock on the Sunday, with three more tugs to stand by in case they were needed as ice-breakers, for the temperature was only just above freezing point.

From Ambrose Light every vantage point on the open decks had been filled with the brides and their kiddies, not too well wrapped up against the cold, all clutching miniature Union Jacks or Stars and Stripes and cheering wildly. A US Army transportation tug came alongside, and from her decks came the strains of *Roll Out the Barrel* played by a section of the unit's band. Then came the traditional fire float and siren welcome, as well as an aerial escort of two fighters, a bomber and a helicopter, and a cavalcade of boats.

The band on the tug struck up *Here comes the Bride*, and the wives knew they had reached their new land – safely. The liner eventually berthed at Pier 90 at 12.40 pm on Sunday, February 10, watched by a great crowd. Customs formalities were eased, and after lunch the brides and children filed ashore in batches and were taken uptown in motor-coaches to New York's largest National Guard Drill Hall in Park Avenue. Their husbands sat in the spacious galleries as the girls filed in on the ground floor and went into wired enclosures, labelled with the name of the state to which they were travelling.

As each girl's name was called, her husband was shepherded down to meet his wife just outside the "cage" and they were then taken together to stations where special Pullman trains waited. If their destinations were local a fleet of taxi-cabs was waiting outside the drill hall. That was the plan. But it did not work out that way.

After about half an hour of orderly reunions some of the husbands in the gallery could stand the strain of waiting no longer, especially when it was realised that the brides were being called forward in alphabetical order. One GI climbed over the balcony ledge and slithered down the supporting pillar. Others followed, and soon the ground floor was a seething mass of GIs, brides, frightened children, screaming babies and harassed officials frantically appealing for order.

To add to the problem there were in-laws *en masse*. Only a small number of brides came ashore that day, the rest using the liner as a hotel for the night. Disembarkation went on all through Monday.

New York itself was suffering from a "brown out" because of the tug strike, for tugs were used to bring all the coal to Manhattan by water. The Mayor had ordered subdued lighting and the cessation of all lighted advertising signs; and all bars and restaurants to be closed by midnight.

Four young fathers would have been particularly anxious to reunite with their brides during those dramatic post-war crossings. For there were four offspring who were actually born whilst enroute on the westbound trip.

On a later "brides" trip one of the priority passengers was Mr (later Sir) Reginald Biddle, for many years Docks and Marine Manager at Southampton. He had been sent to New York to study docking and passenger-handling facilities there, with a view to making improvements at Southampton. One night sleep eluded him completely. So he got up and began to think over the problem. From those thoughts grew the idea and development of the magnificent Ocean Terminal at Southampton, where the liner berthed on almost all of her visits to her home port. Sadly, some years later during the career of the *Queen Mary*'s younger successor *Queen Elizabeth 2*, this beautiful building was demolished to make way for the somewhat less imposing Queen Elizabeth II Terminal. Note, however, that, with its conspicuous roman numeral, this structure is not named after the famous ship, but the current sovereign of the United Kingdom.

On September 29, 1946, the *Queen Mary* docked at Southampton after returning from Halifax, Nova Scotia, at the end of her last trooping voyage. She was demobilized. In her war service she had carried 810,730 "passengers," the majority Servicemen, and steamed an incredible half a million miles. In fact, the overall statistics concerning Cunard's involvement in the War are impressive: the company's ships had carried a staggering 2.4 million wartime passengers, of which 1.2 million had travelled onboard the two *Queens*.

Work then began on one of the greatest reconversion tasks ever undertaken, to restore her to her glory a a passenger liner. Twelve hundred workmen from John Brown's yard came onboard and began the task of dismantling the troop fittings and all the equipment that had been put into her during the war years. They lived just outside Southampton and travelled to the docks every day by bus.

During this "rehabilitation" she had a new stem fitted. After the collision with the *Curacoa* temporary repairs had been made in the Clyde, and then further repairs at Boston. While she was there, a new stem had been made in case of need, and was actually brought over in the liner in 1946 and had lain beside the Graving Dock at Southampton.

The deck rails, honourably scarred with the initials of thousands of American troops, were scraped and planed for final polishing. One section was sent to the American army as a souvenir.

During the War 10,000 pieces of furniture had been taken out of the ship and stored in New York, in Sydney, and in the New Forest. Arrangements were made for this to be shipped home. In New York 200 cases and boxes had been put ashore, in Australia large quantities of public-room furniture and fittings and 2,500 large doors had been stowed away. All these were brought back to Southampton and placed in an aircraft hangar at Southampton Airport at Eastleigh for sorting, renovating and cleaning.

Whilst this incredible task continued, there was a period of time when the interiors of the great ship were but bare shells, as the skilled workers carried out extensive checks on wiring and plumbing, and repaired and restored every inch of panelling, flooring and deckhead. All the paintings were inspected and artists asked to renovate them where necessary. Every inch of woodwork and panelling was examined and checked. At times there were as many as 3,000 workers onboard the liner.

At the same time, aware that the younger *Queen Elizabeth* was superior in many of her internal decorations, the company decided to make a number of alterations in the interior design of the liner to improve the passenger amenities. This was itself a major task, involving the erection of bulkheads, following the preparation of detailed plans.

One of the first things they had made their minds up about was to install a separate cinema. So the starboard gallery and ballroom was turned into a new cinema, seating two hundred people and fully air-conditioned. Plastics were used exclusively in the decor. The old gymnasium became an engineers' wardroom.

A new cocktail bar at the entrance to the dining-saloon and two garden lounges on the promenade deck were created after the popularity of these features had been established in the *Queen Elizabeth*. The port long gallery was created into a new room, divided into four bays by screens surrounded by illuminated jardinières and banks of flowers. A new cocktail-time dance salon was made, and Anna Zinkeisen painted two decorative panels, 25 ft by 8 ft high. These were *The Chase* and *Hunting through the Ages* – colourful, vivid compositions, with mermaids in scarlet jackets and underwater revelry in the realm of Neptune. Later, a shop was erected here sadly hiding these lovely, delightful paintings.

The port side writing-room was turned into a radio-reception office. The shopping centre was made brighter than ever with new fluorescent strip lighting. The Observation Bar, the smoking room, the lounge and the main restaurant were all restored to their 1939 state.

For the Verandah Grill Doris Zinkeisen was asked to restore her mural. She said, "The company asked me if I would do 'some touching up' on the murals. During the War the murals had simply been covered up by some very thin plaster board and the room was used as the anti-aircraft headquarters of the ship. Any Tom, Dick or Harry who wanted to hang up a bit of equipment or put up a notice simply knocked a nail into the wood. When this was removed the company said there were 'some holes in the canvas.'

"Actually I had only just moved in to a new studio and was having the place redecorated and refurnished, as the Air Force had only just moved out. It is on the fifth floor. When the drum arrived it was brought up, and the men promptly knocked down half the balustrade, which just added to the chaos. Anyway, I eventually got the thing opened, and frankly it was just like a piece of lace, there were so many holes in it. It was almost as if the mice had been at it, you know. I had never seen anything like it. I told the company that it was absolutely impossible to do anything with it. If they wanted it I would have to repaint the whole mural. They agreed, so I got a new canvas and began the job all over again.

"I had a hinged stretcher this time, so was able to get the canvas round two sides of the studio, which made the work much easier. I had told the company that I reserved the right to make some alterations if I felt improvements could be made. I did alter some of the figures and added a film star and camera and arc lights. The work lasted right through the winter and spring and deep into summer."

At one time, on a bookcase in the office of an executive of the Cunard Steam-Ship Company in Montreal there stood a polished-wood plaque, bearing a crest of the Lion of Scotland, beneath which was a smaller brass plate bearing the words: "Reconversion of the World's Largest Liners. 2nd October 1946 to 31st July 1947. Q.M. A Tribute to 'Reggie' from 'Mac.'"

'Reggie' was Reginald Smathers, who had entered the company as a boy in the freight department and later transferred to the managerial side. During the War he had much to do with the shore administration of Cunarders. When the *Queens* ended their war service he was selected to go to Southampton to co-ordinate the task of restoration and act as liaison and 'peacemaker' between local management, Thorneycroft's the ship repairers, the trade unions, the sub-contractors and suppliers, the railways, the road-transport services, and all other agencies concerned with this gigantic task.

A tough, dynamic personality, he was the very man for this seemingly impossible position. Two of his proudest possessions in his Montreal home were a cut-glass decanter from "Mac," and a Christmas card bearing the signatures of all the Clydeside foremen who worked with him on that job.

"Mac" was William Macfarlane, the right-hand man to Sir Donald Skiffington. Equally forthright, he was a man to deal with the tough workmen doing the job.

Not only were there 1,200 men brought down from Clydeside for the restoration, but 120 women French polishers. The men lived in a hutted camp at Chandler's Ford, outside Southampton, which had originally been built to house people who had lost their homes in the port's two-day blitz; the women lived in dormitories in the town.

In addition to the Glasgow men there were nearly two thousand others from the repair shops working, as well as contractors' men. This polyglot collection presented many problems.

At one time beer was in very short supply in Southampton, and the local publicans were loath to serve the "foreigners," because it meant that their regular customers went short. The Clydesiders got very restless over this, and their work was suffering, tempers were frayed, and some of them threatened to go home. But Smathers and Macfarlane discussed the problem and eventually got permission, after a long struggle, for it to be served in the men's canteen at Chandler's Ford.

"Keeping the peace" on board the liner was a difficult task. Even in those days there was the problem of demarcation. At the beginning of the restoration there was a trade-union argument as to whose job it was to dismantle the standee beds – joiners or boilermakers. Neither union would agree, and both threatened to withdraw their labour. At one time it was considered it would be better to take the liner away from Southampton, anchor her in Cowes Road, and let the ship's own joiners get on with the task. Eventually it was decided that extra joiners would be signed on for other work, and the ship's joiners removed the standee bunks.

One of the greatest problems was smoking. With three thousand men on board it was necessary to give them "safe places" for smoking. But the men were not content to go to the smoking areas and would have a quick smoke on the job when no one was looking. Two bad offenders were dismissed after repeated warnings. Their union demanded their reinstatement, and it looked as if there was going to be serious trouble.

Smathers persuaded the shop stewards to attend a meeting and got the then staff captain, Gerald Norman Jones, a fervent Welshman and a brilliant speaker, to address them. He told them of all the problems of fire, painting fearsome pictures of what might happen, illustrating it with actual incidents at sea. He concluded, "Do you realize that if we have a fire in this ship not all of us, indeed many of us, would never get ashore?"

There was a moments' silence, and the chief shop steward stepped forward to assure him that there would be no more surreptitious smoking. There were no more serious cases.

It is interesting to ponder the change in attitude and values which has occurred over the past five decades. Not only would this issue never have received such a priority listing at a union meeting now, but the social stigma attached to smoking would, in any case, have reduced discussion of the subject to mere pub talk.

Another major problem was pilfering. In those days of austerity it was very tempting with all the furniture, carpets and leather work. Smathers overcame this to a great extent by having his own police force.

Ship's officers were inspectors, petty officers were sergeants and ratings constables. As each section was well under way a "constable" would be placed on the door and the name of every person who came into that section was taken along with the time of arrival and departure.

The whole ship had to be fumigated, and this was done at holiday periods over thirty hours, with firemen patrolling the quay and a motor-boat patrol round the vessel.

The weather that winter was very bad. The Clydesider's camp was 6½ miles out, and the elderly buses which were used to transport them to the docks had trouble starting in the mornings. The transport manager warned Macfarlane and Smathers that he might be late in getting to work. Smathers reminded him of the urgency of the contract, and the manager kept his engines running all night so that there would be prompt starting.

The women organized a dance to celebrate their first six months of the work, and the "twins" were the guests of honour. Watching the Clydesiders dancing the "Hokey-cokey," Macfarlane remarked, "If some of those bastards worked as hard as they dance we would have finished this job three months ago."

It was not until July 24, 1947, that she sailed on a thirty-six-hour shakedown cruise. As she was returning to Southampton she met for the first time in the splendour of their "colours of peace" her sister off Cowes. On July 31, 1947, she sailed on her civilian post-war maiden voyage, almost eight years since her last voyage as a liner. Onboard were 1,857 passengers, including some who had actually sailed on her eleven years previously, in May 1936.

Then, and only then, was she playing the role for which, with the *Queen Elizabeth*, she had been built; operating the two-ship express service – the service on which Cunard had staked so much, and in which it had so much faith through all adversity.

It had been eleven years earlier, on a late September afternoon, on the day she was launched, that Sir Percy Bates had said:

> The *Queen Mary* is planned for success, and all those who have had a share in her constructions have thought the same thoughts and been touched by the same high imagination.
>
> The testing of our imagination, the proof of our dreams, comes when the ship is engaged on her proper work of sharing with a second ship, the duty of carrying His Majesty's mails to New York every week and maintaining that close connection between the inhabitants of the Eastern and Western hemispheres which is one of the real guarantees of the peace of the world.

The peace of the world had been shattered. But here, now, was the "very proof of the dream." Here was the realization of all that Sir Percy had worked for.

14

The Brightest Star

Week after week, month after month, she was to be in the news. In July 1948 the company made an announcement which stopped one of the world's best free shows in New York and caused great resentment among the people of the city and visiting Americans. They limited the number of friends that any passenger embarking in the *Queen* could take on board to two, and special passes would have to be issued for them.

Prior to this thousands of Americans flocked into the liner every time she was in port, virtually taking charge of the ship, so that the intending passengers sometimes were greatly inconvenienced and it became difficult to get baggage on board. On some occasions as many as 12,000 visitors would be on board in comparison with 2,000 passengers. Incredible parties used to take place, and many times the ship sailed and "stowaways" had to be put ashore by the official launch. Sometimes departure was delayed, as the efforts of the stewards and officers to get visitors ashore took so long.

In January 1949, when she went aground in Cherbourg Harbour in the teeth of a gale while under the command of Captain Grattridge for the first time, she was once more in the headlines.

When she had been pulled free by four tugs the following morning she returned to Southampton for an examination of her hull to ensure that she was in fit condition to travel across the Atlantic. There it was found that a number of plates at the stern had been forced apart and water was seeping in. It was decided that, by the use of concrete, repairs could be made so that the ship could sail. Sufficient sand to make one hundred tons of cement and two lorry loads of quick-drying cement were loaded into the ship and a cement mixer was hoisted aboard and set up on the after deck.

A special squad of two hundred workmen came on board. Some were loaded into the bilges while others formed a chain to pass buckets of cement to where they could be lowered to them by block and tackle at the rate of six a minute.

Without interruption, with other men taking their places for meal breaks, the men worked from eleven o'clock in the morning until breakfast time the following day. In a space of 25 ft long and 5 in high they poured the cement into the ship's bottom to form a concrete base. Eventually, seventy-four hours later, the liner sailed for New York. These "temporary" repairs lasted throughout that year, permanent repairs only being made during a later drydocking.

One of the main problems that had had to be solved before the ship could be built was that of insurance. The Cunard Insurance Fund was closed on March 31, 1954. In accordance with the directions given by the Treasury under the Cunard (Insurance) Act of 1930, the investments and cash balance of the Fund were transferred to the National Debt Commissioners for application for the reduction of the National Debt. The final accounts, published by the Ministry of Transport on May 24, 1954, showed that £880,539 were transferred in cash and investments. Thus the British Government had made quite a useful profit out of a measure which had been strongly criticized when it was inaugurated.

On January 1, 1950, Cunard White Star Line ceased to exist as a company, and ownership of the vessels was transferred to the new company, the Cunard Steam-Ship Company, Ltd. This raised a problem over the insurance. The 1930 Act referred specifically to the Cunard White Star Line. The Government informed the new company that to transfer the insurance would involve some delay, as it would be necessary to introduce an Order in Council and the traditional Parliamentary procedure would take time.

The company decided to approach Lloyd's and the marine insurance underwriters to see if they could cover the amount. This was achieved, and the policies in existence then, provided by the Ministry of Transport, were accordingly cancelled from December 31, 1949. In the meantime the *Queen Mary*'s value had been increased by £450,000 to £5,250,000.

It is interesting to record the figures of claims paid out for damage mainly caused by heavy seas and bad weather.

	£
1941–1944	2,562
1944–1947	12,431
1950–	53,130
1951–	130,293

The steadily rising figures were, of course, mainly due to increased costs of ship-repairing. The 1951 figure included the damage caused after the Cherbourg grounding in 1949.

On March 31, 1953, it was announced that the new marine insurance policies covering the Cunard liners *Queen Mary* and *Queen Elizabeth* were to be increased on each to £10,750,000. The old policies expired after midnight on April 30. This was a record for any individual ship insured in the British market. The policies were each made up of £8,600,000 "insured valued" against full sea perils, including partial loss and repair costs, and £2,150,000 payable in the event of total loss. Initially the whole of the amount was placed at Lloyd's and with British marine insurance companies. The risk was eventually spread over the world market by reinsurance.

This was hailed as a triumph for private enterprise in marine insurance. The company stated that the acceptance of the additional amounts was highly gratifying and indicated the strength of the market. "It is evidence, if this were needed, that from an insurance point of view, the risks of the ships were regarded as being of the highest class, justifying the readiness of the market to grant insurance for such immense amounts."

At that time the *Queen Mary* was docking in New York twenty-four hours late, and her master, Captain Cove, was saying, "It was the worst crossing I have had in many years. There were gales all the time, sometimes reaching 90 mph, and snow, ice and fog."

Until the 1960s and the somewhat unsuccessful attempts by the owners to send the *Queen Mary* cruising to the sun, the distinction between classes was rigorously upheld. Occasionally, passengers from First Class would wander down, uninvited, to the lower decks to witness life in Tourist Class; the reverse was unthinkable. The only occasion when passengers from different classes were officially allowed to wander freely throughout the ship, was on a Sunday morning, when attending the weekly church service. On these occasions, the gates which divided the areas at staircases and landings would be opened, permitting all passengers unrestricted access to "church". There were those, however, who ignored the rules, and set out to have a good time, regardless. Oggy Carss was a student travelling from New York to Southampton in 1947.

"I was down in the hold with a bunch of Tourist [class] people and the cabin would hold four. There was no privacy. You still had to go next door to the bathroom."

Naturally, the temptation to explore was considerable.

"The only time I got up to First Class was on the night that we were going to dock in Southampton. I went up there with a few friends – there must have been four of us who interloped up there from Tourist – and we had an absolute ball. There was an English gentleman with a very beautiful secretary who had been doing business in New York and they took us in hand and introduced us to Harpo Marx. He [Harpo] gave me a cigar and then they took us into the Verandah Grill. They bought all the drinks. First Class was absolutely marvellous."

Though they were never actually advertised, there were certain illicit publications in existence at the time, which actually described "secret" routes around the ship, helping would-be gatecrashers to find their way upstairs undetected. These booklets were most often found through dubious suppliers in New York.

Sometimes, the most unlikely characters would be found in Tourist. Carss continues: "Down in Tourist, my recollection was that it was all rather dark and dreary and the interesting thing down there was that there was one Russian Prince who was travelling Tourist. He [and his wife] always were; they'd be asked to go up to First Class to dine with the Captain."

Some saw things differently. Mary Riviello sailed First Class in September 1950. She longed for something different. She says, "The only thing I must say is going First Class, my brother and I felt that we had missed out on some of the fun; 'cos the Second Class had a little more fun. You know what I mean; it wasn't quite as formal."

First, Second or Tourist Class, rough weather and seasickness continued to be an unhappy part of many traveller's voyage. Some passengers would become hysterical with fear as the vicious North Atlantic flung the ship around. Virginia Schelp crossed in February 1955:

"Well it was very rough and one of the poor women [one of her two cabin mates]... the Mexican lady and I were in our cabin and she became very ill, and of course being Catholic and being very emotional, she called some nuns in; called a priest that was aboard to try and help her get over her seasickness."

On this occasion, as there always had been, there was also romance in the air. One of Virginia Schelp's other roommates had a liaison nearby:

"One of the women [Schelp's other cabin mate] had a gentleman across the hall and he wanted to spend time in our cabin. The Mexican woman and I didn't care for that. So we suggested that she go across the hall to him, and she ended up in his cabin across the hall."

At the end of 1951 Winston Churchill decided to make a trip to America to talk with President Truman. He took with him a large staff of forty, and three Cabinet Ministers – Mr Eden, Foreign Secretary, Lord Cherwell, Paymaster-General, and Lord Ismay, Secretary of Commonwealth Relations.

For his own personal use he had three rooms, a bedroom and a dining-room on the port side of the main deck, while others were turned into offices. Additional telephones were installed so that he could be in constant touch with Whitehall and Downing Street.

The sailing in the liner was first delayed when she was seventy-two hours late in docking at Southampton due to bad weather. The turn-round crew and the liner's crew worked throughout the night to get her ready for her departure. Then she was delayed another day when the port anchor jammed in a hawse pipe during a test. After vain attempts to free it by being towed away by tugs workmen spent 17.5 hours releasing it by cutting out a plate against which it had jammed and then welding it back into place.

On one occasion passengers were somewhat startled to hear the strains of *Rule Brittania*, led by Churchill, coming from his suite. He was leading a choir, which included the three members of his cabinet!

On January 29, 1952, in the House of Commons, Mr Churchill, in a written reply to Colonel Wigg (Socialist, Dudley), said that his own personal expenses in the *Queen Mary* to America and back and Mr Eden's outward voyage did not figure in the costs incurred on his visit as the Cunard Company invited them to be their guests.

In December 1952 the McCarran Act came into force in the United States, aimed at security screening of all foreign seamen before they were allowed to land. The British protested vigorously to the State Department. The new Regulations in the Act, which repealed all previous immigration regulations in the United States, had been vetoed by President Truman but Congress overruled him.

The Cunard Company agreed for a trial period to allow an immigration official to travel in the ship to see if this would speed up procedure. Russell Danielson, an immigration inspector, made the first voyage, and travelled in the liner from New York on the round trip. He screened officers and catering staff on the eastbound trip and deck and engine-room staff on the outward trip to New York. Each man filled in Form 199 with answers to twelve questions. He dealt with one hundred people a day. It would be fair to assume that much of this caution had arisen because of the ever-growing threat of communism, however, as he said: "My questions are not based on communism only. They concern a man's past, possibly as a dope peddler, as a person with a dangerous contagious disease, or who might have been a procurer. My instructions are that this must be done every trip."

It was this fact of having it done every voyage that really incensed the crews of liners. On arrival in New York, if it was not done during the voyage, it meant wasting precious leave time queuing up after the passengers had passed through immigration. After a trial period the American authorities decided that there was no need to have a travelling inspector, and all questioning was done on arrival at New York.

Stories of these questionings are legendary, but a favourite is that of the long line of crew members, greasers, engine-room staff, seamen, stewards, shuffling forward, answering questions. On and on it went, each putting his pass-photograph down on the table in front of the immigration officer, who would ask questions and give it a cursory glance.

Suddenly, a very pretty nurse was next in line. She put her picture down, and the questioning began: "Have you ever been a member of the Communist Party? Ever read any communist literature?"

The inspector's eyes then happened to catch sight of the picture. He slowly put his pencil down, looked up lazily, and said, "Say, you don't have to answer any of this trash. The only question you have to answer is, 'What are you doing for dinner tonight?'"

On this voyage, in January 1953, Cassandra, the witty, impassioned columnist of the *Daily Mirror*, made his first trip and had this to say:

The other day during one of those endless public quiz games a girl was asked, "What would you like most in the world?" She replied, "A voyage to New York in the *Queen Mary*."

Now, until then I had never seen the *Queen Mary*. First of all she is outstandingly vulgar, overwhelmingly voluminous, and impressively voluptuous. Secondly she is a surprisingly old-fashioned wench, for although it is impolite to give the age of this famous mistress of the seas, her keel was, in fact, laid more than twenty years ago. Outwardly she is a very handsome lass, although a good deal too plump to be called an ocean greyhound. Inwardly she is a riot of ostentation carefully executed in the Leicester-Square style of the late thirties. The design and decor of her public rooms, her bars, and her restaurants seem to have been aimed at dollar millionaires from the Mid-west and their opposite numbers in England who proclaim that, "Where there is muck, there is money."

The workmanship is magnificent, the materials used are splendid, the result is appalling; that is if you value good taste. A piece of opulent vulgarity.

There is a strong feeling on board that Winston's our chap and the more beef steaks he tackles the more he will do justice on the other side against some of the smarter sinewy Yankee traders at Washington. And in the beef-steak business certainly nobody can match the victuallers and the chefs of the two transatlantic *Queens*.

Accompanied by his wife, the Prime Minister was on his way to Washington for talks with President-elect Eisenhower. Each day during the voyage he lunched or dined in the Verandah Grill with Mrs Churchill; he was often breakfasting at eight o'clock and busy talking to London by radio-telephone or dictating his war memoirs during the morning.

Shortly after the liner docked in New York at 8.00 am he walked along to the Verandah Grill to meet the Press. He gave what was described as "a comprehensive, reasoned, and witty survey of the crucial issues of the day."

Of the voyage he said, "We've had a pleasant voyage. A hurricane got out of our way very obligingly or else the captain avoided it with his usual skill, and here we are. It's a very pleasant interlude in a busy life to cross the Atlantic in one of these splendid ships."

He was asked by one reporter if he had been screened during the voyage under the McCarran Act for "communistic, polygamous, and atheistic tendencies." He paused for a moment, one report said, "as if weighing the questions seriously" and then answered, "I'm told it's okay." Actually Mr Danielson, the travelling immigration officer, did visit his suite to check on the Britons there, but said, "Naturally I did not bother him. He was too busy."

Churchill returned in the liner later in January, and his suite had not been occupied since he used it on the outward voyage. All the furnishings, including the tables and typewriters which transformed one room into an office, were left for the return trip. Second Steward Douglas Mann was in charge of the arrangement. He had been with Churchill on several of his war-time voyages, including the trip to Malta in the *Franconia*.

On one voyage Captain Donald Sorrell, fifty-nine years old, a dapper little man of 5 ft 4 in, was in command; his second voyage as relief captain. The previous night he had received a message asking him if he could take the giant liner into her pier the following morning with no tugs, no pilots. He replied, "Certainly, I will be delighted," and, as he was to tell naval cadets some years later, "Feeling quite happy about the result." For the whole of the port of New York was without a tug. For five days the port had been almost paralysed by a strike of 3,500 tugmen seeking higher pay.

He knew, too, that there was always a possibility that one day he might have to meet just such a challenge as this. "I had planned three methods as to how I would dock the *Queen Mary* without tugs many years before I did the job," he said later.

By nine o'clock on that morning the liner had made her familiar way up the Hudson river and was lying off her Pier 90, on the other side of the river, hugging the New Jersey shore. Two tousand people lined the New York waterfront, jamming the pier side waiting, watching, like a crowd silently anticipating disaster. Among them were many of the tugboat men who were responsible for this very situation, waiting, hoping for the moment when they could take delight in their disruptive handiwork. Their tugs, squat, tubby craft, of which about eight were needed normally to haul, push, and pull the liner into her pier side from the fast flowing river with a tricky tide and the bustling gusty winds which spring up in a moment, were all tied up. They watched with experienced eyes, watching for the slightest signs that would tell them instantly that was all not well with the liner.

They knew, as the crowd knew, that other ships had tried previously to dock without tugs, and lengths of twisted, mangled pier and sheds bore silent testimony to the results. The Cunarder *Caronia* had damaged a pier. It was true that the French liner *Île de France* had done it successfully, but the *Queen Mary* was nearly twice her size. The morning was hot and muggy – but the main factor was that there was no wind.

Captain Sorrell went down to his cabin and brought back with him an uneven square of faded grey-painted wood with a semicircle of screws on top. This was his own private aid to pilotage. He sent for his chief quartermaster, fifty-five-year-old Jimmy Irvine, who was two inches smaller than himself.

A lifeboat was put out from the *Caronia* to help with the docking lines. Slowly the great liner inched her way towards the pier entrance. By ten minutes to ten her bow began to pass the end of the pier. A moment later the *Caronia*'s boat caught a line and got one end of it on the pier. It seemed as though her first try was to be the right one. But the Hudson river had other ideas.

Captain Sorrell suddenly, but calmly, said, "Quartermaster, you are off course." And immediately he realized that the underwater current had seized her, and the stern was swinging towards the pier as she was being pulled towards the East River.

"Back all, go astern," was the command, and with the line ashore cast off, and another big blast from her whistle, the ship moved out into the river towards New Jersey. As Captain Sorrell said, "I backed out in a hurry."

Placing his block of wood on the front of the bridge, he crouched down behind it and squinted along the rows of screws. Now and again he left it and calmly walked to the bridge end and gazed down at the waters of the river. He was watching the driftwood floating by, waiting for it to tell him when the water was slack.

On the bridge all was calm and quiet. The 976 passengers lined the rails to watch this manoeuvre in these tricky waters. Captain Sorrell now decided to bring his second plan into operation.

Steadily the captain began to give his orders; Quartermaster Irvine repeated them, and apart from the occasional ringing of the engine-room telegraph, there was no other sound on that bridge.

Another blast, and he began to lower his port anchor half-way as a precaution, and several hundred spectators had been moved away from the pier end. This time Captain Donald Sorrell was going to use the tide to his own advantage. His plan was to use the corner of the pier as a pivot, lay the liner prow on it, and 'bend' her round, using the current to ease the stern around.

He began this operation at ten minutes past ten – a little more than an hour since he had begun to dock the *Queen*. Ten minutes later he had got his prow by the end of the pier and a line ashore. Slowly the flood tide started to push her stern upriver, and within five minutes three heavy hawsers from the bow had been secured and the ship's own capstans were pulling them taut. Another five minutes and she was well into the slip. Five more minutes and she was well into the pier, a line from the stern had been secured, and she was warped alongside, with office staff securing the lines. Two minutes later a strong southerly wind sprang up, which, if it had been any earlier, would have prevented the ship docking at all.

By ten minutes past eleven she was tied up and the first gangplank was run out. White-gloved clerical workers from the Cunard offices handled the baggage, as the dockers were supporting the tugmen, and the passengers began to go ashore. Captain Sorrell calmly lit an American cigarette, sipped a weak whisky, put on his plastic rimmed glasses, and said, "I have a lot of paper work to do."

The following day, having made the headlines in the world's newspapers for this achievement, the New York City Board of Air Pollution accused the liner of puffing out too much black smoke, and warned her that if it happened again she would be fined between £9 and £36 ($25 to $100).

Contrary to the generally accepted belief, this was not the first time the liner had docked in New York without the aid of tugs. On October 18, 1938, Commodore R B Irving docked her without the aid of a single tug or a docking pilot. At 5.30 in the morning a large crowd had gathered to see the vessel edge into the dock, and most of the passengers had risen at dawn to see the manoeuvre.

A small motor-boat and a rowing-boat picked up the twelve-inch hawsers at the bow and the stern and passed them to a docking crew waiting on the pier. One hawser snapped shortly after being made fast and for about ten minutes the liner was held by a single hawser and seemed in danger of crashing into the neighbouring pier.

Commodore Irving said afterwards that he gave all the credit to two St Christopher medals attached to his watch chain.

"When I realized that I should have to bring her in alone I took the St Christopher out of my pocket and asked him, "Can we do it?" He said, "Of course." So, swinging him at the end of the chain with one hand and wiping the perspiration from my brow with the other, I did it. I would not like to do it often. Fortunately the tide was just right and there was no wind. It took exactly the same time to dock her as it did with twelve tugs last time we arrived in New York – thirty-four minutes."

In November 1954 Queen Elizabeth the Queen Mother was to return to England in the liner after her visit to America. The Cunard Company decided that the Commodore, Sir Ivan Thompson, should be in command in place of Captain Sorrell. More than a thousand members of the crew signed a protest against this decision, saying: "We consider that in view of the way Captain Sorrell has handled things in the past he should by right stay on board and command the liner on the return of the Queen Mother."

The crew, while in no way feeling any disrespect for the Commodore, said they felt it was an insult to their captain, "particularly as he is a sailor with such a wonderful record," and "is universally liked not only by the crew who come into contact with him daily, but also by the general public in this country and in the United States."

At one time the crew were talking of refusing to take the liner to sea unless Captain Sorrell was on the bridge. The company said that it was usual on such occasions for the senior captain of the fleet to take command. Captain Sorrell spoke to representatives of all departments of the crew and persuaded them to serve under Commodore Thompson.

During the voyage the Queen Mother insisted on visiting all parts of the liner and talking to the crew, always in high-heeled shoes. One gesture, so typical of the way in which she endears herself to people, concerned her visit to the ship's hospital to chat with the nursing sisters. The previous evening her lady-in-waiting had been talking to the physiotherapist, Miss Nancy Varley, and said, "I suppose you will be at the hospital tomorrow?" Miss Varley said this was absolutely impossible, as she had far too many cases for treatment.

The following morning the ship's doctor, Doctor J Maguire came to her treatment-room by the swimming pool, accompanying the Queen Mother.

"I heard you couldn't get along to the hospital, so I came along to see you," she said smilingly, and chatted about her work.

In January 1955 the liner took off two seriously injured Greek seamen from the 7,000-ton Panamanian ship *Liberator* in the teeth of a howling Atlantic gale. Here was a splendid example which showed that, behind the front hall of gold braid and hotel-like service, the crew of the liner, from the captain to the sailors, were absolutely brilliant seamen, capable of tremendous courage and heroism.

It was mid-afternoon when the liner's radio picked up this message from the ship, "Two of our crew have fallen into the hatch. They are mortally wounded. Please ask ship with doctor." The *Queen Mary* was 323 miles away, and although a French liner was nearer, it was decided to let the *Queen* handle the job.

Through the black, dark, stormy night she steamed at full speed, reaching the storm-tossed ship at 1.30 the following morning. The auction pool had been cancelled, and many passengers stayed up, lining the rails, to watch the rescue attempts.

Captain Sorrell, the master, switched on his searchlights to light up the vessel and manoeuvred the liner so as to act as a shield for the tiny lifeboat which was to take Mr Yates, the surgeon, across the waters.

Under Senior First Officer Leslie Goodier with a crew of volunteers, the lifeboat took half an hour to make the seemingly never-ending journey. Mr Yates and a sailor, timing their jump, managed to scramble up the ladder and disappear into the ship. The lifeboat returned to the liner without them, because of the danger of capsizing.

Immediately a fresh volunteer crew was called for, and under Chief Officer P A Read, reached the ship. The injured men were lowered into it, and the surgeon and the sailor came with them. After six attempts the lifeboat reached the liner, and the men were taken to the hospital. All the time the operation had been taking place Captain Sorrell had manoeuvred the massive bulk of the liner in the face of that near-hurricane, to act as a shield and provide some shelter for the lifeboats. On docking at Southampton the injured seamen were taken to a local hospital, where they both recovered.

The passengers made a collection for the boats' crews and collected a large sum of money. Later a number of silver and bronze medals and parchments were awarded to them by the Shipwreck and Humane Society. At the presentation Colonel J D Kewish, the chairman, said, "In my own experience and looking back through the Society records I cannot recall any act of collective courage, endurance, skill and resourceful seamanship which excelled that in which so many of you took part. Captain Sorrell had displayed magnificent seamanship in the fact that he was able to provide a lee and enable two lifeboats to make the journey."

Trouble had been brewing for some time, particularly in the catering department, over conditions of work and living in the ship and during the turn-round both in New York and Southampton. These grievances, some of which were genuine, were inflamed by a number of young stewards who had gone to sea to avoid being called up to do their National Service duty with the armed forces. They were completely lacking in the tradition and spirit of the older men who had helped to build up the Cunard spirit of service.

On June 1, 1955, two hundred men walked off a Cunard liner and two other vessels at Liverpool. It was considered, of course, that the *Queen Mary*, being so well known, could be a key ship in the dispute, which continued for some time, although completely unofficial, with the issues somewhat confused and complicated.

While the *Queen* was in New York Captain Sorrell spoke to a large number of the catering department, and he said when the liner docked in Southampton, "I was given an assurance that they had no intention of walking off the ship at any time. Representations were put forward which I undertook to bring to the notice of the company."

These concerned working hours and daily subsistence allowance received on shore. Extra pickets were sent to the liner, and the following morning one tenth of the crew walked off, having decided not to sail the ship to New York.

The following day, after a series of dockside meetings, another three hundred men walked off, including cooks and deck crew. Passengers who had embarked had to dine off cheese and ham rolls and coffee. The men complained of poor ventilation and overcrowding in living accommodation. The company undertook to send a ventilating engineer as assistant catering superintendent on the voyage if the men would sail. It appreciated the situation, but pointed out that the liner was getting old and that it was difficult to improve the accommodation. However, steps would be taken to do so wherever possible.

The liner became strike-bound. Most of her passengers were returned to London after a breakfast of sausage, bacon and potatoes. The deck and engine men left the ship, because they said that crews of other liners had been brought on board. The company then took immediate steps and obtained an injunction in the Court against the strike leaders and also, on application from Captain Sorrell, summonses were granted against forty-nine seamen, charging them with failure to obey a lawful command.

On June 26 the strike was called off. It was calculated to have cost the shipping companies £2,000,000 and affected 15,000 transatlantic passengers. The round voyages of six Cunard liners were cancelled. Two days later, Southampton magistrates' court granted a conditional discharge to the forty-nine crew members and ordered each to pay £3 costs.

Captain Sorrell said that early on sailing day he twice addressed the deck crew, and on the second occasion gave them a direct order to prepare for casting off. It was not obeyed by the forty-nine men.

Victor Durand, prosecuting, said of Captain Sorrell, "He is a man of complete integrity, much loved by his men, and a man gifted with a great deal of common sense, who handled the situation in a way one can only admire. It was a bitter blow to him when he found he had been let down."

It was said among seamen that Captain Sorrell was never the same again. For, all his life he had devoted himself to the interests of his crews, and on this occasion he felt bitterly let down by them.

At the annual overhaul the company did much to improve the accommodation, within the limitations that major structural alterations, needed to make their cabins equal to those of a modern ship, would be uneconomic. Some tourist-class accommodation was withdrawn and given to leading hands, and in the catering staff's accommodation new furniture was installed as well as more chairs and mirrors.

At the beginning of 1957 the liner went into dry dock twenty-four hours late because of bad weather on the return trip. She was then to become involved in a bitter dispute and to be the focal point of a storm which was to bring the port of Southampton to a standstill.

The liner had gone into dock for her annual overhaul, which normally took between six and seven weeks, but this year was to be a week longer because of the preparation needed for the installation of her stabilizers.

On Tuesday March 5, she was moved out of dry dock and berthed at 107 in the new docks with her bows facing down Southampton Water. At noon on the Saturday the shipbuilding workers went on strike. They claimed that at that time all the repairs and refitments specified when the liner had gone into dock had not been completed. The Cunard Company maintained that by noon the liner was ready for sea. She was due to sail on March 20 with 910 passengers and a further 190 to be embarked at Cherbourg. But the ship-repair workers claimed that she could not sail while the stoppage continued as she was not complete and was therefore "black."

Mr F Long, chairman of the No. 5 area committee of the Confederation of Shipbuilding and Engineering Unions, said that members of the Transport and General Workers' Union would not cast off the mooring-ropes at sailing time and that tugmen would not take her out.

A strong south-westerly wind held the liner firm to the quay-side when she should have sailed, and her departure was postponed. In the meantime the Cunard Company approached the Government and asked for assistance in getting the liner away. Mr Butler, the Home Secretary, who was in charge of the Government as the Prime Minister was in Bermuda, consulted Mr Macleod, Minister of Labour, and Mr Watkinson, Minister of Transport. As a result of these talks it was decided to send Admiralty tugs to help the liner.

It was understood from No. 10 Downing Street that the Ministers accepted the company's view that repairs for all practical purposes were completed before the strike began. The strike therefore was irrelevant to the sailing, and the Government decided to give such help as was necessary to facilitate the liner's departure.

She sailed at 1.35 in the morning with the aid of tugs sent round from the Admiralty dockyard at Portsmouth, after union officials had cruised around them in a launch in the darkness appealing to the crews not to assist the liner.

Later that day ten thousand men in the port were on strike because of this action. The Cunard Company issued a statement saying:

> Our case is that she was ready to go to sea when she sailed. If she had been compelled to put to sea last Saturday she would have had full power in the after engine-room and half power in the forward engine-room. Within forty-eight hours she would have developed full power. On Sunday an official of the Navigating and Engineering Officers' Union [to which officers and engineers of the liner belonged] visited the *Queen Mary* and assured himself that the ship's men were being employed only on making the vessel ready for sea and were not engaged on repairs. When she sailed the liner was on full engine power. At that time her essential documents of seaworthiness and her passenger certificate were in order.

On her return voyage from New York, Mr Tom Yates, secretary of the National Union of Seamen, appealed to the strikers to end their ban on the *Queen Mary*. For during her absence the strikers had stated that she would not be allowed to enter Southampton. He said he had received a radio message from members of the ship's crew from mid-Atlantic demanding urgent action by the union to bring pressure to bear on the brother-unions to cease involving the ship without cause in affairs in which they were not involved, causing unnecessary hardship.

But the liner had to remain at Cherbourg. She arrived there at two o'clock in the afternoon of April 1. In the last two days of the crossing passengers had been told of the events in England and took the changes philosophically, as did the older members of the crew. Younger members were not quite so happy. Arrangements were made with the Mayor of Cherbourg to have a dance in the port for the crew, and a football match was arranged.

The 22,000-ton Cunard liner *Ivernia*, which had been due to go into dry dock at Southampton for her overhaul, was utilized as a cross-Channel ferry-boat for passengers. Her crew were recalled from leave, and she sailed for Plymouth, the passengers going on to London by train.

The biggest task was to restock the liner with food and linen for her next crossing. A miniature airlift was organized, in which Silver City Bristol Freighters flew stores to the liner.

Three hundred barrels of beer were flown over for the Pig and Whistle crew bar. Seven plane-loads of laundry and ship's stores were flown across the Channel, including 80,000 items of linen, table-cloths, blankets, sheets and towels. It was estimated that Southampton lost more than £10,000 through the turn-round in the French port, including £6,500 to the dock authority and nearly £600 to Southampton Harbour Board in dues.

In 1958 the liner went on her 24-hour stabilizer trials in the English Channel. The sea was calm, but Captain George Morris made the liner "rock 'n' roll" by putting one of the four stabilizer fins in reverse. She rolled 18 degrees when steaming at 28.5 knots. The three other fins, projecting 12 ft from the sides of the ship, were brought into operation, and the liner was steady in 35 seconds. While most modern ships have one pair of fins, all three Queens were fitted with two sets of these Denny-Brown stabilizers.

It cost £500,000 to fit them, and the installation was a long task. The Company had thought for some time of fitting the liner with them, but all the experts said that her engine-rooms were so filled with equipment that there just wasn't any room to put the machinery. They examined the plans and blueprints in detail, they visited the engine-room, and shrugged their shoulders.

But the chairman, the late Colonel Denis Bates, said it had to be done if at all possible. He sent engineers and designers to the liner armed with tape-measures. On their hands and knees they measured this way and that way and said that it was still not possible.

It was then suggested that it might be possible if the hydraulic rams working the fins were operated vertically instead of horizontally as was usual. The makers and designers said this seemed feasible and should work. That is how they were installed. The work began some fourteen months before the actual task of installing them.

A tremendous amount of reorganization of plant had to be carried out to make room for the stabilizer equipment. Every time the liner was at Southampton a little bit was done, and occasionally during the actual voyages. Five miles of electric wire cables had to be fitted, as well as 12,000 ft of piping, The actual stabilizer equipment itself was shipped by sea from Leith in Scotland to Southampton.

The compartments in which the fins and the operating gear were housed were so small that all moving parts had to be lubricated mechanically. It was therefore unnecessary for personnel to enter the compartments while the gear was operating. An alarm bell would ring when the fins were returning inboard, and there were strict instructions that no one was to be in the compartments at that time, otherwise they would be crushed to death.

The fitting of the stabilizers was, or course, of tremendous sales value. Previously the liner had been a notorious "roller" in heavy seas, sometimes going over as much as 25 degrees. It was also aimed at saving crockery, as the previous year some 25,000 plates alone had been smashed.

During this overhaul extensive alterations and modernization were carried out in the kitchens, including the installation of electric grills. The company spent altogether around £750,000 – about one sixth the cost of her original construction. This was a tribute to her builders and to the firm of John Thorneycroft who maintained her at overhauls, that the company was prepared to spend so much money on a "new look". This would in fact give the liner another nine years of service, until she was sold to the city of Long Beach.

In 1957 Colonel Denis Bates, the then chairman, was able to say: "Though the War prevented the ships from fulfilling their commercial role until 1947, it is undeniable that the brilliant conception of the Queens repaired the company's finances from the shipping slump of the 1930s and mainly provided the profits, which allowed ordinary dividends to be resumed in 1943 and to reach 11 per cent in 1956."

From her maiden voyage up to mid-April 1960 she carried 935,425 peace-time passengers, and in all – including the trooping career – 1,746,755.

Mr T A Crowe, chairman of the North British Locomotive Co., President of the Institute of Marine Engineers, and a former John Brown's man, told Dundee students of the liner's engines.

"The teeth of the main gearing show no sign of wear, and only minor repairs have been necessary to other parts of the machinery. *The ship never missed either sailing or arriving on schedule owing to a machinery defect.* Conservatism shown in the original design of the *Queen Mary's* machinery has been justified because she has been in service nearly twenty years and has steamed 2,300,000 miles."

It is interesting to make a comparison between the first seven voyages and some of those towards the end of the *Queen Mary's* sea-going career. They indicate, more than any words could describe, how this fine ship maintained her ability to cross the Atlantic Ocean throughout all the years of her life. The last voyages were operating in the winter-time.

		Westbound				*Eastbound*		
Voyage No.	Distance	Time between Cherbourg and Ambrose Channel		Speed	Distance	Time between Ambrose Channel and Cherbourg		Speed
	Miles	Hrs	Mins	Knots	Miles	Hrs	Mins	Knots
1	3,158	108	24	29.13	3,198	111	15	28.74
2	3,158	112	13	28.14	3,198	111	18	28.73
3	3,096	109	05	28.38	3,129	110	15	28.38
4	3,098	104	37	29.61	3,128	105	00	29.79
5	3,087	110	25	27.96	3,129	108	58	28.71
6[1]	3,097	103	12	30.01	3,129	102	20	30.57
7	3,095	107	38	28.75	3,128	106	55	29.26
333	3,088	112	42	27.40	3,120	106	48	29.21
334	3,088	111	27	27.41	3,121	107	09	29.13
335[2]	3,071	117	03	26.24	3,120	108	51	28.66
336[3]	3,088	112	54	27.35	3,088	108	47	28.78
337	3,088	111	12	27.77	3,123	110	36	28.24

[1] First record voyage   [2] Heavy weather   [3] Reduced heavy weather

15

The Great "Floating Hotel"

When Captain Woodruff took the first Cunarder, *Britannia*, on her maiden voyage in July 1840 he was handed his instructions. These began:

> The *Britannia* is now put under your command for Boston. It is understood you have the direction of everything and person on board. We will class the duties on board under the *three* departments viz., The *sailing* being your individual duties in particular, and what regards your Mates and Sailors; the *engineers* and firemen and coal trimmers department. The *stewards* and servants department.

Fundamentally the master's brief has not altered to this day. When the captain of the *Queen Elizabeth 2* takes her out of the Ocean Terminal at Southampton his instructions are virtually the same. He has overall responsibility for the ship and "everything and person on board."

Life onboard the ships, on the other hand, has changed a great deal. With the advancement of the technological age and the communications revolution, society's needs and attitudes have changed. Gone are the need for the art of conversation and the delight in the simple pleasures in life; arrived are the glistening, gleaming ships' interiors, sporting a wealth of modern facilities which seem to grow more and more sophisticated as the weeks go by. Computer learning centres, golf simulators, casinos, self-serve launderettes, wide-screen cinemas, show rooms with automated lighting and digital sound, televisions in cabins (providing both closed-circuit movies and satellite news transmissions), the list is endless. Just as ships' facilities have changed, so too have the working patterns and needs of the officers and staff who occupy them. So has the task of "housekeeping at sea."

Like all shipmasters who command modern passenger liners, the Captain of the *Queen Mary* was primarily a seaman and a navigator, though his duties extended far beyond these two provinces. He would spend hours on the bridge on both sailing and docking days, and if the weather was bad or there was fog and ice about he would be confined to the bridge for long spells, resting in his day cabin, within call of the officer of the watch. Advances in technology have radically altered the life of the Captain – and his officers – on the bridges of today's ships. Primarily this is a direct result of the improvement in the standard and capability of modern navigation equipment. All those decades ago however, sheer hard work and basic calculations were the only way to assure the safe passage of the vessel. Even then, there was occasional uncertainty. Captain Peter Jackson, retired master of *Queen Elizabeth 2,* was a junior officer onboard the *Queen Mary*:

> In those days, when I was first at sea, we had no ... there was no such thing as satellite navigation. There weren't any satellites up for one thing! We did have something called the Decca Navigator and that depended on certain shore stations, but the reception was not too good and therefore it was treated with some suspicion by navigating officers. No, in those days, we all had sextants ... and we worked out star, sun and moon sights. That was the way our navigation was done but when you crossed the Atlantic, you frequently had to go across without sight of sun or anything because you'd have either pouring rain or thick fog.

The system which was used to overcome this difficulty was known as dead reckoning.

"You worked on the speed of the ship and the course that you thought you were steering. Usually you weren't far out and you could do the whole crossing on this dead reckoning situation. But there have been times when even that went wrong."

One such occasion was when the *Aquitania* travelled across the Atlantic, covered all the way by a big depression which obscured the sun, stars and the moon. On approaching Britain, the weather cleared and the officer of the watch was astonished to see land on both the port and starboard sides. He realized that his ship was speeding up the middle of Bantry Bay!

Satellite navigation has now made it possible to instantly pinpoint the position of a ship to an astonishing degree of accuracy, sometimes a mere few feet – and all with just a glance at a small screen. Put simply, the ship's satellite tracker detects the position of three satellites orbiting the globe many miles above. From these three readings, the satellite navigator can instantly calculate its own position; a little like working out the fourth angle of a four-sided pyramid. Despite this sophisticated equipment, navigators are always quick to point out that they are still, to this day, trained the "traditional" way – with a sextant!

In addition to his navigational duties, the captain had to watch over the business side of the ship in addition to entertaining passengers and acting as a genial host to all and sundry. He was expected to hold a cocktail party before lunch and dinner every day except sailing and arrival days, so long as weather and other circumstances permitted. Sometimes he would have younger passengers in for tea.

Without organization, and the proper delegation of duties and team work, it would be impossible for any single man to supervise the whole of the running of a ship the size of the *Queen Mary*, a ship which was, in essence, a small town.

In addition to all this there were, as there are today, difficult passengers. Some passengers have always insisted on complaining to the Captain and will not be placated until he has seen them (failing to realize that the subject of the complaint often has little to do with his direct jurisdiction). Others will make a determined effort to "button hole" the Captain if he takes a stroll along the deck, and try to get themselves invited to one of his parties. His was, and is still, a difficult task, calling for infinite diplomacy, tact and patience.

In the sailing days of the *Queen Mary*, the ship's telephone system was completely manual, requiring the presence of a telephone operator. This operator was frequently instructed to block calls to the captain. Many captains gave strict orders to the telephone operator that no one was to be connected to him without his instructions. As one captain said, "I would never be off the telephone otherwise."

Some masters of the *Queen Mary* were averse to their social activities and cut them to the barest minimum; the first master complained to many of this friends that he disliked the entertaining side. Captain Jackson remembers his apprehension about making a public appearance in the official Master's Welcome Reception:

"I would look at the queue of passengers that were coming along – I couldn't see the end of it! And I had to be there and try to say something of interest to each one, and then the Captain has to get up on the floor and make a speech of welcome to them. I used to dread that night and when it was over, it was like a great weight lifted off my shoulders, albeit it in a temporary measure!"

A great deal would depend on the relationship between the captain and his staff captain, his second in command. The difficulty here was that the staff captain's appointment would change constantly as he moved to relieve in another liner, or went to a cargo vessel as a captain himself. The staff captain of a ship is always responsible for the operational administration of the ship. He is in charge of security and discipline and deals with all problems pertaining to passengers and crew. He also has his share of entertaining to do.

The chief officer on the *Queen Mary* was responsible for the ship's stability and general maintenance as a first-class seagoing vessel. He would calculate the trim of the ship in relation to oil and water consumption, controlled hull maintenance during the passage and would prepare a list of hull repairs and renewals to deck gear during the stay in port.

The stability of the ship was of critical importance. It must be remembered that the *Queen Mary* would gobble over 1,000 tons of fuel oil per day, sucking the thick fuel up from her enormous double-bottom tanks. As the tanks emptied, the ship's keel would become lighter. Something therefore had to be done in order to maintain stability. To achieve this, the empty fuel tanks were filled with salt-water ballast, replacing the heavy bunker oil and thus maintaining an even keel. The ballast water would be pumped out prior to refuelling in port.

The principal assistant to the chief officer was the carpenter. This is a misleading term as it traditionally refers to someone dedicated to the task of working with wood, whether it be creating a new piece of furniture or repairing a broken table. The carpenter onboard a large ship was more than this, and, in addition to the more traditional duties described above, could find himself unbolting cargo doors and lowering the anchor! On the *Queen Mary*, he had four assistants. The chief officer was also assisted by the senior first officer (himself in charge deck crew), and whose right-hand man was the boatswain.

Popularly known as the navigator was the junior first officer, who was in charge of all charts and the navigational aids, and worked closely with the ship's radio officers, particularly where radar maintenance was concerned.

Even for the junior deck or bridge officers, qualifications for working on the Cunard liners were considerable. Captain Peter Jackson again:

"In the first instance, you had to have what we call a Master's Certificate in order to be in the passenger fleet. When I joined the Cunard Company I didn't have one , so I was waiting for my sea time in order to go to for a Master's Certificate and, when I did get it, in 1948, my first ship was the *Queen Mary*. Here was I, a fully qualified Master Mariner, and I was the Junior Third Officer."

Cargo and mail were always the responsibility of the senior second officer, while the junior second and three third officers were responsible to the chief officer for routine drills, such as emergency stations, bulkhead-door drills and fire drills. The junior second helped the chief officer with stability problems, while the three thirds were responsible for the efficiency of the continuously manned fire stations and fire-fighting equipment apart from the engine room.

Apart from these duties, all these officers (except for the captain and staff captain) had to keep the normal periods of "watches" on the bridge each day. These were timetabled in two watches of four hours each. They also had charge of individual lifeboat groups under the chief officer, who was responsible for the boats and life-saving equipment.

Some passengers would often express surprise when they learned that a crew boat drill took place every voyage. This happened every time the liner sailed from Southampton or New York and would usually takes place on sailing day before passenger embarkation. During this drill, every boat would be swung out to ensure that it was in working order; the entire ship's company would have to be at their assigned boat stations.

The officers' social room was the wardroom. According to the traditional political and social structure onboard a liner, there is usually a wardroom for the officers. It is usually managed as a private club and access is only granted to *bona fide* officers wearing the proper uniform. Rules of dress and conduct are strict. Furthermore, guests may only enter at the express invitation of the members. Around the walls of the wardroom on the *Queen Mary* hung many portraits of Queen Mary herself, with the inscription "Presented to the wardroom officers on the occasion of the Royal Visit, 25 May, 1936." There was once a delightfully informal picture of Queen Elizabeth II, waving as she drove through London at the time of the Coronation. There was another of her after her visit to the ship in 1955; and also one of Princess Alexandra. Sir Winston Churchill had a place of honour, and so did Field-Marshal Viscount Montgomery and the Admiral of the Fleet, Earl Mountbatten.

A photograph of the *Queen Mary* on her trials at speed occupied another place of honour, together with the battleship *Queen Mary*. Several past captains were "hung" in the room. Below the pictures of the late Sir Edgar Britten was the inscription "Presented to wardroom officers by the first Captain of the *Queen Mary*." Alongside this was the picture of a captain who did so much to earn her the title "happy ship," Donald Sorrell, signed "happy memories."

A memento of the maiden voyage stood in a corner and was only used on special occasions. It was a silver cocktail shaker presented by a "regular" American traveller, and bore the names of the first wardroom members, all master mariners and all members of the Royal Naval Reserve and most of them destined to command Cunard ships.

Nine radio officers attended to the elaborate wireless-room, controlling communication to every part of the world, and maintaining a permanent watch for emergency calls. It is now strange to contemplate the existence of such a large staff for this facility. Long gone are the telegraphs and radio signals so common in those earlier years. Nearly thirty years after this great liner retired from service, they have been replaced by ultra-fast satellite telephones and faxes. The manning of a large liner's radio office now usually consists of just two operators, working shifts or "watches."

One of the most important people on board was the purser. Over recent years the role of the chief purser has altered somewhat. In those days he combined the duties of the captain's business manager with paymaster, accountant, entertainment manager, passengers' friend and adviser, and editor of the liner's newspaper. In addition to a staff of assistant pursers of both sexes, he would control baggage masters, interpreters, printers and musicians, and was in close liaison with the bankers, hairdressers and shop assistants.

He worked closely with the chief stewards, who controlled all the catering side of the liner – chefs, cooks, waiters, stewards and stewardesses, butchers, storekeepers, barkeepers – and was responsible for all the food and stores. Nowadays, the chief purser's position is more defined and his duties are limited to matters regarding finance, berthing, embarkation and the legal administration of the ship (i.e. passenger manifests, immigration, customs, etc.).

The principal medical officer, in addition to being in charge of the hospital and consulting rooms, and watching overall the general health of first-class passengers and crew, also kept a watch on the quality of the water supply, cleanliness of kitchens and food and of catering staff. He was assisted by another doctor (who attended the tourist and cabin passengers), by nursing sisters, dispensers, sick-berth attendants and a physiotherapist.

It was in 1952 that the Cunard Company decided to see whether there was any demand for a full-time physiotherapist in the liner. After careful advertising and selection they appointed Miss Nancy Varley, a Yorkshire girl, on a trial period of three months. She came to the liner from a hospital in the north. So successful was the experiment that, apart from periods when she sailed in the cruising liner *Caronia*, she remained on the *Queen Mary* until she left the company on her marriage in 1960. Since that time, all the three *Queens* had a physiotherapist onboard.

The physiotherapist was also responsible for the crew, and many a crew member was able to remain at work because of the possibility of having treatment throughout the voyage following some accident or strain. This is a side of industrial medicine which many of the passengers did not realize existed.

Some of the liner's medical officers were very interested in the numerous problems of industrial medicine which occurred in relation to ship's crews. One of these was Dr J Maguire, who was responsible for the introduction of mass radiography for the crew. At first very suspicious of it, they soon realized its importance in protection against tuberculosis, which had been prevalent among seamen in the past, and against which Dr Maguire waged a long campaign by agitating for improvements in crew accommodation.

He was also responsible for the nursing staff wearing the staff-and-serpent emblem, the traditional emblem of Asclepius, the Greek god of medicine, on their epaulettes where before they wore a red cross, and were frequently presumed to be voluntary workers instead of trained nursing sisters.

The crew, apart from those whose duty brought them in direct contact with passengers in a social sense, lived in a world of their own, below decks, and were subject to strict regulations regarding conduct. Any social mixing with passengers was strictly forbidden. No members of the crew, including deck officers, assistant pursers (lady), engineers, officers or nurses, were allowed under any circumstances to attend cocktail parties in public rooms or passengers' cabins. "No fraternization" was the rule. Captain Jackson has very clear memories:

"The navigating staff had their own wardroom, but they were not permitted to mix with passengers in any way. We were not allowed into public rooms; the only people of officer status who were allowed into public rooms were the Purser's Staff. I must admit, in a way, we envied them! But they used to tell us it wasn't all that good because they weren't there for their own pleasure; they were there to act as dancing partners for female passengers."

No member of the crew was allowed to entertain female members of the ship's company in his cabin. This rule was, of course, frequently "broken". Shipboard liaisons of a romantic type were – and are – commonplace. To this day, a "blind eye" is turned to these matters. On a legal note, experienced crewmen would always advise a newcomer never to visit a female passenger's cabin. This could be interpreted as an intrusion. If, however, the passenger visited the crew member's cabin, this was of her own choice and, legally, there was less implication. Officially, no parties were allowed.

The biggest problem with crew life onboard a ship was – and still is – that every single little event, every nuance, every problem was exaggerated beyond its own importance owing to the close confines of the vessel. Matters which would scarcely raise an eyebrow in the "real" world, tend to grow out of all proportion amongst the crew of a ship. Circumstances become rather more difficult than living in a small suburban town, with all the problems inherent in any community of more than a thousand people living under rather strange, out-of-this-world conditions. All the problems of gossip, intrigue, rumour, jealousies, are as prevalent in a liner as in any factory or community, with the added difficulty that the people are thrown together in a relatively confined space for weeks or months at a time. Obviously no such community could live and work harmoniously without a strict sense of discipline, coupled with an understanding for the reasons for it.

Like any ship there were occasions when the rules were broken; when crew members were caught in a breach of the regulations. In some cases the severest penalties were taken against the offenders. In other cases only the common sense and understanding of the staff captain and the captain saved a situation which might have developed and have had repercussions not only throughout the liner, but through other ships.

There was, too, an added difficulty with the *Queen Mary*. No captain of the liner wanted a black mark against his name in his record, for in normal circumstances his next move was to become captain of the *Queen Elizabeth* and then commodore of the line. This often had an effect on his manner of maintaining discipline when on the *Queen Mary*. His attitude generally was to be much stricter than in other circumstances because on his every action depended a vital career move. He had very nearly reached the top of his profession, with all its importance, both professionally and socially.

The social life of the crew revolved around the RMS *Queen Mary* Social and Athletic Club. This organized dances in Southampton, cricket and football matches, darts competitions, coach trips to London, children's parties, concerts and tombola every night in the Pig and Whistle. The Pig and Whistle was the crew bar and recreation room. It had earned its dubious nickname as a result of the age old practice whereby an officer on the old navy ships would send a steward to fetch a pig – a barrel of rum – from down below and bring it to his (the officer's) cabin. The steward was always asked to whistle for the duration of this sortie so that the officer would have a good idea of his whereabouts. Hence the term evolved: go and fetch a pig, and whistle. Anne Logan, a children's nanny onboard the *Queen Mary* during the 1960s, remembers that female members of the crew ventured down to the "Pig" only on rare occasions:

"You never ever saw a female in the Pig. Never ever. No, no! We never went anywhere. But, we went carol singing on the *Queen Mary* that Christmas, in the Pig, that year [in 1963]."

There was also a crew library and cinema and sports competitions with other ships.

The president of the club was the staff captain. He attended committee meetings and maintained overall supervision of their activities by pointing out that this or that suggestion could or could not be carried out and giving the reasons; but it was the members themselves who really ran the club. Each department was represented. Most of their meetings were held late at night, because the members, particularly those on the catering side, did not finish work until late. But their enthusiasm was so great that they thought nothing of deliberating until the early hours of the morning. In the event of sickness in a crew member's family the club would make advances for him to fly home, say, from New York in order that he could be with his family.

On R deck, square, just outside the swimming pool and opposite the main entrance to the restaurant, were two glass cases filled with trophies which the ship had won or was holding temporarily. There was the British Merchant Navy Club, New York Football Cup, presented by the Cunard Line; Thos. Cook and Son's Football Trophy for departmental competition; the Atlantic Steamship Athletic Association Cricket League Challenge Cup presented by Sir Thomas Lipton; a trophy presented by a "very grateful passenger to a wonderful ship and her crew," and bearing the signature "Nancy Astor"; and a *Daily Telegraph* cup for darts.

Accommodation for the crew varied in standard depending on the rank and position held by that person. The officers benefitted from reasonable accommodation, if somewhat dated by today's standards. Cabins for the ratings, however, were not particularly impressive. Anne Logan describes her cabin as very basic: "we didn't have any air-conditioning – we had fans. We lived in two berths, up and down, and we had a basin. We never shut our door, never. We had a curtain and a fan."

Despite these austere conditions, the female quarters were superior, it seems, to the cabins which were occupied by her male colleagues: "the men lived in twelve, fourteen berths." None of these cabins had their own private facilities. Their occupants would share showers with anywhere between twelve and eighteen other crew members.

Curiously, pet nicknames evolved for these funny little crew ghettos. The male crew member's quarters were always known as "Glory Holes", whilst the ladies lived on what was affectionately known as "Fluff Alley".

On one occasion, two days before the *Queen Mary* was due to sail on a voyage a letter arrived on the desk of the catering superintendent. It was from an anxious American mother who was making the voyage. She was very worried about the feeding of her young baby and wanted reassuring that the type of food her baby was used to would be available in the liner.

In fact, so worried was she that she sent a list of the food she wanted for the child during the voyage: this included 18 cans of evaporated unsweetened Libby's milk, 6 cans of Heinz orange juice, Farley rusks (1–2 a day), Zwieback biscuits, Heinz pre-cooked baby cereal (enough for 6 portions), Heinz Junior Baby Foods and fresh food, chicken wings (boiled), beef pot, 1–2 boiled eggs (four minutes each day), 2 ripe comice pears, 2 bananas, 2 sweet red apples and cottage cheese.

After the points had been raised with the liner's chief stewards when she docked, it was felt that the company could reassure this anxious mother that out of their £100,000 worth of supplies in the liner she need have no fears that her baby would not be fed according to her wishes. They could supply everything she asked for.

This was not an unusual problem for the company's catering department to face. It was just a typical, everyday every-voyage problem for the hotel and catering department of this floating city.

On that same voyage a Rabbi came on board twelve hours before sailing and told the chief steward that he wanted all his food pre-cooked by the chef of a south-coast hotel and brought on board. It was pointed out to him that the liner always made special arrangements for kosher food in the ship. He replied that he did not know the cook who had prepared it and he really must insist that he had to know the cook personally. He was asked how long it had been since he stayed at the south-coast hotel and he replied it had been several months previously. Tactfully the chief stewards pointed out that maybe that particular chef was no longer there. The Rabbi then asked if he could have it brought in from a hotel in London. It was pointed out that there would not be time for that before the ship sailed. Eventually the Rabbi was persuaded that the kosher food in the ship was acceptable to Bet Dinn[†]. He made the voyage and was so contented that he travelled back in the liner.

Some passengers would ask for facilities to be provided for a man-servant to cook their meals for them. These were available in one of the small serving kitchens on the appropriate deck near to the cabins.

While dealing skilfully with these various individual problems the catering department had the enormous task of ensuring that the ship is sufficiently stored for each and any eventuality that might arise. During the post-war years of sudden strikes flaring up in the docks on either side of the Atlantic, the company adopted the safety-first policy of the liner having enough food and stores on board for at least one extra complete round voyage. This involved not only the ordering of everyday foods and the more exotic varieties, but also such items as salt-free salts for those on salt-free diets, or de-caffeinated coffee.

Originally bell-boys were used to open the doors of the main restaurant for passengers at mealtimes. Later, commis waiters performed this task. This was due to the enterprise of one particular bell-boy. With his blond hair beautifully brushed and an especially angelic smile, he would stand at the door, beaming at all who passed. Passengers would pause and say, "You look happy today, son," and he would say, "Yes, sir, it is my birthday," and would be given a tip. As he was having a "birthday" every voyage the chief steward felt that this was perhaps over-doing it a little and he was "relieved from his duties."

The matter of housekeeping for the passengers and crew on this massive liner was a fascinating study of method organization, accountancy, common sense and years of experience. The *Queen Mary's* accounts were operated for one complete round voyage. Just as any householder knows how much their family is likely to eat in a week, how much it costs, and how to keep within the budget, so, too, the catering department on the *Queen Mary* had to know that same information, but for a "family" of some three thousand people; and a mixed family at that, with many varying tastes, nationalities and ideas of eating.

The company stipulated a basic rate of money to be spent on first, cabin and tourist class, and the crew. Naturally throughout the years this was amended and modified and, just like any other home, in post-war years, it showed a steady increase as the cost of living increased.

Management kept a sharp eye on these figures and, if the liner was constantly above the rate or showed a sharp rise (or even fall), below the rate there were demands for an explanation. The answer is found in the analysis of victualling. This was a simple matter of housekeeping accounts. The stock remaining from the previous voyage was brought

---

[†] The Jewish community disciplinary court. Since the 19th century, Bet Dinn's powers have been limited to voluntary arbitration and vitualistic matters.

forward and costed; to this was added stores supplied at Southampton, Cherbourg and New York. The gross total less the stock remaining at the end of that voyage gave the cost of the amount of food consumed.

To combat rising prices and the need to adjust purchasing sources owing to a fluctuation in quality, it was possible to adjust the amounts obtained at each port or to alter the menu, always with the compelling underlying rule that the service to passengers was not allowed to deteriorate in any way, and that "quality comes before price."

As the department put it in one of their training lectures, "If you were a first class passenger and you had been served fresh English sole in the Savoy, London, fresh French sole in the George V in Paris, or fresh American sole at the Waldorf Astoria in New York, then you are entitled to have your favourite fresh fish in the *Queen Mary* and, of course, that is our aim, and there is no reason why it should not be served even better than at any of these three hotels."

Each morning at sea the chief steward had a conference with the chef, chief storekeeper and chief butcher at which they studied the stocks on board and their future requirements. The chef submitted his menus for all classes and the items on them were discussed with the storekeeper and butcher just to make doubly sure that they had the material on board in sufficient quantities.

One of the problems was what proportion of first, cabin and tourist-class passengers would choose certain dishes. This was clearly only known by experience, remembering the number of English, American, French and other nationality passengers, their likes and dislikes, the particular season of the year and weather conditions.

At lunchtime many passengers frequently advised the head waiter what special dishes they would like for dinner; these were known as private orders, and were typed and distributed to each kitchen section in the afternoon. This sometimes ran to as many as a hundred special menus varying from caviar, *escargots Bourcuignonne,* charcoal-burnt T-steak *garni* medium-rare, and chocolate sauce for eight people, to one dozen oysters and one small roast grouse for a single diner.

Then, too, there were passengers who wanted meals served in their cabin, or perhaps two four-minute-boiled eggs, brown bread and butter, fresh milk, and a compote of fruit for a younger passenger to be served in the cabin at 6.45 in the evening.

It was at the morning conference that the value of the long experience of the staff would stand them in good stead.

When the ship left port, a request for what was required for the forthcoming voyage was left behind at Southampton so that orders could be placed. The same thing happened at New York. As the company pointed out, "This is not a hard and fast list, for it might be necessary for the chief steward to submit a supplementary requisition on arrival.

A voyage longer than expected, for some reason or other, even to the extent of one more meal to passengers, can call for an adjustment to requirements. At the same time it is our policy to carry sufficient stocks to cover any element of delay, and, indeed, labour situations on both sides during recent years have dictated stocking even more than the normal surplus when such situations have been anticipated."

The majority of stores were bought in Britain, apart from certain fresh foods and typically American stores. Every week the catering department had price lists submitted from Southampton, London, New York, Cóbh, Cherbourg and Le Havre so that it knew the ruling prices.

At the same time the experimental kitchen in Liverpool issued reports on foods it had tested, new types of frozen food, and fresh varieties of other foods. There, these samples were prepared and cooked as if on board ship and a careful assessment made of them.

The catering department would check the chief steward's requisition carefully, bearing in mind the anticipated number of passengers, mainly to ensure that he was not over-ordering and that an undue quantity of perishables which would, of necessity, have to be used up in a single voyage were not being carried.

The requisition was then passed to the purchasing department, which actually placed the orders, bearing in mind quality and price, and dealing in most cases direct with the suppliers.

Some orders were for seemingly incredible amounts. At the peak of transatlantic travel, the Cunard order for meat, for consumption on all their ships in one year exceeded that of any other individual order in Britain. Rigid specifications for quality and weight were laid down; these were then referred to the actual producer.

The Cunard Company has always prided itself on setting a very high standard of service and comfort. For that very reason many travellers, including thousands of Americans, would always travel 'the *Queen Mary* way' in preference to any other. When it came to the procurement of hotel supplies and food, Cunard's attention to detail was incredible.

Faced with the difficulty of maintaining a consistent standard of buying, the company laid down its standards in raw materials, as well as in the finished products and in its service. With great care and precision the catering department drew up a list of everything it used and which specified weight, size, quality, and how it was to be delivered to the ship. For example, shoulder of pork "shall be commercial cut well trimmed (New York style), the skin shall be removed to within about four inches of the shank, the surplus fat trimmed off, and the fat remaining to be evenly tapered to meet the lean at the butt end."

To ensure that these requirements were maintained, every consignment of food delivered to the ship side in New York was inspected and had to be passed by US Department of Agriculture inspectors. If the suppliers failed to maintain these standards the goods were returned. In Britain, the check was carried out by company officials.

These stipulations were applied to every type of food that was loaded into the ship. Fish: for example, sea bass had to be 1.25 lb each; salmon 9 to 12 lb; scallops 8 lb to a gallon; live turtles 100 lb each, and so on.

Vegetables: asparagus had to have 18 to 22 stalks to a bunch ; carrots, all tops off, should be 1.5 to 3 inches; Spanish onions a 2-inch minimum; bananas 12 hands to a bunch, averaging 70 to 80 lb.

The reason behind these rigid rules, apart from maintaining standards, was that the company had found over the years of their experience that these were the best sizes for producing the least amount of waste.

On any given round-trip, the amount of food consumed on the *Queen Mary* was quite incredible. A table illustrating this is provided in Appendix Three of this book.

In 1935, while the liner was being fitted out, Mr T D'Oyly Carte, then chairman of the Savoy Hotel Company, London, wrote to Sir Percy Bates offering his help in finding waiters and expressing his views on the catering that should be provided in large liners.

> The super-restaurant idea is fallacious [he wrote]. There are no super-restaurants; only good, moderate or bad. Restaurants for millionaires are past and done-with. What is wanted is a really good restaurant with really well-cooked food, not necessarily enormous variety, as the trip is short, and really good service.
>
> To get this one must approach the subject from the restaurant point of view as the best restaurants approach it. The staff must be restaurant trained, the waiters, for instance, must not be of the 'steward type'; the cooks must have had restaurant experience and both must be of the type that would be employed at any first-class restaurant and kitchen in Europe, among whom by the way, will be found unfortunately only a very small proportion of suitable British subjects.
>
> The Advisory Committee on Catering Trades to the Ministry of Labour states that by sweeping the country they could only produce not more than perhaps one hundred English-trained waiters, and most of these are in good jobs and would not go to sea.
>
> The steward type are good, probably ideal for the cabin service, but not for the restaurant.

But despite these warnings from such an eminent authority, the company decided that it was possible to take Englishmen and train them to the very high standards that it demanded. This was always their policy. Great care was taken in the selection of men to be waiters, and they attendeds refresher courses during the winter lay-ups along with younger men who were earmarked for promotion.

After the War the two chefs of the *Queen Elizabeth* and the *Queen Mary*, John Pearce and Charles Russell, went to the Waldorf-Astoria and Plaza Hotels in New York for a period to study American methods of running hotels and to refresh their knowledge on the types of attendance which American luxury travellers appreciated. The previous year the two chefs had spent six weeks in several of the leading Paris hotels studying in the kitchens there.

At the one-week refresher courses a very comprehensive study was made of every aspect of the housekeeping side of running the liner and crew members were given an opportunity of learning something of other members' work. They studied victualling, stores requisitioning, and then learnt something of the care and protection of the crockery and glass; seamen's pay, overtime, and leave; crew engagements; menus, diets, carvings.

Visits were paid to the bonded warehouses to learn of the Customs regulations; tours made of all the liner's store-rooms; of kitchens, with talks by the chefs, the bakers, and confectioners on their work and problems; a lecture would be given by the restaurant manager on the duties of waiters, stressing the importance of anticipating passengers' wishes and of cleanliness and politeness. In fact, every section of the catering department's activities were covered.

The engine department of the *Queen Mary* had an incredible sixty-four engineer officers, twenty-two electrical officers and a sanitary officer. These were made up of a chief engineer, staff chief engineer, nine each of the following ranks: 2nds, 3rds, 4ths, 5ths, 6ths, 7ths, and eight 8ths; a first electrician, second electrician, and three each of the following electrical ranks: 3rds, 4ths, 5ths, 6ths, 7ths, 8ths, and two 9ths.

There were 169 engine department ratings, including plumbers, writers, storekeepers, refrigeration-plant attendants, greasers, fireman, trimmers; a total of 257 officers and men.

Robert Johnston, Chief Engineer, was with the ship during her actual construction at Clydebank and sailed in her on her maiden voyage. Several members of his family worked on her during the building. Years later, he commented on the role of the engine personnel: "It is really the senior second engineer who has the most exacting rank in any department on any ship. He compiles the watch lists and sets the watches. He is responsible to the chief engineer for the running and maintenance of the entire machinery installations, submits repair lists, and so on. He is the officer who makes decisions on the watch. There are occasions when any engineer may have to make his own quick decisions when up against a machinery defect, perhaps in the middle of the Atlantic, when even consulting a text book would be of no avail."

All the time the ship was in port some of the engineering officers would be on duty with maintenance work, inspections and supervising the work of contractors who were onboard to carry out repairs.

The day before sailing day, sixteen hours before departure time, heating and warming through the turbines began. This was a task which had to be done gradually and with great care, otherwise tremendous damage could be done. It involved such mysterious processes as running the main condenser sea-water circulating pumps; condensate distilled water pumps to be put into service; forced lubrication oil pumps to start and the main engine gland sealing steam to open up. During this warming up process the main engines were turned every half-hour by mechanical gear.

Two hours before the actual sailing time the main engines were tested and tried to the satisfaction of the chief engineer. This included the bridge and engine-room telegraphs, main engine thrust alarms, main engines to revolve ahead, and astern steering gear and whistles.

Fifteen minutes before scheduled sailing time all telegraphs were rung to stand by and all engine-room electrical and mechanical clocks were checked by the master clock on the bridge. All the time until the pilot was discharged, a double watch of engineers was on duty. Then "Full Ahead" was rung on the telegraph, and the bridge would ring the engine room to ask for 174 revolutions. But the engines would take three hours to work up to this speed. When approaching a port it would take three hours to reduce speed in preparation for taking the pilot on board. The engineer officers had a number of specialists among them; the oil-fuel engineers, for example, who were responsible for transferring oil fuel from the storage tanks to the settling tanks ready for use. Among their duties were the gauging, recording and calculating of fuel consumption, as well as preventing spills of oil fuel during loading, a task which could take up to twenty-four hours.

One of the most important duties was that of the water-treatment engineer, who was actually part-chemist, as the water from neither Southampton nor New York was suitable for the high pressure boilers of the *Queen Mary*. He would have samples of the water drawn off and tested, and where necessary add chemicals to ensure that it reached the high standard of purity demanded.

Supplementary to these tests taken chemically, the main condensers were fitted with electric salinometers, which were very sensitive to contamination. A sea-water leak from the main condensers could cause havoc. Each of the four condensers had 13,700 tubes through which sea water was circulated to condense the exhaust-turbine steam. If any one tube developed a pin-hole, contamination of the exhaust steam would take place.

In all the thousand in one variety of stores carried in the liner each voyage, none was more important than the humble sawdust. For, to stop a leak temporarily until the ship arrived in a port, sawdust was injected with the sea water, and, as there was a vacuum of twenty-nine inches on the steam side of the tubes, the vacuum would pull in a small particle of sawdust to seal the tiny hole. In port the tube defect would be properly rectified.

In spite of the most conscientious maintenance of machinery installation, steam or boiler water losses amounting to about two hundred tons every twenty-four hours would occur. Four large evaporators would work continuously for replenishing the losses, making double-distilled perfect water from the sea.

In each of the five boiler rooms, there was an engineer officer, and his prime responsibility was to keep the level of the water in each of the six boilers correct. Although feeding the boilers was automatic, to assist the engineer officer a fireman was detailed to watch the water, his eyes glued to the water gauges. It was this officer's duty too to ensure that everything was working satisfactorily, and that fuel was burned and not wasted.

Just as a domestic chimney became dirty, so the twenty-seven chimneys or uptakes of the *Queen Mary* boilers would get dirty also; they would have to be cleaned in port, some in New York, some in Southampton. But every night at sea, to minimize the deposit of soot, the smoke tubes of the uptakes which led to the funnels were steam-blown. This was a noisy operation, carried out by the ship's firemen and supervised by the engineer of each boiler room. All smoke that is emitted to the atmosphere passed through stationary vanes in each of the funnels. It was swirled by these vanes, which extracted 8% of the heavy particles, particles which would otherwise pollute the air, and these were washed back to the sea.

In the two generator rooms, the engineer officers had an equally busy time on watch. Besides having seven turbo generators to look after, there were a multitude of pumps in operation, such as ballast, hydraulic and domestic to mention only a few; morning and evening the first class swimming pool had to be filled and emptied. Always, in all sections of the department, there were gauges to watch, control panels, indicators, revolution counters, engine thrust and lubricating-oil alarms, and always everything had to be recorded.

One of the important "unseen" tasks was, of course, that of keeping the ship on an even keel. There was a gauge called a clinometer – this pendulum gauge showed the angle of list of the ship. The engine-room second engineer had to keep a close watch on this, regulating the list by filling, transferring or emptying special tanks. When it is remembered that five hundred tons of washing water alone were used every twenty-four hours, plus a thousand tons of fuel oil, and that there might be a wind of gale force, it is clear that to keep the *Queen Mary* on an even keel called for close attention and much work.

While passengers sedately sat in steamer chairs or worked in the gymnasium or slept after late-night dancing in the Verandah Grill a quiet, unobtrusive man would wander around the ship with a watering can in his hand. He was Eric Littaur, gardener-at-sea. In more than one hundred locations in the liner he tended some twelve thousand plants, placed at eye-catching points. Hydrangeas, begonias, fuchsias, lilies and bulbs of every description, with coleus and ferns and palms, formed boxes and banks of colour on stairways, deck squares, and along corridors, as well as in public rooms.

Twice a day he would water them and watch over them with an expert eye. His task was more difficult than that of any land-bound gardener, for the ship on her 4½-day voyage encountered a wide range of climate.

High up on the sun deck this sailor-with-secateurs had his store – many glass-fronted refrigerators filled with a profusion of fresh-cut flowers, including many exotic or tropical blooms.

Besides the plants, he cared for all the fresh flowers brought onboard at Southampton and New York and all flowers sent to passengers. It was nothing unusual for him to get a telephone call in mid-Atlantic from someone in Denver or San Francisco asking for a bouquet to be made up for a passenger. This was perhaps one of the aspects of his work which he enjoyed the most.

In his seagoing career he cared for flowers for the Queen Mother ("She loves them"), Sir Winston Churchill ("He never takes the slightest notice of them, though Lady Churchill does") the Duke and Duchess of Windsor ("She brings her own vases"), Lord Beaverbrook ("always insists on having them in his state-room when he comes on board, then rings the bell and says, 'Get those damned things out of here'").

Many times he spoke to passengers who had world-famous gardens and who would ask his advice and often send him cuttings for himself. On leave? He spent all his time in his own garden – on shore.

The majority of passengers leaving the liner at Southampton probably never spared a thought as to what happened on board once they turned their back on her. As their Ocean Liner express rushed them through the English countryside towards London it never occurred to them that some forty-eight hours later the ship would once again be heading down Southampton Water.

The speed with which the liner was turned round in New York was even quicker, a little over twenty-four hours. At one time the stay in the two ports was more or less the same, but it was changed after the crew had asked for a longer period in Southampton, saying they preferred to work harder in New York and have more time ashore in Southampton. It must be remembered that in the days when the *Queen Mary* was in service, docking fees, tugboats and other services cost a great deal less than in the harsh financial battlefield of the 1990s. Although ship's crews then considered twenty-four hours to be a fast turnaround, this would be regarded as sheer luxury by today's standards. The *Queen Elizabeth 2* "turns around" in a little over 8 hours in New York - and Southampton!

The turn-round procedure was based on long years of experience and was virtually organized on the lines of a carefully planned military operation. Whatever the time of night or day that the *Queen Mary* arrived, stevedores were there waiting to descend into the holds as soon as she tied up, to begin unloading the heavy "not-wanted-on-the-voyage" baggage, the sacks of mail, and the American cars that tourists brought over. The baggage was swung ashore in slings on to the quayside and carried upstairs to the baggage inspection room of the Ocean Terminal on conveyor belts.

At first light in the morning, if it was a late-night arrival, the laundry vans would begin to drive up to the ship's side, unloading hampers of clean linen, sheets, pillow cases, towels, table-cloths, and so on, which had been laundered while the ship was away. As soon as the passengers began to leave their cabins, either to have a final meal or to watch the approaching coastline, stewards would move in and strip the beds and collect the last of the soiled towels. This linen was all packed up ready to be landed and laundered, and at the same time the catering staff would do the same with their linen.

Meanwhile the task of re-storing the ship was well under way. The chief steward had left behind on the ship's previous departure, a requisition for this coming voyage so that the purchasing department could begin to place the necessary orders. A quick conference was held in the chief steward's cabin on arrival so that any last-minute alterations could be made to this in the light of later developments. In an few hours the food and wine would arrive at the ship's side ready to be loaded into the store rooms. Once the passengers had left, an army of cleaners moved in with brushes, brooms, mops and vacuum cleaners to smarten up the whole ship, while window cleaners were busy at their task, electricians checked the electric light-bulbs and painters touched up here and there.

In those days, every member of the crew from the master downward would have one voyage off on leave after five voyages. Now the leave party returned and those going on leave departed. Again, times have changed. On modern ships a different leave pattern operates for most of the ship's company. Crew, staff and officers are usually retained onboard for a period of four or five months continuously, proceeding on vacation then for anywhere between four and six weeks.

Fuel oil, the very life-blood of the ship, was pumped into the ship's storage tanks from oil tenders, which came alongside on the water side of the ship. So cleanly and quietly was this done that many passengers did not even know that this work had already begun.

Small groups of men in dirty raincoats with notebooks and pencils in their hands, bowler hats on their heads, would wander about, noting work that had to be done, either within the next day or at some future date. Here and there a panel was removed and some one would fiddle about with a complicated tangle of wires; here and there one would hear the noise of a drill.

Despite all this activity, the liner was but a ghost of her real self during a "turnaround". Once the passengers had left, it was as if her soul had been taken away. It was as if her very heart had stopped beating the moment the main engines stopped. This was not unique to the *Queen Mary*. A ship's atmosphere does not originate from her carpets, walls or furniture; nor from her engine, electric lights or the propellers, nor from the galley or the pianos or the cinema.... The life of a ship emanates from her most precious cargo – passengers and crew; people.

The *Queen Mary* lay alongside the quay, to all outward appearances a giant liner, floodlit, with lights on in port-holes and along the decks. But she was an empty house. Inside, there was an unnatural stillness. She seemed no longer a ship at all, with the creaking of wood and a hundred mysterious sounds and noises as she rode the waves, a living breathing creature.

This turn-round operation was nothing compared to the annual overhaul, when the whole ship, from masthead to hull bottom, was given a spring clean that would be the envy of every household. Everything was cleaned, painted, checked and inspected, from main engines to loose covers; from chairs to lifeboats; from radar to hairdressing equipment; from cutlery to cabins. Twice a year, the liner was withdrawn from service for an overhaul. In the summer, this was for ten days for a quick dry docking and inspection and survey and refurbishing.

It was during the winter six-week overhaul that the real spring clean took place. This engaged some 2,000 men of 30 trades in a carefully planned task.

As soon as the liner had docked and the passengers had departed all the linen was stripped, 120,000 pieces of it, plus 8,000 blankets, and landed for laundering and checking. The lifeboats were prepared for survey and overhaul. The public rooms and staterooms were stripped of their carpets and furnishings, and all of this was placed in a central store onboard, 3,500 pieces of furniture being later landed and examined and repaired by 250 men in a workshop.

In the central store 13,000 curtains, bedspreads and loose covers, and 2,400 stateroom carpets and 60 public room carpets were sorted and checked before being cleaned and renovated.

The liner then moved into drydock, and even as the water was being pumped out the men were busy in small punts scrubbing off slime and marine grass from her underwater hull.

As soon as the main engines had cooled and freshwater connections had been made for the sprinkler and fire-protection systems and the drydock was dry, surveyors and ship-repair men would begin to inspect the hull from the dock floor to see that all was well.

Then a maze of scaffolding was erected from the dock floor, from which each of the 32-ton propellers and the 140-ton rudder were examined.

She looked for all the world like some fantastic monster, some Gulliver enmeshed by the Lilliputians, as these small humans crawled and swarmed and swing about the body that was her hull.

The 16-ton anchors were lowered to the dock bottom, and every link of the 350 tons of chain cable was examined, scaled and painted. Seven tons of anti-fouling and anti-corrosive paint were applied by 120 painters, working on the staging, and more than one ton of paint was applied to the superstructure, funnels and masts. All the navigational equipment, gyrocompasses, echo-sounders and radar installations were checked by skilled men, as well as the radio equipment.

When all the interior had been stripped, painters and polishers moved in; parquet floors were examined and repaired; veneers were re-polished; metal work refurbished; mirrors re-silvered; thousands of tiles in the swimming pool were checked, as well as the deck coverings throughout the ship. Not an inch was missed; not an item overlooked.

All the catering equipment – ovens, mixers, machines of every sort and kind – was checked and tested; stock taking was carried out for the 54,000 pieces of china and earthenware and 40,000 pieces of plate. Cutlery was cleaned and silverware was polished.

All the main and auxiliary machinery was surveyed and over-hauled, from the 257,000 blades of the main turbines to the main gearing and shafting, condensers, manoeuvring valves, to the tiniest, smallest connection and through all the maze of boiler tubes. The electrical installation throughout the ship was tested, from the main dynamos to the smallest electric light bulb in an indicator, as well as miles of wiring and thousands of points. So it went on, 600 telephones, 5,700 locks, 35 passenger and goods lifts, painting, polishing, cleaning, scrubbing, refitting, repairing, remaking, checking.

Then gradually the jigsaw puzzle of the pieces was put together again; the ship moved to her berth and awaited those passengers who would once again bring her to life, and soon she would take her place, refitted and refreshed and in every sense restored, on the North Atlantic.

16

"Anything to Declare?"

The process of customs clearance and the role of Customs officers worldwide has not changed greatly in recent decades. Ships are inspected and passengers and crew subject to random checks on both sides of the Atlantic. The Customs officer's lot is not always a happy one. Regarded with deep suspicion and often disliked by passengers and crew members, his job is to protect and serve the Crown. Few seem to realize that it is actually in their own best interests and of their country, that the Customs officers exist in the first place.

When the *Queen Mary* docked at the Ocean Terminal in Southampton, passengers would go ashore and have their baggage cleared in the baggage hall by the staff of H.M. Customs. At the same time, Customs officers – who would go onboard while she was coming up Southampton Water – would be taking duty from the crew and sealing all the bonded stores, shops and showcases in the liner.

But that was not the end of the work of the Customs officers. All the time that the liner was in port, at any time of the night or the day, a rummage squad could suddenly appear in the ship. They were authorized to search anywhere: engine-room; officers' accommodation; the public rooms; behind pictures or panels for smuggled goods; wherever their experience dictated or acting on "inside information."

The *Queen Mary*, partly because of the number of crew and passengers she carried and partly because of her quick voyage, became a big channel for smugglers just after the end of World War II. At that time, Britain was still undergoing a difficult time of rationing and of continuing shortages. America, on the other hand, was practically free from these restrictions. Particularly plentiful there were toilet requisites, tinned meat and fruit, silk and nylon stockings, and various other commodities considered to be luxuries in Britain, but fairly commonplace on the western side of the Atlantic. Strangely enough, these items also included birdseed.

Birdseed retailed at about 20c per lb in America; it was from 16s to £1 in Britain; there was an import control in force and a 10% duty on the retail price. The Revenue authority allowed 5lb a time to be brought in by individuals as a concession. Small fortunes were made by some crewmen, who brought in the seed in large quantities packed in food parcels, in their used laundry, in their spare shoes, and even loose in their pockets.

It was when almost every other member of an entire crew began declaring an extraordinarily large amount for one budgerigar or even half a dozen hens that the Waterguard branch of the Customs began to keep open a "weather eye".

Prosecutions followed, but soon the ever-resourceful smugglers found other articles in short supply, such as lipsticks, cosmetics, and finally artificial-silk stockings – the nylon 'racket' went on for years. It may at first seem like a very unlikely item with which to generate so much illegal income, but stockings were indeed a luxury item, much sought after in Britain in those lean post-war years.

Nylons were subject to import licensing restriction, but the crew were allowed to bring in six pairs of nylons each trip without an import licence. However, every time the *Queen Mary* came into Southampton, in addition to the legitimate seven to eight thousand which the crew of more than twelve hundred (including more than a hundred women) could be expected to declare, from two to three thousand were seized.

The smuggling stories are numerous.

A favourite hiding place for them was in the strong cartons made by food exporters, the corrugated cardboard divisions of which were replaced by nylons. Sometimes the original contents were removed and the cartons crammed with stockings, with a piece of tin or lead to made up the usual weight. Alert Waterguard officers soon got to know whether a carton's weight was genuine or not, and a fine and confiscation followed on the occasions when their suspicions were proved correct. Oil drums were used for the same purpose, being thrown overboard and recovered by confidants ashore operating from a launch in the guise of dockers.

It was about this time that the Waterguard began stationing officers on the crew gangway day and night and also having quay patrols, for the smugglers were throwing packets of stockings overboard in watertight containers during darkness, then diving overboard and swimming with them to an adjacent quay or choosing a time when the tide would take them to a waiting accomplice ashore.

The rummage crews changed their tactics every trip. Sometimes they would do a mass attack on the ship, sometimes seal off one portion, such as the engine-room, asking everyone to remain there while a search was made, or concentrate on the officers' quarters, for there was one occasion when a large quantity of dutiable goods was found in the day cabin of a man who was relieving master of the *Queen Mary*. They had been hidden there by a steward, who thought that no Customs officer would dare to search the captain's quarters!

Two young United States students came ashore one trip on a sunny but cold afternoon, eiderdowns draped round their shoulders. Naturally, their appearance aroused suspicion. When questioned, they said they were "feeling the cold" after coming from New York. This in itself would have been a reasonable answer. The giveaway was that they were wearing only thin trousers and open necked shirts, while their baggage, which had been examined, contained warm clothing. A penknife was used delicately to undo a few stitches at the corner of one eiderdown and something pink and silky revealed itself. In each eiderdown in six compartments, and instead of normal stuffing were found one thousand pairs of artificial-silk stockings. They had been placed there by a gang operating from America.

Firemen, greasers, and assistant stewards, pantrymen and assistant cooks, seemed to be the main carriers of the big racketeers.

The *Queen Mary*'s vast engine-room was actually searched on four successive arrivals at Southampton for a large quantity of stockings which was thought to be hidden there. But nothing was ever found, although Customs were convinced that quantities were taken off every trip.

One night the ship was being searched as she came up Southampton Water and a preventive officer found a large quantity of stockings carefully concealed in one of the bunks in the firemen's quarters. While questioning the four occupants he heard a rustle of paper behind him. He swung round. The large opened parcel of nylons had disappeared. The preventative officer noticed the open port-hole, but all four strenuously denied getting rid of them. Little did they know that at that very moment a Customs cruiser had been following the liner, and her crew had seen stockings fluttering down from one of the *Queen Mary*'s port-holes along the liner's working alleyway.

Some of the ship's boiler-room firemen were observed by the Waterguard Customs officers to be enjoying particularly lavish lifestyles. They would be seen wearing particularly expensive Savile Row suits and occasionally staying at the most expensive hotels in town during shore leave. Some would also be seen mixing with businessmen who were obviously strangers to the district. It later turned out that these "businessmen" were, in fact, stooges of the big-time operators.

One day a metal object was washed ashore in Chichester Harbour in Sussex. Recovered, it was found to be a liner's ventilator measuring nine inches by six inches, eight feet long, and sealed at both ends. At first it was thought to be a bomb or a mine, but the Waterguard opened it and found tightly packed inside 250 pairs of nylons, which told the authorities that dutiable goods were being dropped overboard from ships passing through Spithead outbound and inward.

Then, off Calshot at the entrance to Southampton Water, just after the *Queen Mary* had passed in, a piece of wood mounted with a tiny red light was spotted floating in the water. This was fished out, and to the wood was attached a strong piece of cord at the other end of which was a waterproof container so weighted as to make it float just below the surface. Inside were three thousand pairs of stockings.

There were a handful of crew who went to sea only for the purpose of smuggling. Such a man was a civil engineer down on his luck who managed to get to sea and looked after one of the waiters' sleeping quarters and mess rooms. He always had plenty of money.

On one trip he was questioned; he declared a great deal of dutiable goods and paid duty, but the preventive officers were not satisfied, and decided to have a thorough search of his quarters, and while doing so saw that he was repacking his bags after emptying them out for inspection. They noticed that he was putting light-weight jars of face cream and other toilet preparations on which he had paid duty at the bottom of the bag and heavy goods, like tinned foods, on top. Once more he was made to unpack, and the officers began to examining the jars of face cream.

As they probed the contents of the jars the steward asked them to stop; he did not want them spoiled on account of the fact that they were presents. They were indeed; inside the jars under the top layer of face cream the officers found eight hundred valuable gold necklaces, a quantity of gold watches, and gold jewellery all neatly packed in grease-proof paper. Some of the smaller items were hidden in lipstick holders. He was fined £1,000 and lost his job. How long he had been doing this is not known; all that was established was that he worked for a gang, but he would not reveal who were the employers on whose behalf he decided to go to sea.

These are just a few of the many cases concerning the *Queen Mary*, investigated by the Waterguard Division of H.M. Customs during that hectic six-year period 1947–52; and it must be remembered that there were many more which were not publicized or which received the attention of Customs Special Investigation Branch.

There was the waiter who declared cigars and nylons and a medium-sized Teddy Bear for his youngster, but the toy was unusually heavy. In the head, arms and legs were stuffed 120 pairs of nylons. That toy cost the waiter £150 in fines, with an alternative of four months' imprisonment.

Another waiter, from Bournemouth, declared eight tins of boned turkey in a small carton; this time the weight was too light for officialdom, and the tins were opened. They were stuffed with 88 pairs of nylons and 320 cigarettes. Small pieces of lead had been put in each tin to ensure correct weight, but they had not been sufficient. Confronted, the waiter admitted that he had bought a tin-canning machine for £3 10s, which he kept in New York, and did his own canning. It cost him £150.

Ballpoint pens were not fashionable and certainly not particularly cheap in those days, and so the smuggling of fountain pens became part of the 'racket' until one seaman was heavily fined for having more than one hundred of them strapped round his arms and thighs. They must have bothered him, for it was his awkward gait and difficult movement of his arms when opening his bag for inspection that aroused suspicion.

Another shortage in post-war Britain was soap powder. A young man in the *Queen Mary*'s catering department was seen to have an abnormal amount of soap powder during one disembarkation, and again it was the weight which was the giveaway. The packets were heavier than usual. The first one opened revealed pairs of nylons carefully hidden beneath the powder; the other packets had been similarly packed and then neatly stuck down again.

Another strange place of concealment for stockings was devised by a *Queen Mary* crew member who managed to fold a dozen pairs round each leg under his socks, while he increased his chest measurement by wearing several under his shirt.

One of the worst cases, and believed to be part of the operations of one of the "gangs" which operated with members on board, but directed by what could be termed "master minds" in New York and in London, was that of an assistant cook, who had hidden cartons containing 2,399 pairs of nylons underneath vegetables in one of the *Queen Mary*'s refrigerators. He had also hidden more loose pairs in a potato-peeler, and another 720 pairs in cartons under meat in the butcher's shop refrigerator. That man was fined £300 and sent to prison for two months with an option of a further three months in default. The money was paid in a few days.

The older hands among the crew were resentful once during the peak of the smuggling period, when the *Queen Mary* was having an extra quick turn-round. An assistant cook, long suspected as a smuggler, caught red-handed, insisted that a man named "Willie" in the crew had asked him as a favour to mind a large carton of "food" in a refrigerator. Needless to say, the carton contained nylons. The Customs officers, with the cooperation of the master, had the whole crew mustered and the suspect was taken round and asked to identify "Willie." This he failed to do, and eventually admitted his guilt, but many of the crew, as a result of the muster, lost a great deal of valuable shore leave.

Once, when the *Queen Mary* was lying in Cowes Roads waiting to come up with the tide, the rummage crew had reason to make a search of unusual hiding places in the neighbourhood of the bridge. In the radar housing they found 242 pairs of artificial-silk stockings, 100 cigarettes, and half a pound of tobacco. The stockings were in a parcel tied round with soft white string. No one claimed the parcel, but searching the radio officer's quarters, they found a similar piece of string in one of the operator's cabins. Questioned, he pointed out that the string was quite common in New York. Then the officers found a piece of paper showing figures apparently indicating stocking sizes. Further questioned, the operator admitted that he was just trying to make a few pounds for himself and realized his foolishness. It was all the more unfortunate for him in that he was on the point of retirement and had an unblemished record of forty years at sea. The fine he had to pay ate into his retirement fund.

There were several small gangs mixed up in the nylons "racket," and one was perhaps the most successful until carelessness or possibly "wind-up" caused one of the members to make a slip. Seven men were involved – a *Queen Mary* steward, a well-known travel agent's interpreter, a baggage man on duty in Southampton docks, a taxi-driver, a tailor in New York, a Southampton railwayman, and a Marylebone shopkeeper.

The hunt began in 1949 when a trunk was found abandoned in an embarkation shed at Southampton alongside which the *Queens* berthed. It was found after all the passengers had been "cleared" and contained seven thousand pairs of nylon stockings. Inquiries were made by the Customs officer but they got nowhere; then another trunk, addressed to "John Miller, London," was abandoned, but diligent inquiries in London and in New York elicited the fact that he was dead. It did lead the officers eventually to an address in the West End, to a Southampton hotel, and to a member of the gang.

Eventually the case was built up. It was found that the nylon-filled trunks were put upon the liner in New York by an agent working for the New York member of the gang; the steward altered labels and gave fictitious names; the travel man somehow acquired pieces of Customs chalk and marked the trunks himself as having been passed by Customs and when necessary switched labels again; the taxi driver and railwayman removed the trunks by road or train as directed by the "brains" in London; and the latter disposed of the contents. This went on for many months until the second abandoned trunk was found and, with the contents of the first trunk, provided the King's Warehouse with 16,649 pairs of stockings, of a duty value of £3,500.

Two of the gang turned King's evidence and prison sentences followed. That was the end of large-scale organized smuggling.

Throughout this period it was taking Customs officers in the baggage hall so long to question many gift-laden travellers, assess the duty, and collect it, that boat trains were liable to delay, passengers by road were being held up, and generally the work of the port of Southampton was in danger of being disrupted. It was decided, therefore, to send two preventive officers to New York in the *Queen Mary* and the *Queen Elizabeth*; every trip their task eastbound was to interview passengers and to collect duty. Each passenger was given a receipt to notify baggage officers ashore that they had been examined by Customs and paid duty, but they were still subject to further examination. The work was speeded up enormously by this means, and between £6,000 and £10,000 in duty was collected each voyage.

This went on for two or three years until only one Customs officer made the trip, but the individual officers were not too happy about this arrangement, because each officer was glad of a second opinion when assessing duty and there were times when there was a difference of opinion between officer and passenger. Eventually the service was withdrawn, but it had served its purpose.

Many people wondered what happened to all these goods seized and confiscated from duty-evading *Queen Mary* crew and passengers. They would be taken to the Queen's Warehouse and in due course sorted out, valued, and then taken to a central depot, where annually an auction sale was held. To this came reputable dealers, who bid for the goods and then disposed of them to retail shops with whom they dealt regularly. Who knows but that more than one person who had attempted to evade the law, had his or her goods seized, and paid the penalty, actually bought from a shop in due course the very goods which brought them the humiliation of a fine or even a term of imprisonment?

But it was not only eastbound that smuggling occurred. The United States had to be equally as vigilant as the United Kingdom. Lucy and Syd Lerner made a crossing from Southampton to New York in 1967 towards the end of the *Queen Mary*'s working life. On that journey, they brought their new Mercedes car over the Atlantic with them. They recall clearly those first familiar words of the customs officer: "Please step aside." They continue:

"They took the rugs out, and it took them about two hours [to inspect the vehicle] while we were standing there. We had guests waiting for us on our arrival. Anyway, at the end of the two hours, the officer came over and said 'Put everything back the way it was.' He apologized for the delay. I said: 'What the Sam Hill were you looking for.' He said 'Drugs.' I says: 'Do we look like we're drug pushers?' He says: 'No you don't, but there are some drug dealers that will attach a package to your car and then they'll pick it up wherever you are.' He then said: 'Don't feel badly because we just did this last week to the Duke of Windsor.' That was the cute part of the story."

One aspect of the *Queen Mary*'s operations, and indeed of other liners operating on the North Atlantic, was the presence on board of immigration officers. Their job was to exclude the undesirable from the particular country they served. This service to the travelling public was not confined to Great Britain; Germany and the Netherlands would also put IOs on board in certain circumstances.

Before the 1939–45 War it had been the practice for some years to send immigration officers to Cherbourg, Le Havre and Cobh to meet British

Atlantic liners and examine their credentials during the remainder of the passage to the terminal ports, Southampton, Liverpool, and occasionally London. Following the return of the *Queen Mary* and *Queen Elizabeth* to commercial service after the War, an immigration officer crossed to New York every trip and examined passengers on the eastbound voyage.

The service was given at the request of the Cunard Line who were responsible for the officer's fare and his maintenance. The Treasury, probably somewhat reluctantly, authorised a modest allowance to the individual officer for what might be called "reciprocal hospitality." Furthermore, Cunard approached the Home Office and asked that an immigration officer should travel regularly between New York and Southampton on the homeward voyage to "clear" those of the passengers disembarking at the home terminal port. This was approved and worked very satisfactorily since, with the system being maintained well into the career of *Queen Elizabeth 2*.

From across the Atlantic in the old days came, among the tourists and business visitors, the share pushers and the card-sharpers, and it was the vigilance of the IOs which in large measure frustrated their designs.

The bulk of the alien passengers dealt with by IOs during the later years of the *Queen Mary*'s illustrious career were well-to-do American tourists, diplomats, politicians, professional men and women, while the British passengers were usually businessmen or Service personnel. But there were others, such as stowaways, people genuinely left behind on board in New York seeing friends off, and unemployed folk of the entertainment world seeking work over here. Then there were the tragic cases, like travellers coming to England to seek relatives in the old homeland or in transit to Baltic countries for the same purpose, and all without sufficient means of subsistence while they made their search.

With aliens travelling in the *Queen Mary* it was not always be possible for the IO to keep strictly "to the book". He would have to use his own judgement, treat each case on its merits. He would have to sum up (as he must still do on the *QE2*) as quickly as possible on the strength of a brief scrutiny of the passenger and his documents and a few well-chosen questions whether he should immediately admit him or subject him to a more detailed examination.

Many ruses would be adopted by doubtful aliens to make themselves appear respectable and admissible; if they were coming to take a job as likely as not they would pose as tourists; if they had committed crimes abroad they would not disclose the fact; if mentally unbalanced it would not necessarily be obvious in a brief interview. But if the officer had suspicions or thought that the passenger was not medically fit he would ask the individual to go and see him when the *Queen Mary* eased up in Cowes Roads and the Port Medical Officer came aboard. If the latter confirmed the IO's suspicions, the passenger would be refused permission to land.

A friend of the original authors, who made many trips in the *Queen Mary* as travelling IO, had several unbalanced people to deal with – more than a few with a 'royalty' complex, seeking an interview with the Queen on some personal problem. He had passengers who gave "Buckingham Palace" as their address when presenting the landing card.

Then there were the men who said that they had appointments with famous statesmen and that this was the reason for their voyage. Needless to say, Sir Winston Churchill was a favourite victim.

This particular officer remembered two rather tragic cases in the *Queen Mary*, although the *Queen Elizabeth* and indeed, more recently, the *Queen Elizabeth 2* have both had their share too. There was the distinguished-looking, dignified, yet sad-looking gentleman of Romanian birth who presented an affidavit which bore visas of various countries but which made it clear that he was only allowed to stay in those countries a very short time. He was granted permission to enter Britain for one week; that is all the IO would allow him in view of the other endorsements. When the Romanian saw the IO's stamp on his document he thanked him courteously, but said ruefully, "It is a sad world; you see, not so very long ago I was Prime Minister."

Then a certain colleague of the IO, who was a West Countryman and was a much-travelled officer of the Royal and Merchant Navies before he entered the Immigration Branch, had the shock of his life when a stateless person appeared before him, travelling to England on an affidavit sworn before an attorney in the United States, but speaking with a strong Cornish accent and revealing his birthplace as Redruth. This man had emigrated when the tin mines closed down in Cornwall in 1922, become a naturalized American, but on the outbreak of World War II had returned to his homeland and enlisted in the British Army. Returning to the United States in 1945, he found he had lost his American citizenship because of protracted absence and had not reacquired British nationality. In the man's own words he was therefore a "stateless Cornishman."

Stowaways were always a big problem, such as the enterprising Dutchman who boarded the *Queen Mary* at Cherbourg from a tender, made straight for the liner's hospital, and confronted an astonished nursing sister as the liner came across the channel and had the effrontery to ask, "What about my medicine?" The only visit he had had was a visit from the IO, detention under the care of a master-at-arms while the liner was in port, and trans-shipment back to Cherbourg next voyage.

When leave to land was refused, the carrying company which brought the alien was responsible for removing him or her, under directions given in writing by the immigration officer concerned. The liner's master was responsible for seeing that this was done and that the refused passenger did not escape while the ship was in port. This particular responsibility in the *Queen Mary* was always delegated to the chief master-at-arms.

The travelling IO's job in the *Queen Mary* was not only unique, it was a tremendous responsibility. When he left New York, he was three-thousand miles from a supervising officer to whom he could refer. He needed all his tact, sympathy, firmness, knowledge of the world, of human foibles and frailty, to do his job to the satisfaction of his superiors and the travelling public. That they were so tactful was well-evidenced from the remark made by one particular "prisoner" during the 1950s who was quoted as saying: "You know, I've been refused entry to many countries in the world, but never so pleasantly as on board the *Queen Mary* this time."

The turn-round in New York was short, which sometimes was merciful when in summer the humidity is extremely high and shade-temperature is in the eighties or nineties. It was not easy to rally "customers" on the first day out and before they had settled down.

Then there was the weather: it is not easy to sit at a table hour after hour and examine passengers when there is a howling gale and the ship is rolling or pitching. And those who travelled in her before stabilizers were fitted will remember just how badly the beloved *Queen Mary* could roll. On more than one occasion, the IO's stamps, the passengers' passports, and indeed several of the passengers went over too.

Some first-class passengers would occasionally fail to make the interview before the ship docked, either through seasickness or just lack of thought. Less frequently there were the near-alcoholics, like the gentleman on the *Queen Mary* who was the only first-class passenger not seen by the immigration officer when there was only a limited number of passengers and the weather was miserable. At last, contact was made with him by telephone and he agreed to meet the IO. He failed, however, to turn up, and telephone calls to his cabin were unanswered. Eventually the IO went to his cabin to find the occupant standing in the middle of the room, somewhat worse for wear, with his trousers wound round his ankles. "Been trying to get to see you for days," he hiccuped, when his visitor revealed his identity, "but I've been trying to get my trousers up all the time."

In New York, the immigration officer was always allowed to live onboard; when he went ashore he would be issued with a temporary crew card describing him as Assistant Purser. He could do what he liked ashore as long as he was back onboard by sailing time. The dreadful possibility of missing the ship always loomed over him – with 2,000 uncleared passengers onboard, the majority arriving at Southampton, and him left behind at the mercy of the Consul General.

If the *Queen Mary* (or indeed her sister *Queen Elizabeth*) was ever held up in port by strikes or by bad weather, a new problem would present itself to the immigration officers, for many Americans would naturally want to return to their country by other means. Permits to land would have to be prepared for them, and this usually resulted in minor administrative complications and a strain on the department's resources.

Possibly no other immigration officer found himself in a more difficult position in the *Queen Mary* than officer Roche, later to become HM Immigration Inspector at London's Heathrow Airport. He sailed in her one year, on New Year's Day in a gale. Somehow, with extra tugs, Captain Grattidge and his pilot, Captain Jack Holt, got her out and into Southampton Water and through the Solent to the Nab Tower, passing on her way two coasters hove-to because they could make no headway on their passage to Cowes.

The *Queen Mary* hit the full force of the gale as she rounded the Nab Tower; lifelines were rigged along the promenade deck and down the companionways, and she pushed on and duly anchored inside Cherbourg breakwater. By this time the wind had reached eighty miles an hour and showed no signs of abating, and the process of embarking passengers, baggage and mails by tender was a protracted business. To add to everything, the *Queen Mary's* anchor fouled a submarine cable left by the Germans and she ran aground and so remained all night.

The following morning tugs pulled her off, the great ship swung free, and she headed out for the open sea. One of the two Customs officers making the trip turned to Roche and said, "We'll probably return to Southampton for survey. It'll be fun for you with all those Cherbourg to New York passengers onboard, won't it?" He was right; she was heading back to Southampton and Roche had six hundred aliens onboard who had no intention of visiting the UK but were being taken there forcibly, many without the necessary papers, most of them with all their holiday money spent, and many with individual personal problems which would be his care.

Roche realized he could not interrogate all six hundred in, say, six hours' crossing and that extra IOs would have to come down by tender to meet the liner and, with the Captain's permission, he was able to telephone for assistance. Then, working closely with the purser, he had a message broadcast asking all passengers who wanted to go ashore at Southampton to notify him and he prepared a list for his colleagues whom he hoped would come down to help him. Only one was sent down, and the two officers had their work cut out.

In the first place, Mr Malik and the Russian deputation to the United Nations were onboard, also a deportee whom the Home Office thought they had seen the last of, and a charming, penniless Irish-American, who had been refused permission to land from the previous voyage after he had been banned from every bar onboard for obtaining credit with no money to pay.

For four days, while the *Queen Mary* was patched up with one hundred tons of concrete, Roche sat in the liner's long gallery stamping temporary shore passes, refusing leave to land to a few unsatisfactory passengers, and slipping home for half an hour each evening to see his family in a Southampton suburb; his wife's greetings became chillier at each visit, until she echoed the words of a famous statesman, "For God's sake go."

At last the *Queen Mary* left, and, with no Cherbourg call to make, kept well in to the English coast and went almost flat-out for New York. A bitter, cold winter voyage it was, with hardly a soul venturing on deck unless duty called, and not made easier by continued signals from the company's newest ship, the *Caronia*, which was taking the Azores in her stride and enjoying temperatures of 90 degrees in the middle of January.

The *Queen Mary* reached New York a day ahead of the *Caronia* and, when the latter ship arrived, her crew and officers made many offers to the ship's company of the *Queen Mary* to come aboard and enjoy the hospitality of the youngest member of the fleet. But it was not very tactful of the member of the purser's staff who greeted Roche as he came onboard from the *Mary*, "Oh look – look what the cat's brought in; another fellow from the ten-day ship," for it was exactly ten days from the time of her original departure from Southampton to her arrival in New York.

The forgoing gives a brief idea of the duties and the problems, of a travelling immigration officer working during the busy transatlantic career of the *Queen Mary*. Some of their work was naturally classified and could not be recorded. When necessary, the IO would work closely with the immigration department in New York and at Cherbourg; from time to time he would be able to give them a "tip-off" on a suspect. On rare occasions a US immigration officer would make the trip across just to see the UK officers at work, but eventually the American authorities decided that there was no advantage in making this a regular procedure and, indeed, preferred the interrogation when approaching, at, and after arrival in New York.

Needless to say, the *Queen Mary*'s immigration officer would work closely with the purser and his staff, and when he got ashore in Southampton would also work closely with the Waterguard Division of Customs and even more so with Scotland Yard's Special Branch, which had officers at all passenger ports. The officers would constantly be on the look-out for undesirable aliens and criminals attempting to escape the country.

There was an IO who made several trips in the *Queen Mary* and developed a great affection for her. On the 21st anniversary of her launching, when making the Atlantic crossing, he threw a party for the officers in his cabin, crowded as many as possible into his bathroom, and then, even to the extent of cracking a bottle of champagne, "launched" into the bath a miniature *Queen Mary*.

17
Turnaround – A New Home

The *Queen Mary* continued to sail across the Atlantic. She was, however, ageing, and by the mid 1960s was thirty years old. Ships do not live forever. They grow old and have to be replaced. And so it was with the *Queen Mary*.

Since the late 1950s, the rapidly developing air travel industry had been taking its toll on Cunard's transatlantic schedule; in one year, 1958, a hard fact hit the management head-on: the number of passengers crossing the Atlantic by air equalled those taking the journey by ship. In short, a large percentage of Cunard's passengers were now flying instead of sailing. This situation was to intensify over successive years. Cunard's hitherto bustling trade was slipping into a worrying decline. The company realized that dramatic steps would have to be taken in order to preserve their flagging business.

For some time, Cunard had been working enthusiastically on the concept and design of a replacement for the *Queen Mary*, a massive 75,000 ton vessel known on the drawing boards as *Q3*. After years of debate, set against the backdrop of a dwindling Atlantic trade, the company was forced to concede that the project was dead before it even lifted off the ground. Colonel Bates had died in September 1959, and was immediately replaced by Sir John Brocklebank, an expert in cargo shipping. When asked what would have happened if *Q3* had ever been built, Sir John was to write just one word: "disaster".

With the realization that any replacement ship would need to cruise as well as "cross", *Q3* was abandoned. In time, Cunard would conceive of a slightly smaller vessel, designed to accommodate passage through the Panama and Suez Canals, a vessel which was fully equipped to cope with all possible forms of passenger sea travel. This vessel would become the *Queen Elizabeth 2*.

Hand in hand with the decision to abandon *Q3* came some sweeping moves designed to increase the working efficiency and profitability of

Cunard. From 1963, the traditional summer drydock refits for the *Queen Mary* were combined and rescheduled to a winter lay up. With fewer passengers making trips during the colder weather, it made sense to use this period of the year for technical and refurbishment work, whilst re-instating another summer voyage. The result was increased revenue during the summer and a reduction in the cost of drydocking.

Cunard was not, however, content merely with a superficial revamp of the annual itinerary in order to reverse its financial decline. In 1964 the company announced the appointment of a new chairman who would replace Sir John Brocklebank. Ironically, Sir Basil Smallpeice's previous appointment was on the board of BOAC, one of the very companies whose jet aircraft had contributed to the gradual decline of the shipping industry. The new chairman's brief was simple: Cunard must survive and profit, regardless of how many drastic measures must be taken. Sir Basil wasted no time in commencing a radical examination and restructuring of the company.

To assist in the evaluation of the struggling company, he called upon the services of a team of management consultants to advise on organizational improvements. He also secured the Economist Intelligence Unit (EIU), to conduct a concise study of the seagoing travel sector. Their reports unanimously concluded that, without drastic re-organization, Cunard would shortly be in deep trouble.

This reorganization was to comprise significant changes in three main areas: administration, marketing and tonnage.

Firstly, the management of the ships was moved from Liverpool to Southampton. Cunard's administration was then divided into five main sections under the leadership of Managing Director Philip Bates, the son of the late Colonel Bates. Commercial, hotel, technical, accounting and personnel; the creation of these five divisions was a wise exercise in streamlining for a company whose infrastructure had, over the years, become increasingly cluttered in the wake of complacency; complacency borne of the golden era of Cunard's Atlantic travel when it seemed as though nothing could halt the progress of the world's oldest and most famous shipping line.

The consultants' reports also suggested a wide-scale re-evaluation of the current trends in the travel industry. No longer could Cunard ride on a wave of nostalgia, depending solely on the regular ferry routes between the Old World and the New. The need for sea travel was disappearing rapidly and if Cunard was to survive it would have to adjust its operation for a public who wanted to travel for pleasure as well as those who still entertained the concept of transatlantic transporters.

The idea of sending the two giant *Queens* on cruises to the sun was seen as a possible salvation for the great ships though, in reality, it turned out to be anything but. This type of voyage would decorate her annual transatlantic schedule until the end of her career, in an attempt to sustain a year-round working programme.

The first such cruise undertaken by the ageing *Queen Mary* was the Christmas Cruise of 1963, voyage 425, Southampton to Las Palmas.

Anne Logan, now a stewardess on the *Queen Elizabeth 2,* was a children's nanny on that very first cruise. She recalls, "It was a *News of the World* cruise. The newspaper ran a competition and the prize was the Christmas Cruise on the *Queen Mary*. We had thousands of children. It was murder!"

She went on to recall other aspects of life onboard. "We used to muster on Boat Deck for boat drill. It wasn't like it is now. There'd be two lines of stewardesses and the leading stewardess would be stood there with him [the Staff Captain]. They'd walk up and down and he'd ask you about the drill, the signals, this...that...whatever he felt like. And she'd stand there with a stern face, because the leading stewardess was the bee's knees. She ruled the roost."

There was, however, some fun to be had at Christmas:

"We went carol singing that Christmas in the Pig [and Whistle, the Crew Bar] – that was my first Christmas at sea. Whilst we were down there, on that Christmas Cruise, Cliff Richard came down and filmed some of *Summer Holiday* with Susan Hampshire."

On February 12, 1966 she sailed on a one-month cruise from New York, voyage 477, which included stops in Las Palmas, Tangier, Piraeus (Athens), Naples, Cannes, Palma, Gibraltar, Lisbon and Madeira, before returning to New York on March 23. Cunard issued a special illustrated brochure for the occasion and were particularly lyrical in their advertising copy:

> For twenty-six glorious days, the splendid panorama of the Mediterranean's hardy, friendly people and colourful cities will pass before your eyes. Enjoy the simple beauty of flower-filled Las Palmas...breathtaking Tangier, intriguing cross-roads of European and African life....Athens, where you can relive the glories of the Golden Age...Naples, gateway to the Eternal City of Rome....Cannes on the French Riviera, gay favourite of the international set...Palma, on the Magical Isle of Majorca...the stalwart symbol of strength, Gibraltar...Lisbon, a delicate, beautiful lady in lace...and finally, the picturesque port of Funchal on Madeira.

By today's standards, prices were miraculous! Fares ranged from a mere $960 for a berth in a shared inside "B" Deck cabin without bath, to $8,700 for a suite for two people on Main Deck. Shore excursions, under the auspices of the American Express company, were extra.

Other cruises were short hops, reminiscent of the party-type voyage which ran out of the United States during the depression of the 1930s, and which provided an escape into liquor-licensed bliss for Americans inflicted with the restrictions of the prohibition. These "booze cruises" were probably the only deliverance from bankruptcy for the ship owners. In the 1960s Cunard sought to soak up some of the British pleasure trade by offering similar mini-cruises out of Southampton. The itinerary was simple:

Voyage 479

Wed April 6	*Depart :*	Southampton	(pm)
Sat April 9	*Arrive:*	Las Palmas	(pm)
Sun April 10	*Depart:*	Las Palmas	(pm)
Wed April 13	*Arrive :*	Southampton	(am)

Three decades later, this seems hardly the kind of itinerary to make the mouth water. In the Britain of the 1960s, however, where cruising was still the exotic travelling playground of the rich, this route was perceived as something rather special. A near-affordable way to leave home shores, lie in the sun, enjoy being pampered on one of the most glamorous – and famous – liners in the world and, above all, to have done something that one's friends and neighbours hadn't.

On the Western side of the Atlantic, the more cruise-wise American market was far from forgotten:

Voyage 476

Fri Feb 18	*Depart :*	New York	(pm)
Sun Feb 20	*Arrive:*	Nassau	(pm)
Mon Feb 21	*Depart:*	Nassau	(pm)
Wed Feb 23	*Arrive:*	New York	(am)

It must be remembered, however, that neither of the old *Queens* were designed for hot weather voyages; neither had been equipped with adequate air-conditioning and conditions inside a ship sailing in hot climates could become intolerable without proper ventilation. This had already been experienced during the old ship's trooping days during the war. The *Queen Mary*'s cruising programme, like that of her younger sister, also suffered because she was not able to transit either the Suez or the Panama Canals. This limited her cruising activities to the Atlantic and the Mediterranean. Cunard attempted several superficial changes in the ship's structure, in the hope of attracting a new clientele; these included transforming the Cabin-Class Main Lounge into the Flamenco Room, a location which was entirely at odds with its surroundings. With its walls flaunting a superficial disguise of white trellis, mock Spanish brickwork and bullfighting posters, this room, which had once been the place for elegant late-night conversation over port, cigars and needlepoint, was immediately devoid of any real natural purpose and ambience. It simply did not work. Worse still, much of the room's original artwork was obscured in this effort to adjust the saloon for the cruising passenger.

In 1964, the Cabin-Class Lounge was converted into a room for teenage passengers and entitled the Beachcomber Club. The Observation Bar (traditionally first-class only) broadened its invitation to include guests from tourist class. These physical modifications were all part of an attempt to elaborate on the cruise concept and attract a completely new clientele to the ship. It is always sad to witness changes which compromise the very character of a beautiful ship. All too often, ship owners are driven by a fear of revenue loss, to rebuild, demolish, alter and re-conceive areas of their vessels which are fundamental to the very life of the ship. True, the *Queen Mary* was at great risk and steps had to be taken to preserve her trade; Cunard was – and is – after all, a business which had to survive in an increasingly competitive market. Did this justify, however, ruining large areas of a ship which itself constitutes a significant part of British history?

Another type of change had already taken hold back in the 1950s when various policies were updated upon the realization that many passengers were defecting to the air. For example, in 1959 the company decided to permit tourist-class passengers to use the First-Class swimming pool. This allowance was made almost apologetically, with the proviso that the tourist-class passengers could only use the pool for a particular two-hour period daily. This would enable the pool to be washed and cleaned before being occupied by the first-class passengers.

As it turned out, all these changes would be in vain.

Air travel continued to rob the ocean-going market of its passengers, and the transatlantic trade moved even further into decline. By 1966 approximately 4,000,000 passengers were crossing the Atlantic by air compared with a mere 650,000 by sea. The 1966 NUS (National Union of Seamen) strike caused big problems for Cunard. The Union was demanding an impossible increase in wages – no less than 17%. The Ship-owner's Shipping Federation considered the demand to be outrageous and, together with the British Prime Minister Harold Wilson, appealed to them not to strike. The NUS were determined however. The industrial action continued and the *Queen Mary* and *Queen Elizabeth* were crippled; strikebound. The strike was like a cancerous sore weeping all of life's fluid from the great ships. At this point in time, they both needed more than this sorry and negative jolt out of existence. Yet the strike continued, hammering a giant nail into the coffins of both the *Mary* and the *Elizabeth*.

Cunard lost millions in a matter of weeks.

The writing was on the wall and the end of an era was upon the maritime world. On May 8, 1967, Captain William Laws, master of the *Queen Mary,* opened a sealed envelope. The contents was a message from the Chairman of Cunard which spelt the end that so many had hoped could have been avoided, but which was now inevitable:

It is a matter of great regret to the Company and to me personally, as it will be to friends throughout the world, that these two fine ships, the *Queen Mary* and the *Queen Elizabeth*, must shortly come to the end of their working lives. They hold a unique position in the history of the sea, and in the affections of seafaring peoples everywhere. But we cannot allow our affections or our sense of history to divert us from our aim of making Cunard a thriving company and no other decision will make commercial sense.

Neither of the two great old Cunarders was paying their way; it was estimated that the *Queen Mary* was losing around $2,000,000 a year. She would be withdrawn from service in October that year. Though the decision to end her seagoing career had been made, the question remained as to the exact nature of her fate. Cunard made no secret of the fact that her scrap value was around $2,000,000, though a considerably higher price would have to be paid by any prospective owner with intentions to operate her as a business venture. Cunard were naturally not prepared to sell her to another shipping line, as this would have resulted in her being operated in direct competition with her original owners!

Hundreds of suggestions were received, some feasible, others utterly fantastic. Several cities and organizations made approaches to Cunard and a wide range of ideas was submitted for the *Queen Mary's* future. Liverpool wanted to use her as a giant floating youth hostel in the River Mersey; a British Labour Member of Parliament hoped to have her modified so that she could house homeless families, Japan wanted to buy her and use her as a floating maritime museum; a group of industrialists from Atlanta, Georgia, wanted to use her as a floating trade centre. Sir Basil Smallpeice himself hinted that the ship could find her way to Gibraltar as a concrete-berthed hotel. Strangest of all, one man from Little Rock, Arkansas, wanted to weld the *Queen Mary* and the *Queen Elizabeth* together to make the world's largest catamaran!

In the end, there were just three serious contenders: New York, Philadelphia and Long Beach, California. Long Beach had been interested in taking charge of the vessel as early as 1966 when the Long Beach Harbour Commission wrote an initial letter of enquiry. On July 24, 1967 seven delegates from the City of Long Beach flew to London and made a bid of $3,450,000 for the ship. But how could a small "city" such as Long Beach (which had a population of around 350,000 in 1967) compete with international giants like New York and Philadelphia? The answer: oil.

Crawling out from the city, under the ocean floor, lay a vast reservoir of oil, with thousands of pumps continually drawing up thousands of barrels of "black gold." On each barrel, the oil companies paid a royalty that was split between the State of California and the City of Long Beach. This latter share alone ran to several millions of dollars each year. There was a complication, however. According to State Law, the City of Long Beach could not spend this revenue on anything except harbour and waterfront improvement. If Long Beach was to purchase the *Queen Mary*, the State Lands Commission would have to be convinced that the acquisition of this ship would indeed be seen as a "waterfront improvement".

Some years earlier, Long Beach had begun negotiations with the California Museum Foundation to construct an $8,000,000 maritime museum in Long Beach. In fact $6,000,000 had already been put on reserve for such a project. It would seem logical to combine the two projects and construct the maritime museum onboard the *Queen Mary*. The museum foundation and the city would be able to save millions on the cost of construction – after all, the "building" would already be in existence – and what better setting for such a venture than inside the world's most famous floating creation! Sir Basil Smallpeice gave Long Beach ten days in which to obtain approval from the State Lands Commission and to finalize its offer – his generosity was partly due to the fact that the conversion of the *Queen Mary* into a museum would ensure the preservation of the ship's character.

The project received strong support from Janet McCoy, Director of the Office of Tourism and Visitor's Services for California, and J Howard Edgerton, President of the California Museum of Science and Technology. Even State Governor Ronald Reagan endorsed the plan. The State Lands Commission gave its approval and four Long Beach officials flew to London to meet with Sir Basil and close the deal. On August 18, 1967 the contract was signed and, with a signature, a new career was decided for one of the most famous floating vessels ever.

On September 16 the *Queen Mary* sailed on her last westbound crossing to New York and a few days later she set off from that port on her 1001st and last transatlantic voyage, travelling eastwards and carrying 1,200 passengers. Her departure was an emotional one, as was the crossing itself, and many Americans who had known the ship both in peace and in war made sure that they were onboard for this momentous trip. The atmosphere was one of partying and riotous revelry; where strict class distinction and separation had for so many years prevailed, all three were now intermingling for parties, receptions and all-night dancing. The crowds turned out to greet her when she arrived, firstly in Cherbourg and later in her home port of Southampton on September 27. In fact, many people had participated in a special package deal that brought them from England, across the channel to Paris and then back to Cherbourg to join the ship for the final Channel crossing. During that last short trip, the souvenir hunters were all busy, and hundreds of small items were taken: ashtrays, teaspoons, knives, side plates. Upon arrival in Southampton, the passengers were forced to assist with discharging their own baggage as the crane drivers had decided to go on unofficial strike. The crowd sang *Auld Lang Syne* and a stowaway was exposed, a New Yorker Thomas Barry, who eventually paid his fare. When questioned he said, "I thought she should not make her last trip without a stowaway."

One passenger who crossed the Atlantic in that dramatic period of uncertainty and change during the twilight of the *Mary's* career was Doreen Hughes. She was a young mother who travelled westbound with her husband and two young children. They were emigrating to the United States. She has clear recollections about the atmosphere onboard.

"I remember it was very close to the end and everyone was extremely depressed. Most of the staff were very depressed about the fact that she was coming out of the water."

She goes on to describe something very unusual:

"It sounds strange to say it now, but I had a particular tube with my daughter's cawl [inside it]. She'd been born with a cawl covering her head. This is rather strange and apparently if you are, you never drown. But the bottle broke and I had a thought that the ship would never be destroyed. I remember thinking at the time "this boat will never be broken up. She will float somewhere else."

The *Queen Mary's* last official voyage for the Cunard Line was a cruise to Las Palmas, Canary Islands, which took place during the first two weeks in October. In 31 years she had steamed 3,794,017 miles and carried more than 2,114,000 people. The original building cost had been £5 million. It was estimated that she had grossed approximately £132 million.

The original agreement was that Cunard should deliver the ship to her new owners in Long Beach with just a skeleton crew. They were not in favour of the idea of taking passengers on such a long trip on a ship which simply had not been designed for world cruising. Long Beach officials, however, were insistent that the great ship should make a grand entrance, complete with passengers. The voyage was advertised as "The Last Great Cruise" and would be her longest-ever peacetime voyage including the ports of Lisbon, Las Palmas, Rio de Janeiro, Valparaiso, Callao, Balboa and Acapulco. The cruise would entail crossing the Atlantic to South America, rounding Cape Horn and crossing the equator twice. Worse still, she would be sailing through the tropics; this would result in a great deal of discomfort for her passengers as a direct result of the lack of air-conditioning. Cunard refused to actually book the voyage (though they did assist in the planning), and so a New York travel agency was engaged for the task, the Fugazy Travel Bureau.

At 9.42 am on October 31, 1967 she slipped out of her berth in Southampton for the very last time, commencing voyage 516, under the command of Captain John Treasure Jones. The band of the Royal Marines played *Auld Lang Syne* and fourteen Royal Navy Helicopters flew in anchor formation above as a special salute.

Predictably, there were vast crowds present. Captain Jack Holt, the ship's pilot, took her down Southampton Water as she flew the special pennant which signifies that a ship is going out of service. An armada of boats of every type, shape and size sounded their whistles, trailed streamers and flew flags whilst they followed the liner down the river. All 1,000 passengers lined the rails including one of the new owners, Vice Mayor Robert Crow of the City of Long Beach, and, as a guest of the new owners, the wife of Captain Jones. The Royal Yacht Squadron signalled "I am sorry saying good-bye – very best wishes."

Best wishes were also extended to the passengers by the Captain himself. The message from Captain John Treasure Jones was printed clearly in the special programme issued to all passengers:

> Captain J. Treasure Jones R.D., R.N.R., Rtd., on behalf of Cunard Line Ltd, the City of Long Beach, California, Diner's Club, Fugazy Travel Bureau Inc, the Ship's Company, the Cruise Director and his staff, extend to you a warm welcome and express the most sincere wish that your stay on board will be a happy and memorable experience.
>
> It is our endeavour to ensure that you enjoy every minute of your stay with us, whether your inclination is to throw yourself wholeheartedly into the numerous events we have planned for you, or just relax and "take things easy".
>
> So share with us this wonderful adventure of a holiday afloat in the *Queen Mary*.

One item that had been removed from the ship was the personal standard of Queen Mary, which had hung on the main staircase. The flag was later deposited in the vaults of Cunard's bank, to be incorporated later in the new supership *Queen Elizabeth 2*.

Among the more unusual items stowed for the trip were two bright-red London double-decker buses, which were going to America for promotional purposes, though they would also serve an unusual purpose during the voyage itself. They were secured to one of the after decks.

At every port she called, Captain Treasure Jones and his crew were treated like superstars and the piers were crowded with hundreds, if not thousands of people. Fleets of small boats greeted her and circled her day and night whilst she was at anchor.

There were numerous complaints regarding the service on this trip, however, as the ship was understaffed; indeed many of the crew had been unenthusiastic about taking the journey in the first place. Her ship's company numbered 860.

It was obvious from the start that any complaint requiring a detailed or long-term response would be in vain. After all, now that the ship was leaving commercial service, who would there be to follow the matter through? The cruise information booklet even included a special notice:

> Should, however, any passenger find anything not to their liking we would ask that they make their comments known to the Purser, Chief Catering Officer or Cruise Director, or to the Fugazy representative onboard in order that their complaint may be dealt with promptly.
>
> Passengers will bear in mind that in the circumstance of this final voyage of the ship there will be no opportunity of investigating complaints after the voyage is completed.

There were also some awkward moments. To conserve fuel throughout this long journey, only two of the four screws were to be used, giving a respectable cruising speed of 22 knots, but it soon became evident that rough weather and the drag of the two non-functioning propellers would reduce the speed considerably and cause the *Queen Mary* to miss the high tide at her very first port of call, Lisbon. Without a high tide, she would not clear the bar in front of the harbour. She had to be slowed even more so that her arrival would coincide with the next tide 12 hours later.

The next leg was a short one, a mere 700 miles to Las Palmas. Then, after refuelling, the *Queen Mary* headed out on her first long haul, 3,500 tropical miles to Rio de Janeiro. First-class passengers, many of them elderly, sweltered in airless cabins designed for the North Atlantic run. Even worse off were the crew members below decks. One fish cook collapsed in the heat of his cabin and could not be revived, even when his inert form was brought up to the ship's hospital and packed in ice compresses. He died of a cerebral haemorrhage caused by heat stroke. He was the only person who did not survive the trip, though there was one passenger, 68-year old Siri Hueg of Long Beach, who broke her hip in a fall and died the day after the ship docked in her home town.

Geoffrey Coughtree, now a cabin steward on the *Queen Elizabeth 2,* recalled conditions on this last voyage:

"It was a very hot voyage, because the air-conditioning was practically nil. We were allowed to wear shirts and things, you know. We had all the portholes open. It was an interesting experience because a lot of people had come back just for nostalgic reasons. We had about 800 [passengers] – something like that. And of course, they had to make a laundry on there because it was such a long voyage. They made a laundry in the tourist class Dining Room. There were a lot of adverse comments."

Neither the *Queen Mary* nor the *Queen Elizabeth* normally had a laundry onboard. All sheets and linen were landed in New York and Southampton at the end of each voyage. Upon the next arrival one of the two ships would collect the clean laundry which had been previously left there by her running mate.

Not all who started the cruise finished it. During the three day stopover in Rio de Janeiro, some of the wealthier passengers made for the modern air-conditioned hotels ashore and one couple, Mr and Mrs Edward Dunlap of Long Beach, abandoned ship altogether. Mr Dunlap had developed phlebitis in his leg. They returned home to California by air.

After leaving Rio, the *Queen Mary* headed south along the coast of South America. Hot weather was soon only a memory and staterooms and cabins had to be heated! Everything moveable was tied down in preparation for rounding Cape Horn as the ship passed by the Falkland Islands, and then Tierra del Fuego, the half-Argentine, half Chilean island that lies at the tip of the continent at a latitude as far south as Labrador is to the north. An icy rain was falling as the ship came in sight of Cape Horn, but some of the passengers were forming a queue on the open decks – for a bus! Dr Orville Cole, the Long Beach physician who was to organize and become the first president of the "*Queen Mary* Club", had asked permission to sell tickets for a "ride" aboard the two double-decker buses as the ship rounded the Cape, so that passengers could later claim that they had gone around the Horn on a London bus. The proceeds went to a school in Valparaiso, Chile. Both buses were completely sold out. Valparaiso was a "twin city" to Long Beach. Another passenger, "Dutch" Miller of Long Beach, captain of the city's extensive lifeguards, jumped into the ship's swimming pool for a few strokes so that he could say he had swum around Cape Horn!

The weather was surprisingly calm as the *Queen Mary* headed north along the coast of Chile, but by the following day, she had run into rough weather. An abstract from the ship's log:

a.m.   "11.00   Posn. 53° 00'S 75° 02'W Ship's Co. mustered at Emergency Stations wearing lifejackets. W.T. and Fire doors, GSV's and Emergency dynamos tested. Special parties exercised – followed by Boat Drill.

Noon   Very rough sea, heavy NNW swell. V/L pitching easily and spraying Fd. overcast with rain.

On the eighth day after leaving Rio, she reached Valparaiso. Here, the Mayor of Long Beach, Edwin Wade, joined the ship. As she continued north towards stops at Callao in Peru and Balboa at the pacific end of the Panama Canal, Wade grew increasingly worried. He could feel the ship heating up again, and he knew that the 60 newspaper reporters who were due to come aboard for the last leg, from Acapulco to Long Beach, would have to accommodated in the only cabins that were left – the sweltering cabins far below on C and even D decks.

No sooner had the reporters come aboard than the Dunlaps, who had arrived in California by air, held a press conference describing the dreadful conditions aboard – a "nightmare of rats and cockroaches," a mutinous crew, a death among the passengers, a threatened amputation of Mr Dunlap's leg. The stories by the hot and bothered reporters did nothing to counter this near-libellous report. One English reporter, Ivor Davis, sent a story that appeared in the London *Daily Express* under the headline, "The Queen that Died of Shame". When, however, the *Queen Mary* reached Long Beach on December 9, 1967, 40 days and 14,559 miles out of Southampton, the US Public Health team who inspected the ship said that she was very clean and that there was no sign of any rats at all.

When the *Queen Mary* was 500 miles off Long Beach, an aircraft flew out and dipped very low over the liner, bombarding her with fresh chrysanthemums and carnations. Sixty-five miles out, the first of the vanguard of small craft, organized to greet her at the oil port, arrived and escorted her for the remainder of the voyage. She was accompanied from daybreak by every imaginable sort of waterborne craft, from rubber life rafts with outboard motors, to yachts. A plane skywriting "Hail the Queen" was the next addition to the welcoming committee, followed shortly afterwards by US Coast Guard cutters, more yachts, barges, cabin cruisers, dinghies as well as the nuclear cruiser *Long Beach* - around 10,000 craft in all. The aircraft carrier *Bennington* had a great streamer down the side of her upper decks bearing the message "Welcome *Queen Mary*" as she lay alongside one of the naval dockyard quays.

Captain John Treasure Jones looked on the amazing sight from his bridge. He steamed until two miles off shore at Newport Beach, then to the eastern end of the breakwater at Long Beach, then west along the breakwater five miles to point Fermin, where he turned around and returned to the harbour entrance and picked up his pilot to enter the harbour. As a group of passengers on deck raised their voices in *Auld Lang Syne*, they were joined by bands, shipboard whistles, and horns and a thunderous round of cheering. Perhaps most memorable were the hundreds of passengers who were gathering small items from around the ship – forks, spoons, ashtrays, even deck chairs, in fact anything they could find – and throwing them over the side. Far down below, small boat owners and their charges would rush for the sides of the *Queen Mary* in the hope of grasping some souvenir of the great occasion.

Just after 11.00 am, the first dripping lines attached the liner to the dockside. Mayor Edwin Wade was ready for the symbolic ceremonial handover to the new owners. With him was Vice Mayor Crow, resplendent in his London-bought bowler hat. He had left the ship in Southampton and flown to Long Beach so he could be there to greet the ship upon arrival.

Captain Treasure Jones was introduced to the leading figures of the city and was then presented with a 3-foot-long key to the city of Long Beach, made from flowers and the city flag. In return (as is customary), he presented the city with the Cunard house flag, together with the ship's Blue Ensign.

Geoffrey Coughtree remembers the end for the crew:

"When the ship got to Long Beach, we were all being flown home in stages. I was one of the last to leave; I think I was there for four days. It was just getting like a ghost ship. Where we'd had [two or three] watchmen patrolling the decks, we had just one policeman walking round three of those huge decks. All the linen was out in the alleyways – it looked awful. I'll always remember when I got into the bus to go to Los Angeles Airport, I couldn't look back at that lovely ship, thinking we were leaving her behind. Although [if they could not have kept her in Britain] America was the right place for her to go. She played a great part between the two nations and really kept us together."

The formal handing over ceremony on December 11 was later described by Captain Treasure Jones:

> It was most impressive, though it was delayed somewhat waiting for the British Consul General, whose chauffeur was wrongly directed. We were in direct telephone communication with Cunard in London, who instructed us to go ahead and sign the ship over to the City of Long Beach. On completion of the signing, the ship's register was handed over to me by the British Consul General to return to England and the *Queen Mary* was from that date taken off the Register of Ships. Its engines having been disconnected from the propellers, the *Queen Mary* was now classed as a building.
>
> The British Ensign and Stem Jack and Cunard House flags were then hauled down and the United States Ensigns hoisted at both mastheads. This was a most moving ceremony and we all felt a big lump in our throats. thus ended the ship *Queen Mary*, but a new *Queen Mary* will emerge which, I think, will be honoured and revered in the history and glory of RMS *Queen Mary*.

The officials of Long Beach were very impressed with the condition of the liner and said that Cunard had kept her in first-class condition. Perhaps the last word should be given to the Long Beach official who said, "We shall treasure the *Queen Mary*."

18

Long Beach

Today, the *Queen Mary* lies at Pier J, Long Beach, California. The setting is spectacular: 1.5 miles across the water is the downtown Long Beach skyline. From the other side of the harbour, she sits against her Lilliputian backdrop, regal in every sense of the word. A true Queen, no longer ruling over the ocean waves, but instead casting her countenance like a veil of optimism across a town which was, until fairly recently, the scene of dispute and dissatisfaction concerning the great ship. It is as if she determines to defy all who seek to relocate her, auction her or pension her off.

Those who would have her removed from this perfect situation demonstrate a remarkable lack of vision, for they ignore the enormous potential which she offers, as both a leisure attraction and a tool of education, a gateway to knowledge of an important part of this century.

Her Long Beach location places her within easy reach millions of people in the greater Los Angeles area. In addition, the city and the attraction both receive millions of visitors, both from out-of-state and from foreign shores, each year.

The *Queen Mary* is therefore in a position to draw from a huge population of potential visitors. Pier J is only 25 minutes from Los Angeles International Airport – nearer to the airport than downtown Los Angeles. Indeed, even before the ship was open to the general public, Long Beach had recouped, through tourism, a substantial part of the price initially paid for the liner, since hundreds of thousands of visitors streamed past her berth, many stopping in the city to shop, eat and drink.

Converting the *Queen Mary* was an enormous job that extended over several years, far longer than first anticipated. This was largely due to the absence of any really comprehensive working blueprint. The decision to purchase the ship had been made at a very late stage. Consequently, shortage of time had prevented sufficient market research and impeded the development of a sound business plan.

The contract for the ship's overall technical conversion was awarded to Rados & Sons Engineering of San Pedro, Los Angeles. Rados employed over 130 architects and engineers and had an impressive track record in marine engineering, including aircraft carriers, cruisers and commercial cargo ships. The company took the wise precaution of placing a group of engineers onboard the *Queen* before her arrival in Long Beach in order to carry out various tests and surveys. Their concern was understandable: the conversion of the *Queen Mary* was one of the biggest maritime undertakings to date. As Robert Rados, Company President pointed out, the ship drew more water than an aircraft carrier, her superstructure was 12 storeys high, and her power plant could provide sufficient electricity for the entire city of Long Beach. A complete engineering analysis was essential in view of the inevitable complexity of the task.

Soon after her arrival in California, proposals for the *Queen*'s future were announced to the public. The plans were complex and comprehensive. They included shops, six restaurants, a convention centre capable of handling 1,100 delegates, a walk-through theatre showing films of the ship's career, and mock-ups of senior officers' cabins. The bridge and radio room were to be renovated as public attractions, that would show visitors how the navigational and communication equipment worked. A guided tour of the lower decks would be a major feature and would include engine and boiler rooms, steering gear and propeller shaft. This tour would give visitors the opportunity to see one of the *Queen Mary*'s propellers and engines actually working, albeit at a speed of 1 rpm and "housed" in a special water space of 150,000 gallons.

The biggest attraction was to be a combined maritime museum and aquarium, which would house an elaborate display of exhibits valued at approximately $3 million and occupy no less than 40% of the ship's internal capacity. This museum would be built in the colossal engine and boiler areas deep down in the bowels of the ship. Its intended title was the "Oceanarium" and proposed exhibits covered such topics as pollution of the sea, sea mammals, crops from the sea, propulsion and oceanography today.

First however, all loose flammable materials had to be removed, including 700 tons of fuel left over in her vast double-bottom tanks after her last great cruise from Southampton.

It had been decided that dry-docking would take place in the Long Beach Naval Shipyard which was under the command of Captain C M Hart, USN. The yard had been founded in 1943 and therefore dry-docking the *Queen Mary* happily coincided with its twenty-fifth anniversary. Quite apart from being the only naval shipyard in Southern California, this facility was one of the largest employers in the area, providing work for some 8,500 civilians in addition to military personnel. At first, this seemed like an ideal situation; however, there would be problems.

The forthcoming conversion raised some serious questions as far as the unions were concerned. The *Queen Mary* was now officially classified as a building and clarification was therefore necessary regarding the boundaries of duty between Naval Shipyard personnel and land-based workforces. It had been agreed that the naval personnel would carry out only those jobs which necessitated the ship being out of the water, i.e. in dry dock. However this was disputed by the maritime unions who set up a picket line in protest. The result of this industrial action was that the dry-docking, originally scheduled to begin on February 22, 1968, was delayed by six weeks. It was not until April 6 that the *Queen Mary* was finally squeezed into dry dock No. 1, the Morrell Dry Dock.

This monster dock is 1,093.7 ft long, 142.3 ft wide and 44.2 ft deep. It takes only three hours to empty this basin of some 59,000,000 gallons of water and, astonishingly, just one hour to refill it again. An official publicity sheet at the time boasted that the dock's floor and sides were 25.5 ft thick and contained enough concrete to pave a highway from Long Beach to Bakersfield, California.

Once in the dock, the ship had around 320 tons of paint removed – enough to make her float 1.5 inches higher in the water! At the time the work started, no-one realized exactly how much paint had been applied to the huge hull over the years. On some sections it was quarter of an inch thick. It was even possible to detect the original red lead painted onto the steel in the 1930s. Over this were countless layers of white, interrupted by just one streak of grey, indicating the *Queen*'s wartime livery.

Also in the dry dock, three of the *Queen Mary*'s propellers were removed, the fourth remaining in position, so that future visitors could observe it rotating slowly below the waterline. To permit the passage of thousands of curious sightseers past this particular part of the ship, a 100 ton box-type viewing gallery was fitted to the side of the hull. The four massive stabilizer fins were removed, no longer required to protect passengers from the turbulent swells of the icy North Atlantic. Dry dock also provided the opportunity to permanently close and seal any redundant ducts and openings in the hull, reducing the risk of leakage and flooding.

A press release of the time confidently claimed that this dry-dock operation had prepared the liner for another 25 years flotation. On May 18 she made the sluggish return journey to pier E, to continue refitting.

Meanwhile, plans for the new museum together with artists sketches were revealed in the local newspaper together with a new estimate of the cost - a cool $14 million. It was to be the start of a tale of confusion which would persist for some years, a story which would involve ever-changing management and humiliating squabbling over the future and design of Long Beach's new attraction.

Since her arrival in California, the Long Beach authorities had devoted considerable effort to finding a suitable operator to run the *Queen Mary* following her conversion. In May, it was announced that the Diners Club corporation had become major contenders for the management contract, and were hoping to acquire the lease for the ship's overall operation.

Work carried on through 1968. One of the major structural alterations was the removal of her three original funnels. They were so old and decayed by years of exposure to the elements that they began to collapse as soon as they were lowered onto the concrete dock. They were replaced by "dummies" later in the conversion. The boiler and engine rooms became vast demolition sites, as thousands of tons of machinery and fittings were ruthlessly stripped and removed through gaping holes in the hull. The company which was hired to perform this ghastly task was Lipsett and Co. Coincidentally, Lipsett had been responsible for scrapping the *Queen Mary*'s arch-rival, the *Normandie*, nearly thirty years earlier in New Jersey.

With the vast potential viewing public and the unique opportunity offered by the world's most prestigious liner, it made good sense to appoint the French underwater explorer Jacques Cousteau as executive designer for the Museum of the Sea. Cousteau himself believed that the United States was the only country with sufficient resources to build a museum of this size and the project held a special fascination for him. He wanted the museum to be designed in such a way that visitors would become personally involved in the adventure of the sea and appreciate how their lives are bound to it. The major part of the museum was the design of the Living Sea Corporation of Hollywood under the direction of its president Jean Michel Cousteau, son of the oceanographer. The contract for the museum's construction was won by a joint organisation, Smith-Amelco.

The *Queen Mary* conversion was taking far longer than expected and Long Beach council was becoming increasingly concerned at the ever-spiralling cost of the project, now forecast to be somewhere in the region of $30. The city, however, argued that the *Queen Mary* would attract other investors to the area, thereby offsetting this extra expense. Meanwhile, opening day was now expected to take place in July or August 1970.

Press releases of the time revealed elaborate plans for the new museum, provisionally titled "Jacques Cousteau's Living Sea". They vividly described complex multi-projector systems which would display a myriad of slide-shows and moving pictures; fog screens, ice sculptures; even animated models of fish and divers which had been constructed at the Centre d'Études Marines Avancées, in France. Visitors would enter the Living Sea via a specially created tunnel simulating the effect of flying through outer space, past planets and stars. This journey would conclude when the "space ship" landed on earth in the midst of a jungle of mist, pools, ice and fog. The plans were ambitious and public relations personnel were quick to point out that whilst the museum's bulk trade would be the enthusiastic amateur visitor, the museum would also be suitable for "serious" students of marine science. Waterfalls, giant rotating towers, huge oceanographic displays, films, multimedia shows, animations, rides; all these fantastic creations were to be installed into what remained of the ship's lower decks. And all the time, the management wranglings continued.

Jack Wrather was a well-known entrepreneur, noted for his interests in the entertainment industry which included the worldwide rights to the popular television programmes "Lassie" and "The Lone Ranger". His interests, however, extended well beyond television. It was Wrather who had financed and built the hotel at Disneyland, a particularly shrewd investment. Furthermore, his corporation had serious interests in oil.

The year 1969 signalled a dispute between Wrather and Diners Club. Wrather alleged that Diners had broken an agreement to award them the contract for the hotel operation and other commercial services. Instead, they had awarded the sub-lease to a rival company Sky Chef. Eventually, the dispute was resolved by allowing Wrather and Sky Chef to operate as a joint venture.

In February 1970, Diners Club announced that it would be withdrawing from the project altogether. Diners had been taken over by the Continental Insurance Company, who, recognizing the rapidly spiralling cost of the *Queen Mary* project, (now estimated at over $50 million), had instructed them to terminate all interests with the exception of the famous Diners Club card.

As the months wore on and the work slowly continued, technical problems mushroomed at an epidemic rate. In hindsight these obstacles should have been anticipated from the outset: turning a 31 year-old ship into a fixed structure which complied with all the requirements of a national building code was not an easy matter. Air-conditioning, for example, was not a part of the *Queen Mary*'s design. The ship had originally been built to sail across the cold waters of the North Atlantic, where air-conditioning was never a necessity. Without this facility in Southern California, however, the owners and operator would have been hard-pressed to make a success of the new project.

Another aspect of the operation which caused some difficulty was the fact that the liner had to be completely rewired, so that she could be linked to the city's electrical grid. The *Queen Mary* was British-built, and therefore had a 240 volt supply. Everything onboard had to be replaced with the standard American 110 volt system. New sewage systems were necessary; new telephones... the list seemed endless, all the ship's systems had to be rebuilt. Hand in hand with these difficulties came the frequent union squabbles. No-one seemed able to decide who was going to carry out the work in the various areas of the refurbishment.

Contractors laboured steadily to complete the various onboard attractions. The Engine Room Display, the *Queen Mary* Story and the rotating propeller display were all progressing slowly, as was the Museum of the Sea, though it now seemed improbable that it would be complete in time for opening day, now put back to July 1971. Considerable attention was also paid to the ship's exterior, including the full restoration of all paintwork and the refurbishment of her 24 lifeboats.

While all this was happening, the boarding ramps and gangways that would form an integral part of her permanent berth at Pier J were also being built. Later there would also be parking for around 4,000 vehicles and a solid rock breakwater which would cost just over $1 million.

On February 27, 1971, nine tugboats jostled the *Queen Mary* away from her fitting quay at Pier E and laboriously towed her to her permanent home at Pier J. It had been necessary to dredge a special channel through the Long Beach waters, in order to allow this short "cruise". This task in itself had cost around $100,000. Thousands of spectators turned out for the historic event, some camping out overnight in order to secure a good seat. Predictably too, hundreds of small boats lingered in the water to witness the event.

For some time now Long Beach's *Queen* had been without a leaseholder or management. That changed in March 1971, when it was announced that the ship's lease had been taken up by the Speciality Restaurant Corporation, who would now be responsible for the development of all areas except the hotel.

The Speciality Queen Mary Corporation was a subsidiary of Speciality Restaurants Inc., a Long Beach based company with substantial assets and whose other establishments included the Ports O'Call restaurant, the Rum Runner and the Yankee Whaler, all of which were located at Los Angeles Harbour, San Pedro. The president of Speciality Restaurants was the entrepreneur David C Tallichet Jr, owner of the prestigious Reef Restaurant which occupied a site adjacent to the *Queen Mary*. Speciality Restaurants Inc. employed over 1,500 people and boasted gross sales of $20,300,000 for 1970. Plans for the *Queen Mary* included banquet rooms and six fast-food centres. Fast-food outlets on the *Queen Mary*? When this news spread through the maritime world, historians and shipping enthusiasts were incensed. If the Long Beach City Council wanted to attract tourists to the *Queen Mary*, then surely it would be better for them to see the vessel as she actually was; as she earned her fame and immortality, and not as some grotesque modern tourist trap?

It seemed that nothing could settle for too long with the great old ship; as if she wanted to thwart the efforts of all who tried to take her over and make her something she was never intended to be. The late William Winberg, former curator and manager of the *Queen Mary* archives, was probably the world's leading authority on the vessel's Long Beach career. He painted a graphic picture of the confusion:

"... Diners Club was taken over by the Continental Insurance Company and they said, "Get rid of everything except for the credit card." So they pulled out and the City of Long Beach was left holding the bag. They brought in a company called Speciality Restaurants to do the shops and restaurants ... then a non-profit group was formed to run the tours. The ship was divided up into territorial battle zones as far as who would operate what sections and, of course, the non-strategic areas were just kind of abandoned and left to rot."

Despite the confusion, several of the *Queens's* large public areas had been developed and refurbished. The First Class Restaurant on 'R' Deck was modified and renamed the Grand Salon. Making ingenious use of wasted space, the designers took the opportunity to cover over the funnel hatch adjacent to the Grand Salon and create a large area which became the Windsor Room. The Main Lounge on Promenade Deck was reborn as the Queen's Salon. The Observation Bar, (Promenade Deck Forward) was enlarged by enclosing outside deck space and incorporating it into the existing Bar area.

The first tours of the *Queen Mary* began in Spring 1971 and throughout that summer the Long Beach authorities – to their relief – steadily began to recoup their enormous investment. The museum, officially named Jacques Cousteau's Living Sea, opened on December 11. The organizers were understandably delighted with the initial results – on that first day attendance figures exceeded 4,000.

Reactions were mostly favourable, though some thought the whole thing a big white elephant. The "Living Sea" occupied a massive area below decks, roughly located aft of midships and in space previously taken by boilers and turbines. Not all the space gutted by the workforce had been fitted, however, and on the leaflet handed to visitors this was shown on the cutaway map as "Future Exhibit Development." Sadly this would come to nothing; the area would remain a vast, cavernous, deserted space.

Negotiations regarding the development of the hotel section of the *Queen Mary* had been underway for sometime. Ultimately, PSA Hotels Inc. a division of Pacific Southwest Airlines, was awarded this contract and refitted and refurbished around 400 cabins. Specifications called for all replacement furnishings and decor to be accurately representative of the *Queen Mary's* cabins during her heyday. The Hotel Queen Mary opened in January 1973.

During 1972, more public areas were redesigned and refurbished. New restaurants were built: the Lord Nelson Prime Rib, on Promenade

Deck; Lady Hamilton's Restaurant, also on Promenade Deck and Sir Winstons – the premier dining salon – way aft on the starboard side of Sun Deck. Part of the long gallery on Promenade Deck was converted into a conference room to meet the need for areas for functions and meetings on the *Queen Mary*.

The most controversial development, however, was the conversion of the Verandah Grill. The Grill had enjoyed an unrivalled reputation of excellence throughout the *Queen Mary*'s seagoing career, yet Speciality Restaurants converted this beautiful room into a fast food snack bar. Gone were the comfortable dining furniture, tasteful fabrics and Doris Zinkeisen's lavish canvasses which, together with impeccable service and an impressive pageant of clients, had earned the Grill the reputation of the finest floating restaurant in the world. In their place were formica tables, plastic seats and milk shake dispensers. This irreverent and pointless destruction was regarded as sacrilege by *Queen Mary* devotees. Interestingly, despite the radical change in product offered here, the operators retained the name "Verandah Grill".

During 1972, the *Queen Mary* took a gross revenue of nearly $7,000,000. Yet, despite this commercial success, unrest and disagreement continued behind the scenes. Undeterred by the resentment caused by the "refurbishment" of the Verandah Grill, Speciality Restaurants now proposed to convert the First Class swimming pool to a discotheque. This met with a suitably hostile reaction and was regarded as a direct demonstration of the lack of understanding and appreciation of this valuable legacy of ocean-going art deco.

Bill Winberg regarded many of the structural changes throughout the vessel as unnecessary.

"They figured they would have millions of people coming down here every year; you need to expand access to areas like the engine rooms and various public lounges so you could get all those anticipated people on the ship at once ... those people never came. That's why you had to make all of the different changes. A lot of them weren't necessary, very definitely. They could have left areas "as is"; a number of people have said they should have just left the ship as it was for maybe a year and had people come down and see it as it was and then made the changes. That's a possibility."

Winberg was perhaps a little optimistic. Some structural changes were definitely necessary. For one thing, the regulations which govern a land-based building in California (which is how the ship was now classified) were entirely different to those which applied to a ship at sea. As such, thousands of modifications were necessary in order to bring the *Queen Mary* in line with the Californian building regulations.

That the taste of the general public is generally fickle, may partly explain why the Living Sea Museum, hitherto the star attraction onboard the *Queen Mary*, seemed to lose its appeal throughout 1973. Revenue declined, and continued to do so the following year. A dramatic increase in marketing and advertising was needed. There had been allegations, however, that Long Beach officials had been involved in the misappropriation of Oil Tideland money and that some $14 million had been illegally diverted to the *Queen Mary* project. With such allegations in the air, it was highly unlikely that sufficient funds would be released. The financial situation was to deteriorate considerably in the following years and, together with perpetual bickering between the various rival companies onboard, resulted in the sad demise of the museum. Jacques Cousteau's Living Sea closed in 1981.

With little apparent coordination or management it seemed as if the entire *Queen Mary* project was floundering. Furthermore, in February 1974, the Hyatt Corporation took over the Hotel Queen Mary from Pacific South Western.

The City of Long Beach, realizing that the *Queen Mary* could not survive under a combined management any longer, concluded that they would have to bring in one operator to take complete control of the entire site. Accordingly they bought back the separate leases and, in 1980, the Wrather Corporation, driven along not only by Wrather himself, but also his energetic board, including President of Wrather Hotels, Dick Stevens, took over the complete operation of the ship and the adjacent area. The Wrather Corporation was a complex organization which included the *Queen Mary* (and the surrounding multi-acre site), various entertainment properties, extensive gas and oil properties, Wrather Hotels, Wrather Port Properties Ltd and, at the time, an option to purchase the Marina City Club in Marina del Rey.

A press release of April 1981 stated:

> In 1980, Wrather signed a lease agreement with the City of Long Beach to manage and operate the *Queen Mary* and adjacent 55 acre property. This property includes the 365 room hotel facility aboard the *Queen Mary*, the world-famous *Queen Mary* Tour and the English theme village located shipside (which will be renamed Londontowne), and all *Queen Mary* restaurants and shops.

Wrather commissioned a Santa Monica company, R Duell and Associates to landscape and design his new English village. Among their prior notable achievements were the huge theme parks, Magic Mountain, Great America and Six Flags.

Wrather also intended to develop a further 240 acres, which would include an additional 1,500 hotel rooms, 1,200-slip marina and a sailing school in addition to more shops and restaurants. The new waterside complex was to be named "PortAdventure" and the first phase alone would cost $22,000,000. Jack Wrather claimed:

PortAdventure will be a significant Southern California destination and attraction complex. It will feature land, sea and air attractions with an emphasis on family fun. Our goal is to make PortAdventure a place for the whole family to spend a day or an entire vacation.

The most novel addition to the site was a huge dome containing the famed Howard Hughes aeroplane *Spruce Goose*. Built not of spruce, but birch wood, this massive plane flew only once (piloted by Hughes himself) before being laid to rest in a massive hangar. The *Spruce Goose* had been donated to the Aero Club of Southern California by the Summa Corporation in 1980. Wrather reached an agreement with the Aero Club for the two organisations to assume joint management of the enormous aircraft. The Aero Club would be responsible for moving the plane and building the exhibition. Wrather was keen to establish the *Spruce Goose* as a theatrical show, rather than a static exhibition piece. To achieve this he hired producer Edwin D Ettinger to devise the entire flying boat presentation. Ettinger, the former Marketing Director for Disneyland, had extensive experience in creative design. His credits included Sea World and the Universal Studios tour.

Spruce Goose's home was to be the world's largest geodesic dome, some 130 ft high, 425 ft in diameter and costing $4,000,000. It would be specially constructed by Temcor, the Torrance-based dome manufacturer and designer. As Wrather said:

> The Hughes Flying Boat and *Queen Mary* share a unique history, so it is appropriate that they be featured together now. The flying boat was originally conceived as a means of carrying war supplies across the Atlantic during World War II when menacing U-boats were threatening ocean liners such as the *Queen Mary*.

With typical bravado, Wrather injected the entire project and all those around him with an infectious enthusiasm and stimulation. Extensive renovation work was soon undertaken. The Lord Nelson and Lady Hamilton Restaurants were refurbished and emerged once again as the Promenade Cafe. The ship's superstructure was repainted (the first time in 10 years), decks were recaulked, repegged and repolished, railings varnished, bulkheads repainted and brasswork cleaned. New carpets were custom-designed to Cunard's original colours and ordered from Wilton in England. The *Queen Mary* Tour was restructured and designed by Pasedena-based architects Smith and Williams. Wrather even commissioned Bob Moline, jingle composer and President of Tell the People productions, to write a song, *PortAdventure by the Sea*, which would herald the start of the PortAdventure enterprise. Spirits were high and it seemed to all of Long Beach that the *Queen Mary* would benefit greatly from the new management.

The Wrather years were in fact very successful for the *Queen Mary*.

Part of this was due to the astute thinking of the marketing division. Part of their approach was to devise a number of "package" tours, which included not only the *Queen Mary* but other notable Californian attractions. For example, through the period May 14, 1983 to March 31, 1984, for the modest price of $371 holidaymakers could enjoy three nights onboard the *Queen Mary* (including a "Captain's" tour of the ship), admission to any two local attractions (Disneyland, Knott's Berry Farm, Universal Studios, Marineworld, Sea World or San Diego Zoo), or a full day cruise to Catalina Island and four days car rental with unlimited mileage. At that time, it was estimated that the *Queen Mary* site was generating around $5 million a year positive cash flow. The president of the organisation at the time was Joseph Prevratil.

No ship can sail without a captain. Despite the fact that she is landlocked a "captain" has always been considered an essential ingredient to the *Queen's* life at Long Beach. During those lively Wrather years of the early eighties, the Master of the *Mary* was Captain John Gregory. In reality Gregory had almost no seagoing experience. He was, in fact, a retired air force officer, hotel manager and minister. However, the owners had selected him carefully. He looked – and sounded – the part. Interestingly, Gregory had purchased his captain's uniform in "Quartermaster's", a Long Beach uniform shop, and his cap badge had been donated to him by the Cunard company. Gregory had been ordained as a minister in 1951. As such he was frequently called upon to conduct marriages in the ship's Wedding Chapel, constructed on the site of the former second class smoking room. A natural public relations ambassador, Gregory, despite his lack of orthodox maritime training, would nevertheless perform his social duties with the grace and ease of the most experience seagoing skipper. He was in fact the ship's 34th Captain.

The new managers even appointed a cruise director, to coordinate all onboard entertainment events. This was Michael Crowe a veteran of Norwegian Caribbean Line. His plans called for the installation of a ship's library and movie theatre, in addition to traditional shipboard games and activities such as bridge, shuffleboard, backgammon and deck tennis.

In the mid 1980s Jack Wrather died. The corporation was not able to make a consistent success of the *Queen Mary* operation, as they had insufficient funds to sustain an adequate maintenance, and the ship slipped into a gradual decline. It was then that the Disney Corporation appeared on the scene. This was no coincidence: Walt Disney and Wrather had been close friends for years. Disney now wanted to purchase the hotel at Disneyland, but could only do so by additionally acquiring the lease for the *Queen Mary* and *Spruce Goose*. So in 1988, Disney signed a four-year contract for all three, with an option to extend beyond 1992.

Although large funds were allocated to the ship, resulting in an improved maintenance programme, better safety standards and the refurbishment of the hotel, historians and *Queen Mary* aficionados were again disappointed. Disney undoubtedly made practical improvements, though it became apparent that commercial enterprise, and not historical authenticity, was the principal motivation.

Devotees balked when the funnels were repainted with a cheaper, brighter red, instead of the authentic "Cunard" red. The hot Californian climate made it necessary to improve the ventilation on Promenade Deck. Instead of repairing the original cranking mechanism for opening and closing the large windows, however, the glass panes and the cranks were simply removed. Specially designed replacement panes were ordered to partially cover the window area, allowing the breeze to circulate. The replacement windows, however, were manufactured to incorrect measurements and had to be discarded.

Disney was also looking at expansion, particularly a project which was alternately referred to as "Disney Sea" and "Port Disney", and which would have involved a massive swelling of the entire site and investment of billions.

As Winberg later recalled:

"Competition started between expanding the Anaheim property [at Disneyland] or expanding here, [*Queen Mary*]. I did a lot of work with the Disney imagineers ... they fell in love with the ship. They loved this place. Number one because of the history and, number two, because it was different from anything they'd ever done before with Disney. So we were all encouraged by that... they hadn't really committed on what they wanted to do yet [with the *Queen Mary*], but they didn't want to do a lot of capital improvements because they knew DisneySea was probably coming along and that would bring literally millions of dollars. So what they did was to try to put in entertainment packages instead of physical rides. So it was an entertainment push on the short term, leading to the long term. That was the real reason behind "Ghosts, Myths and Legends."

"Ghosts, Myths and Legends" was an attraction which included a short dramatic presentation by professional actors and described in detail how the *Queen Mary* was allegedly haunted. An effective little cameo in the overall scheme of things, it cleverly enabled Disney to exercise a new marketing ploy which in turn attracted new patrons to the site. In fact, the ship gained a great deal of free publicity because of the ghost stories. As Winberg said "I'd go out on sales calls and the first question out of people's mouths was: 'You work on the *Queen Mary*? Have you seen a ghost?'"

One of the most popular aspects of a visit to the *Queen Mary* was the Engine Room tour. Presented by the Standard Oil Company of California, this tour took the visitor down to the very depths of the great liner and demonstrated the real heart of the ship's mechanical workings; the "Shaft Alley" showing, as the name suggests, the 27 inch propeller drive shafts; the aft steering station, containing the massive hydraulic gear needed to move the 140 ton rudder; the propeller room, especially constructed to enable the visitor to walk "outside" the ship's hull and see the massive 18 ft diameter, 35 ton bronze screw, in a special water compartment of its own.

Another interesting and popular area was the area immediately aft of the wheel house on Sun Deck. Many of the smaller ships' areas were recreated here in "display cabinet" format to give the visitor an idea of just what the ship looked like in its heyday. These included the ship's hospital, troop accommodation as used during World War II and typical restaurant table settings as they would have appeared when the ship was in service. What was previously the Officer's Wardroom (or lounge bar) was changed into a display of "mock" officers' cabins.

By the early 1990s, however, the ship had still not started to make the kind of profit required and, on March 6, 1992, Disney announced that they would terminate their lease on September 30 that year. In December 1992 Disney left (having already granted the ship a "stay of execution" by remaining past September as "interim managers"), and the *Queen Mary* was alone and, seemingly, unwanted. Prior to their departure, Disney repainted the outside of the ship and carried out many repairs to the teak decking and mahogany panelling.

The Port of Long Beach was faced with a difficult decision. Scrapping was out of the question for several reasons, not least of all the disturbance and removal of asbestos which would have been both prohibitively expensive and an enormous health risk. Just as 25 years previously, tenders to buy or operate the ship were invited. Several countries entered the fray, but it was rumoured that she was too weak to be moved and that such action would cause her to break up or sink in her berth. Many of the Long Beach locals and fans of the ship from the surrounding area (and indeed from foreign shores) began to campaign for the ship's preservation. Interestingly, many of these were people who were far too young to have remembered the great liner in her heyday. On the other hand, these younger people had grown up with the ship in their back yard all their lives. They had never known a Long Beach without the *Queen Mary*. Ultimately, they were successful. Ownership of the ship was transferred from the Port of Long Beach Harbour Commission to the City Council itself, who decided to find a new lessee.

Joseph Prevratil was approached by the City and asked to investigate the feasibility of reopening the ship as a tourist attraction. Prevratil was a former senior member of the Wrather Corporation. It is probable that, up to this time, the most profitable period for the liner in Long Beach was under his management in the early eighties. He was a logical choice.

In February 1993, the R.M.S. Foundation Inc. took over complete management of the *Queen Mary* for the City of Long Beach. The R.M.S. Foundation had been formed by Prevratil, along with Robert Gumbiner of F.H.P. Health Care. Saving the *Queen Mary* certainly ensured Prevratil's popularity and respect within union circles. Under his leadership, the R.M.S Foundation established four principal areas of business: the Hotel Queen Mary, the tourist attraction, food and beverage and merchandise. With this streamlining, Prevratil hoped to revitalize the liner and turn negative equity into hard profit. But this would not be easy. The *Queen Mary* had lain fallow for months since Disney pulled out and, inevitably, neglect had taken its toll. An enormous amount of work had to be done to restore the hotel rooms and public areas to a standard which was acceptable to the modern tourist industry. Furthermore, the *Queen* was soon to lose a good friend and marketing ally: the *Spruce Goose* was sold to a private owner in Oregon, dismantled and shipped out, leaving the giant dome empty and without purpose.

Good news arrived in spring. The Director of the United States National Park Service announced that on April 15, the *Queen Mary* had been placed on the National Register of Historic Places. The great ship had officially been recognized as a property of important historic value and a cultural resource worthy of protection and preservation.

Prevratil's task was – and still is, by any reckoning – overwhelming. The enormous amount of work which must be carried out on a daily basis to ensure the ship's maintenance and upkeep is, to put it mildly, daunting.

Prevratil has been successful, however. In its first year, the R.M.S. Foundation generated around $12 million revenue, though sustaining a loss of $4.2 million. In 1994 revenue was up to $17 million with a loss of only $500,000. He subsequently anticipated that in 1995 profits would be around $5 million on a turnover of nearly $21 million. He was close – 1995 yielded a profit of $4 million.

One significant key to the success of the project seems to have been sensible control on admission and hotel prices. During the Disney years, the day tripper had to pay around $17 to board and tour the ship. Prevratil's price is just $10. Hotel rooms too are sensibly priced at an affordable $75 upwards, although the better rooms and suites are considerably more expensive.

The five-year lease held by the R.M.S. Foundation was originally to expire in 1998. However, the need for further financing prompted Prevratil to seek a far longer lease, thereby providing better security for prospective investors. The situation was threatened by a group of Hong Kong investors who made an aggressive bid to purchase the giant liner for some $20 million and relocate her to Hong Kong Harbour. Long Beach rejected this proposal by a 7-1 vote, deciding that the ship still had much to offer the South California tourist industry. In any case, moving the ship would necessitate a multi-million dollar refit in order to make her seaworthy once again.

On July 25 1995, following extensive negotiations, the City Council unanimously approved a 20-year lease for Prevratil and the R.M.S. Foundation to operate the *Queen Mary* and *Spruce Goose* Dome complex. Not that the new lease will be an easy ride. For one thing, it calls for a rental payment of at least $300,000 a year or a percentage of gross receipts, whichever is greater. Once the rental surpasses the $300,000 mark, the payments escalate on a sliding scale: 3% of $17.5 million or the revenue of the *Queen Mary* and its adjacent Marketplace shopping village, 4% of revenues of $17.5 million to $23 million and 5% of more than $23 million.

The business structure which quietly ticks behind the *Queen* and the Dome is well crafted and finely tuned. The R.M.S. Foundation is a non profit-making organization. It must qualify for a 501 C3 classification under American tax laws. However, it is vital to generate revenues with which to fund maintenance, renovation and development. These revenues, which include items such as rental of the *Spruce Goose* Dome and the enormous cash profits from the adjoining car park, cannot be made by the charitable organization on the same tax rating. The *Queen Mary* and *Spruce Goose* Dome are therefore leased by the city to Queen Seaport Development Inc., a profit-making corporation which then subleases the *Queen Mary* to the R.M.S. Foundation. In this way, cash can legitimately be generated by a commercial company which then supports the ageing ship under the Foundation. By remaining under the umbrella of a charitable organization, the *Queen Mary* also has the advantage of attracting notable patrons, including Prince Michael of Kent.

The *Spruce Goose* Dome has enjoyed new success over the past two years. Various ideas were touted following the departure of the huge wooden aircraft. In early 1995, Raymond Novelli, President of Presidential Air and owner of a nation-wide membership campground company, began negotiations with Prevratil that would have led to the complete redevelopment of the Dome, converting it into the country's largest country and western music club, renamed the Sundance Dome. Never a man to do things half-way, Novelli intended to invest millions in the project, anticipating enormous returns from the regular twice-weekly shows, featuring country music's biggest stars.

Negotiations broke down in 1995 however, and the Sundance Dome never was. Instead, the Dome has become a new sound stage for some of Hollywood's greatest new epics. "Batman IV", in the series of movies featuring the caped superhero, was filmed within Temcor's colossal creation. Prevratil is realistic about this type of enterprise. Whilst it does not offer the same appeal to the visitor as the huge plane once did, it is producing precious funds which are helping shape the future of the *Queen Mary*. The rental of the Dome for "Batman IV" resulted in $700,000 profit.

There are other key enterprises. Next to the *Queen Mary*'s port bow is "Mega Bungee", a 220 ft tower from which the courageous (or just plain crazy) throw themselves on the end of a giant elastic band. Bungee jumping may have little to do with the world's most famous North Atlantic Liner, but, as Prevratil is quick to point out, "Mega Bungee" is the *Queen*'s biggest revenue-earning lessee or concession and helps to maintain the great ship.

Other profitable outlets onboard the *Queen Mary* include the California State Lottery, the Photo Booth on Promenade Deck (where guests may pose with steamer trunks and a make-believe backdrop) and the convention facility. A large number of rooms are available for business promotions, incentive groups and company meetings.

Despite doubts in some quarters, Joseph Prevratil and his company are keen for the *Queen Mary* to survive and succeed.

All of the on-site revenue-generating devices point to a cash flow which could help pave the way to the complete restoration of the *Queen Mary*. And Prevratil is determined to see the restoration through. He is, however, realistic. His severest critics hound him almost daily demanding that he returns the vessel overnight to the way it was in the 1940s. All of us – including Prevratil – wish that this could be so.

"I do want to restore the *Queen Mary* back to more what it was like, because I believe that there is a growing interest in historic attractions and that is definitely on the upswing. I think there has to be a greater emphasis on historic restoration because it is my opinion that both the tourist and the local person will come to see the authentic restoration of what it [the *Queen Mary*] was, rather than trying to make it something it wasn't."

But Prevratil knows that, for a full restoration to take place, the *Queen Mary* must first succeed as a profitable business venture. Then, and only then, can hard cash slowly be invested in the lengthy process of rebuilding, carpeting, painting, replacing and general refurbishment.

Devotees should take comfort in the restoration of the teak decking around Sun Deck which began in early 1996. Furthermore, the Verandah Grill is no longer a fast-food outlet but is being reconverted back to its former glory. Prevratil anticipates that this particular project will be complete in early 1997. The First Class swimming pool too, is set for extensive refurbishment, including the addition of a turkish bath with attendants, a project costing $250,000.

There are those, of course, who enjoy perpetuating myths about the ship's physical structure and well-being. Prevratil has become used to fending off these suggestions:

"The scare story about two years ago that the *Queen Mary*'s hull was in bad shape and about to sink; that the rivets had all dissipated – none of those things are true. That was all part of a PR effort to get rid of it."

There were also those who genuinely campaigned to have the *Queen Mary* moved from Long Beach; members of the community who regard her as an eyesore and as a "white elephant". Prevratil, however, feels that now the ship is beginning to make money again, there is now less of a desire to have her removed from Long Beach.

Not that "getting rid of" the ship would be that easy. The removal of thousands of tons of machinery in the early 1970s together with the many other modifications that have been made during her years as a tourist attraction, have weakened the structure. Safe though the *Queen Mary* is as a "building" in California, towing or moving her across an ocean would be a practical impossibility, not to mention prohibitively expensive. The massive empty boiler rooms and deserted engine areas would require strengthening at a cost of millions of dollars before any kind of seagoing journey could remotely be considered.

1994 was the 60th anniversary of the launching of the *Queen Mary* and September of that year was filled with "gala" events onboard the ship. All kinds of activities entertained and enthralled the visiting public including Scottish Bagpipe bands, an exhibition about Clydebank (the ship's birthplace) and even a re-christening of the ship by HRH Prince Michael of Kent.

1996 too was a year of celebration. June 1 saw the "Night of Nostalgia", a star-studded gala dinner-dance event attracting celebrities, *Queen Mary* veterans and the paying public. Proceeds from this event went directly to the restoration of the flooring of Piccadilly Circus shopping parade on Promenade Deck.

A project such as the *Queen Mary* is potentially subject to change and new ideas. In December 1996, *Lloyd's List* revealed a proposal by a group of Japanese investors to move the ship to Tokyo Bay for 2 or 3 years to be a hotel and tourist attraction there. Doubtless there will be numerous other suggestions in future years.

We can only continue to marvel at this wonderful ship, a living tribute to a magnificent era of ocean travel. More than just a ship; she is a symbol of victory and achievement. Victory over the most awful social depression in history, when merely to complete her was a feat unequalled in the maritime world; victory over the politicians and public figures who did not want her built in the first place; victory over Hitler's U-boats as they sought to pursue and destroy her, without success; victory over so many of her peacetime rivals, ships from other countries who were equally as determined to capture all the trade during the heyday of transatlantic travel; victory over her French counterpart, the *Normandie*, for it was the *Queen Mary* who was the final Blue Riband victor of the pair; victory over those who now would have her destroyed, or sold as scrap. She is a noble reminder of an era when the construction of this magnificent liner was singularly the greatest triumph of 1930s industrial Britain. A timeless masterpiece which continues to delight, educate and thrill millions each year.

19

Postscript

The great, solid block that was the headquarters of the Cunard Steam-Ship Company still stands on the Liverpool waterfront, beaten by the same wind and the ever-lashing rain, bleached by the sun and still overlooking the grey-brown waters of the Mersey River. These days, the building is owned by an insurance company.

In a nearby street, the famous White Star Building is also occupied by a financial institution.

Imagine: this was, indeed, the very heart of a shipping city where, standing in the windows of that building, one could see ships of all nations passing by in procession at tide-time.

Will Liverpool ever again reclaim its fame as a seafaring port? Probably not. At least, not in the foreseeable future. The city's heritage can never be removed, however. It is indelibly etched on the landscape, in the minds and souls of the generations of men and women who have strolled down the weather-beaten docks, across the small footbridges and pathways that now festoon the newly renovated warehouses.

Clydebank is still a happy little town not far from Glasgow. The John Brown's Shipyard went on to create more maritime masterpieces, notably the *Queen Elizabeth* and the *Queen Elizabeth 2*. More recently it became the U.I.E. engineering works, responsible for the creation of colossal oil rigs and drilling platforms.

A few of the original redbrick buildings still stand, including the gentlemen's toilet and shower rooms. The huge cranes hang over the uneven ground like giant alien birds, watching all below. One has recently been named Louis's Leap, after a sorry suicide incident a few years ago.

The original slipways have all but disappeared, though one can still catch a glimpse of the cracked remnants at low tide. Adjacent to the site of the old ways is a small hill, strewn with wood; piles of timber rubble, resembling railway sleepers; thick lumps of lumber, old, hacked, broken and very waterlogged.

A curious breeze whips the air here, almost deliberately conspiring to remind us that on this very spot, on a rainy day in September 1934, thousands of people gathered to witness an historic event. Defying all odds, and the wishes of so many political enemies, a huge steel structure began it's slow descent into the river and began a life that would charm and bewitch the world and generations to come.

Appendix One: Facts and Figures

Contract placed	December 1, 1930
Keel laid	December 27, 1930
Work suspended	December 11, 1931
Work resumed	April 3, 1934
Launched	September 26, 1934. Ceremony by Queen Mary in presence of King George V and Prince of Wales (Edward VIII)
Left Clydebank	March 24, 1936
Trials	April 15–19, 1936
Maiden voyage	May 27, 1936
War service	March 1940 to September 1946. Carried 810,730 passengers and steamed 661,771 miles
First civilian post-war sailing	July 31, 1947
Length overall	1,019 ft 6 in
Breadth	118 ft
Height	124 ft, keel to top structure
Draught	38 ft 10.5 in
Gross tonnage	81,237
Number of decks	12
Passenger capacity	First class: 704; cabin class: 751; tourist class: 583
Officers and crew	1,285
Cargo space	44,690.5 cubic feet
Radar	Two units, with range from few yards to over 40 miles
Anchors	3. Each weighed 16 tons, with 990 ft of chain cable
Lifeboats	24, motor, each carrying 145 people
Name letters	QUEEN MARY on bow, 2 ft 6 in high, covering 55 ft
Rivets	Over 10,000,000
Portholes and windows	2,000
Public rooms	38
Funnels	3. forward: 70 ft 6 in high; middle: 67 ft, 6 in; aft: 62 ft, 3 in
Whistles	3, each weighing one ton, which could be heard 10 miles away
Watertight bulkheads	18
Rudder	140 tons
Engines	4 sets of single-reduction geared turbines developed 160,000 shaft horsepower and drove 4 propellors. 2 sets forward drove the port and starboard outer propellors and 2 sets after drove the port and starboard inner
Propellors	4, each 32 tons and 18 ft diameter

Boilers	24 water-tube, burning oil fuel in 4 boiler rooms, supplied steam to main engines at a pressure of 400 lb per square inch at a temperature of 700°F. 3 auxiliary boilers provided steam for all ship's services at 200 lb pressure. 160,000 tubes in installation.
Turbine blades	257,000
Oil consumption	1,020 tons every 24 hours at 28.5 knots. Carried 8,630 tons.
Power stations	2, producing sufficient to illuminate city with 300,000 30-watt lamps
Light fittings	12,000
Clocks	700
Telephones	600
Radio stations	2
Crow's nest	Up 110 steel steps in foremast. 130 feet above waterline, roofed, electrically heated, telephone to bridge.
Carpets	10 miles
Cutlery	16,000 pieces
Crockery	200,000 pieces
China and glass	100,000 pieces
Sheets	30,000
Table-cloths	21,000
Blankets	5,600
Towels	210,000
Electric lamps	30,000
Safe deposit	350 miniature safes
Drinking water	468 tons in 4 tanks
Flags	48. 23 from foremast, 25 from mainmast
Kennels	Port side, sports deck. Accommodation for 26 in separate kennels.
Fire hydrants	378
Swimming pools	2. Each took 25 minutes to fill or empty. First-class: 107 tons of water Cabin-class: 105 tons of water
Sun deck	4.5 times round equals 1 mile
Fastest ever voyage	Left Cherbourg (westbound) 2.24 am Auust 4, 1938. Reached Ambrose 1.30 am August 8. 3,097 miles at an average of 30.94 knots. Best day's run, 790 miles at 31.60 knots. Fastest ever voyage (eastbound) Left Ambrose 1 pm August 10, 1938 Reached Cherbourg 7.37 pm August 14. 3,128 miles at an avg of 31.72 knots. Best day's run 738 miles at 32 knots
Refrigeration capacity	60,000 cubic feet. The *Queen Mary*'s plant would meet the needs of 15,000 average homes.

Appendix Two: The Ship's Company

Officers, Staff and Crew onboard the *Queen Mary*

DECK DEPARTMENT (Total 190)

Master	1
Staff captain	1
Navigating officers	8
Radio officers	12
Carpenters	1
Assistant carpenters	4
Bosun	1
Bosun's mates	3
Masters-at arms	8
Fire patrol	6
Storekeeper	1
Lamp trimmer	1
Quartermasters	6
Able seamen	57
Ordinary seamen and boy seamen	8
Purser	1
Staff purser	1
Assistant pursers	16
Assistant pusers (ladies)	4
Baggage masters	3
Interpreter	1
Printers	5
Musicians	20
Photographers	3
Telephonists	4
Surgeons	2
Nursing sisters	4
Physiotherapist	1
Dispenser	1
Hospital attendants	3
Officers' stewards	3

CATERING DEPARTMENT (Total 829)

Chief steward	1
Second steward	1
Restaurant managers	2
Bedroom stewards	81
Waiters and commis waiters	204

Officers' stewards	32
Night stewards and asistants	36
Deck and public room stewards	39
Kitchen staff	158

FEMALE STAFF (Total 73)

Stewardesses	44
Nursery stewardesses	3
Bath attendants	10
Shop assistants	7
Swimming pool attendants	2
Hairdressers	6
Turkish-bath attendant	1

The remainder of the "catering" department was made up of pantrymen, bell-boys, boots, linen storekeepers, chief storekeeper and assistants, barkeeper and assistants, clothes pressers, utilitymen, gardener, writers, lift attendants, barbers, P.T. instructors, swimming pool attendants. masseur, and Turkish-bath attendants.

ENGINE DEPARTMENT (Total 254)

Engineer officers	64
Electrical engineer officers	22
Sanitary engineer	1
Boiler-maker	1
Plumbers	6
Engineer writers	2
Leading hands	3
Storekeeper	1
Assistant storekeepers	3
Refrigeration attendant	1
Electric greasers	6
Deck and main greasers	45
Firemen	42
Trimmers	46
Trimmers' peggys	8
Cinema operators	3

Appendix Three: Provisions

The following is a list of the enormous quantity of foods and provisions which were consumed on any given round trip of the *Queen Mary*, during the height of her career. All quantities are approximate.

Biscuits	1,100	lb
Cereals (breakfast)	500	lb
Cereals (breakfast packets)	1,000	lb
Beans, peas (dried)	950	lb
Flour of all kinds	20,000	lb
Macaroni, spaghetti, noodles	550	lb
Oatmeal and rolled oats	450	lb
Dried fruits	1,300	lb
Fish (canned)	1,150	lb
Fruit (canned) No. 10 size	1,350	cans
Fruit (canned) No. 2½ size	1,300	cans
Mustards (various), peppers, spices and herbs	150	lb
Salt	2,400	lb
Conserves, fruit	45	lb
Honey and Ginger preserved	35	lb
Jams and Marmalade 1 lb	1,050	jars
Jams and Marmalade 7 lb	30	gall
Jellies (various)	115	lb
Syrups (various)	30	gall
Juices, fruit, and vegetable No. 10	850	cans
Juices, fruit, and vegetable No. 5	1,900	cans
Nuts (various)	550	lb
Pickles and olives	800	bottles
Sauces, ketchups, and chutneys	900	bottles
Salad oil	160	gall
Turtle soups etc	475	pints
Cup chocolate and cocoa	41	lb
Coffee (various brands)	1,700	lb
Sugar (cube, granulated, etc.)	7,500	lb
Teas (various)	1,100	lb
Vinegars	200	pints
Vegetables (canned and purée)	3,500	cans
Strained foods, infants	300	cans
Essences	25	bottles
Bacon	5,150	lb
Hams	2,500	lb
Cheeses	1,800	lb
Butter	5,900	lb
Eggs	70,250	
Cream	3,250	qts

Milk (fresh)	24,250	pints
Milk (evaporated)	600	gall
Margarine and lard	2,250	lb
Fish (fresh and shell)	19,500	lb
Fish (smoked)	1,450	lb
Salmon (smoked)	425	lb
Sturgeon (smoked)	50	lb
Snails	300	
Scallops and clams	125	gall
Apples (40-lb boxes)	300	boxes
Apricots (dessert)	100	lb
Bananas	1,450	lb
Blueberries	100	lb
Grapes (choice)	1,500	lb
Grapefruit	90	boxes
Lemons	35	boxes
Limes	1,000	
Melons (various)	2,800	
Nectarines	300	
Oranges (various)	8,000	
Tangerines	100	lb
Peaches	500	lb
Pears (various)	1,150	lb
Strawberries and other soft fruits (in season)	2,250	lb
Pineapples	75	
Fresh frozen fruits	1,500	lb
Ice cream	4,000	qts
Choice loins, beef	19,000	lb
Choice rib beef	1,250	lb
Choice fillets beef	1,150	lb
Beef (various)	2,000	lb
Beef (corned)	1,500	lb
Lamb (including joints)	10,000	lb
Pork (corned)	850	lb
Veal	1,850	lb
Offals (various)	3,650	lb
Tongues (corned and smoked)	1,250	lb
Chickens (broiling)	1,900	lb
Chickens (squab)	175	lb
Chickens (Guinea)	115	lb
Chickens (Roasting)	6,500	lb
Chickens (Poussin)	90	lb
Poulardes de Bress	900	lb
Poulets de Grain	600	lb
Pigeons (various)	425	lb
Turkeys (Tom)	5,950	lb
Turkeys (Hen)	225	lb
Turkeys (Smoked)	50	lb
Sausages (breakfast etc.)	2,150	lb

Vegetables	41,000	lb
Vegetables (frozen)	8,750	lb
Potatoes	55,000	lb

Other specialities, such as caviar, foie gras, etc., were carried as well as special stores to cover kosher requirements, special diets, Japanese stores etc.

On each round voyage the wine, spirit and tobacco stores carried onboard were:

	Bottles	½ bottles
Champagne	2,400	1,440
French Sparkling Burgundy	300	180
Red Bordeaux	960	720
White Bordeaux	720	480
Red Burgundy	600	600
White Burgundy	420	300
Rhone	60	72
Rhone Rose	240	-
Alsation	60	-
Rhine	600	480
Moselle	300	288
Rhine and Moselle Sparkling	180	-
Chianti	-	132
American Wines	36	-
Empire wines	192	-
Port	168	-
Sherry	480	-
Cooking wines	144	-
Liqueurs	672	-
Cognac, Fine Champagne etc	180	-
Cognac (3-Star)	300	-
Armagnac	24	-
Rum	360	-
Scotch	2,400	-
Irish whiskey	120	-
American whiskey	1,200	-
Canadian whiskey	480	-
Gin	1,200	-
Aperitifs, Vermouth, etc	2,504	-
Ale and Beer	6,000	-
Stout	2,400	-
Lager	12,000	-
Lager (draught)	6,000 (gal)	-
American beer and ale	2,400	-
Cider	240	-
Mineral waters	48,000	-
Cordials	360	-
Cigarettes (No.)	1,500,000	-
Tobacco	240 (lb)	-
Cigars (No.)	15,000	-

Appendix Four: Comparisons

From early days until fairly recently, shipowners were fond of using the sheer size of their vessels as a means by which to impress and, ultimately, attract the public to sail. One way of conveying the ships' dimensions was by means of the visual arts. Quite frequently, the artist or poster painter would deliberately depict the surrounding tugboats and fireboats as being very small, thereby exaggerating the size of the liner featured in the picture. Another was by the use of written comparisons. Predictably, the massive *Queen Mary* would provide virtually limitless scope for any inventive commercial artist. Amongst the visions concocted at the time was the striking study of Columbus's entire fleet of ships comfortably sitting in the First Class Restaurant on the *Queen Mary*, shown earlier in this book. Another famous painting showed the *Queen Mary* straddling London's Trafalgar Square and its environs.

Cunard actually went to the extent of publishing a special book, the *Book of Comparisons*, which illustrated the incredible dimensions of their new vessel by means of artist's impressions combined with descriptive paragraphs. For reasons of historical interest, the figures used here have not been updated or corrected; these are quoted verbatum as they were first published.

- If her total passenger list was carried in railway sleeping cars it would take 65 American Pullman sleepers or 166 British Railways sleeping coaches to accommodate her.
- If she were placed in Fifth Avenue with her stern against the Empire State Building her length would extend to 38th Street.
- If she were placed along the Strand with her stern at Charing Cross Station yard, her bows would be at the Savoy Hotel.
- Her main engines generate as much horse-power as would be required for fifty American passenger locomotives.
- Over 10,000,000 rivets were used during the construction of the *Queen Mary*. Placed in a heap, they would make a pyramid totalling 25,000 cubic feet.
- The forward funnel of the *Queen Mary* is 70 feet in height from the Boat Deck (a foot higher than the Egyptian Obelisk in Central Park, New York). The diameter of each of the funnels is 30 feet and would permit 3 modern locomotives, placed abreast, to pass through – or to enclose the hull of the first Cunarder, the *Britannia*.
- There are three acres of deck space for recreation on the *Queen Mary*, equal approximately to the ground area within the Yale Bowl and New Haven, Conneticut.
- Seven turbo-generators deliver nearly 10,000 kilowatts per hour. This electrical energy is sufficient to meet the lighting and public service needs of a city of 150,000 people or such cities as Tulsa, Oklahoma, Des Moines, Iowa, San Diego or Jacksonville, Florida.

Bibliography

Ellery, David; *RMS Queen Mary: The World's Favourite Liner*, Shipping Books Press
(Waterfront Publications imprint) , 1995

Hodd, John, (compiled); Slaven, Anthony and Moss, Michael S; *The History of Clydebank*,
Parthenon, 1988

Howard Bailey, Chris; *Down the Burma Road*, Oral History Team, Southampton Local
Studies Section, 1990

Hutchings, David F; *RMS Queen Mary: 50 Years of Splendour*, Kingfisher Publications,
1986

Johnson, Howard; *The Cunard Story*, Whittet Books, 1987

Lacey, Robert; *The Queen of the North Atlantic*, Sidgwick and Jackson, 1973

Mackenzie-Kennedy, C; *The Atlantic Blue Riband: Evolution of the Express Liner*, William
Sessions, 1993

Maguglin, Robert O; *The Queen Mary: The Official Picture History*, Wrather Port
Properties

Maxtone-Graham, John; *Crossing and Cruising*, Charles Scribner's Sons, 1992

Maxtone-Graham, John; *The Only Way to Cross*, Macmillan Publishing, 1972

Miller, William H. and Hutchings, David F; *Transatlantic Liners at War: The Story of the
Queens*, Arco Publishing, 1985

Prior, Rupert; *Ocean Liners: The Golden Years*, Tiger Books International, 1993

Ship Building and Shipping Record, issues 1967

Other books available

RMS Titanic: A Modern Legend, revised edition
David F Hutchings
Best-selling book on the *Titanic,* revised for an eighth printing.
Paperback 273 x 215mm   48 pages   illus: 177 b/w, colour spread   ISBN: 0 946184 29 1   £7.95

HMHS Britannic: The Last Titan, second edition
Simon Mills
Titanic's forgotten sister ship launched in 1914, requisitioned as a hospital ship and sunk off Greece in 1916.
Paperback   273 x 215mm   64 pages   illus: 80b/w, 5 line, 2 maps   ISBN: 1 900867 00 1   £9.50

RMS Olympic: The Old Reliable
Simon Mills
The first liner to exceed 40,000 tons. *Olympic* was first of her class to be built, but her story has been overshadowed by the ill-fortune of her two sister ships *Titanic* and *Britannic.*
Paperback   273 x 215mm   64 pages   illus: 76 b/w, 2 line 3 maps   ISBN: 0 946184 79   £8.95

RMS Queen Mary: The World's Favourite Liner
David Ellery
A pictorial history with a unique collection of almost 300 black and white photographs and a selection of very rare, early colour pictures.
Hardback 273 x 215mm   176 pages   illus: 296 b/w, 11 colour   ISBN: 0 946184 84 4 £22.25

RMS Lusitania
Triumph of the Edwardian Age
Eric Sauder and Ken Marschall
Paperback   273 x 215mm   48 pages   illus: 111 b/w   ISBN: 0 946184 80 1   £7.95

Shipping Albums 1
Merchant Ships of World War II: A Post War Album
Victor Young
A collection of 80 original colour photographs of more than 60 WWII-built merchant ships seen in ports around the world up to the 1960s and 70s. Records of a type of ship and a style of seafaring gone forever.
Hardcover   240 x 215 mm   72 pages   illus: 80 colour   ISBN: 1 900867 01 X   £14.95

SHIPPING
BOOKS   *Publishing for the ship enthusiast*
PRESS

Index